Denman Waldo Ross

The Early History of Land-Holding Among the Germans

Denman Waldo Ross

The Early History of Land-Holding Among the Germans

ISBN/EAN: 9783337403157

Printed in Europe, USA, Canada, Australia, Japan

Cover: Foto ©ninafisch / pixelio.de

More available books at **www.hansebooks.com**

THE EARLY HISTORY

OF

LAND-HOLDING AMONG THE GERMANS.

BY

DENMAN W. ROSS, Ph. D.

L'idée formulée par les faits représente la science.
CLAUDE BERNARD.

BOSTON:
SOULE AND BUGBEE.
1883.

Copyright, 1883,
BY DENMAN W. ROSS.

UNIVERSITY PRESS:
JOHN WILSON AND SON, CAMBRIDGE.

PREFACE.

This volume is the result of an investigation into the early history of land-holding among the Germans. The investigation was begun in the year 1875, and it has been continued, with occasional interruptions, since then.

The collections of early records were, most of them, read through. Passages bearing upon the subject of the investigation were noted. They were then carefully classified; passages establishing certain facts being grouped together. A general theory was then formed, to bring the facts thus collected into a natural order and relationship. This theory is now offered to readers and students for their consideration.

In order to reach a just judgment of the theory, three inquiries should be made: — 1. Are the passages of the records, which are described or referred to, correctly interpreted? 2. Have any passages in the records been overlooked, which are inconsistent with the theory offered? 3. Are the facts which have been ascertained well arranged and fully described?

Although much labor has been spent, during a long period of time, in order to reach a truthful, consistent, and lucid statement, the result is still unsatisfactory to the writer, in many respects. It will be unsatisfactory to the reader also, without doubt. An entirely satisfactory statement still remains to be made. Perhaps it may never be made. The records are in many cases inconsistent; and in regard to certain points we have no records whatever; nor is there much chance of any being discovered.

Nevertheless, we believe that it will always be possible to advance in the knowledge and understanding of our subject. Perhaps the time may come when we shall no longer be able to gather new facts, though such a time must still be far off; but the time will never come when we can make an exhaustive general statement, which will involve no error of any kind. It will always be possible to make a more simple, a more lucid, a more truthful statement. It must be remembered that we advance in science not so much by presenting new views as by correcting old ones. In other words, we advance not so much by establishing our theories as by modifying them. Absolute truth is far away from us, and unattainable. The most we can do is to approximate towards it; and we do this by giving up the statement of to-day for another, which will bring facts a little more nearly into their true and natural relationship. We advance in this way very slowly, but surely;

having always something new to say involving the best of what has been said.

Consistently with this idea, we hope, after some years, to rewrite this book, or to write another book upon the same subject; to exclude all that has been said amiss, to include all that has been rightly said, and many things besides which ought to have been said. Instead of creating many things, we will perfect one if we can. As Balzac tells us in one of his letters, "Il faut refaire, recorriger, mettre tout à l'état monumental."

CAMBRIDGE, June, 1883.

CONTENTS.

Theory 1–109

Sources of Information 111–122

Notes and References 122–252

Literature of the Subject 252–264

Index 265–274

THE EARLY HISTORY

OF

LAND-HOLDING AMONG THE GERMANS.

THE life of the early Germans, considered from an economic point of view, was pastoral rather than agricultural. Agriculture was resorted to more or less; at first from time to time, and afterwards regularly; but the wealth of the people, and their chief means of subsistence, consisted of live-stock, and the land was used, most of it, as pasture-ground for flocks and herds (¹). *Pastoral life.*

The freemen settled neither in villages nor in towns, but apart from one another in isolated farmsteads,— *Einzelhöfe*, the Germans call them (²). *Isolated farmsteads.*

The extent of pasture ground which the freeman occupied round about his farmstead was determined by the number of his flocks and herds. As among the Latins, the *pecuniosus* was also *locuples* (³). If a man owned much stock, he occupied a great deal of land. If he owned a little stock, a small amount of land was enough for him. There was plenty of land; so every man occupied as much as he wanted. The ani- *Pasture ground.*

mals grazed in herds, under the care of herdsmen, who drove them out from the farmstead and brought them back again (⁴).

Grass land. While most of the land was occupied as pasture-ground, a part of it had to be reserved for its grass crop. The climate of Germany is cold. Snow lies upon the ground, in most places, during many months of the year. At that time there is no green herbage anywhere. It follows that, if flocks and herds are to be maintained, grass must be cut and stored away for winter. Every man required, therefore, besides his pasture ground, a certain extent of grass land. The amount of grass land which the freeman occupied was determined by the number of animals he had to maintain through the winter.

Agriculture. Although the early life of the Germans was pastoral rather than agricultural, agriculture was resorted to more or less. In Cæsar's time, among the Suevi, it was resorted to by everybody in turns. While some of the people went to war, the rest engaged in agriculture. Thus, we are told, neither war nor agriculture was neglected. This seems to have been the custom, also, in the time of Tacitus; not particularly among the Suevi, but among the Germans generally (⁵).

Slaves as cultivators. The cultivators were, as a rule, slaves. The freemen seldom engaged in agricultural labor, unless they were obliged to do so. They spent most of their time, when not at war, in hunting;

the rest in idleness, eating, drinking, or sleeping, at entertainments or assemblies (⁶). In early society, people do not willingly resort to agriculture, until they have servants whom they can oblige to do the work for them. The work is too hard, and takes too much time. Stock-raising affords an easier means of subsistence. The transition from the pastoral to the agricultural life has almost always been effected by means of slavery. This was certainly the case among the Germans. Whoever reads through the early laws, formulæ, and documents, will be convinced of this (⁷).

At the same time a class of dependent freemen *Dependent freemen.* or clients was coming into existence almost everywhere, — a sort of plebeian order, intermediate between the class of independent freemen and the class of slaves. It consisted of men living under patronage or over-lordship. It consisted of men who, having been freed from bondage, were unable to escape from dependence, because they had no arms, no stock, no land; of men who, having been separated from their kindred, and the protection which the family or clan relationship afforded, were afraid to live alone, to hold their own against the world; or of men who thought that they were more prosperous as dependants than as free-lords. It was a fortuitous assemblage of persons of divers descent, nationality, race. Being freemen, they could leave their respective patrons and lords when they pleased; but before doing so they were obliged to pay back all that they had received, or an equivalent thereof. This they were seldom able to do. So, although they were politically free, they were economically unfree. They were then debtors, bound in servitude to their respective lords and patrons. In this position they were often obliged to take lots of land, to cultivate these lots with their own hands, and to pay to their lords a part of the produce of their labor. Their condition was often little better than that of the slaves. It appears to have grown worse and worse as time went on; until, at last, the two classes, the class of slaves and the class of laboring freemen, were very nearly merged together. We may describe them together, as one class, — the class of serfs. It comprised the bulk of the population of Western Europe during the early and middle ages ([8]).

Dependants politically free, economically unfree.

Dependent freemen as cultivators.

The class of serfs.

The amount of land which the freeman occupied for tillage depended upon the number of cultivators, or serfs, he had at his farmstead, or in houses of their own near by. As Tacitus tells us, arable lots were occupied according to the number of cultivators, — *agri pro numero cultorum . . . . occupantur*. A certain measure of land, what Tacitus calls an *ager*, — what is known in later times as a *hida, mansus, huba,* or *colonica*, — was assigned to each cultivator. Two *agri* were assigned to two cultivators; ten *agri* to ten culti-

The agri, or arable lots.

One lot assigned to each cultivator.

vators; twenty *agri* to twenty cultivators; and so on (⁹).

When the *agri* marked off were equally fertile, they were distributed among the cultivators; one to each man, usually by lot: but it seldom happened that the *agri* were equally fertile. The land upon which they had been marked off was apt to be more or less diversified in surface, and the soil was better in some places than in others. *The agri distributed by lot.*

The *agri* were then of unequal value, and quarrels were apt to arise in regard to them. As each of the cultivators paid a portion of the produce of his lot to his lord, and all those who were of the same rank or consideration paid the same portion, as a rule (¹⁰), inequalities between the lots were a just cause of dispute, and they had to be corrected. *The agri not always of equal value.*

The only way in which the lots could be equalized in value, without being made unequal in extent, was by a redistribution in sections. The land upon which the lots had been marked off was, therefore, divided into sections,—what Tacitus calls *spatia camporum* (¹¹),—approximately rectangular, we may suppose, and, so far as possible, equally fertile in every part. Each section was then divided into as many shares as there were lot-holders in the land, and each man received one share of each section, as many shares as there were sections. Thus an almost *The agri often redistributed in sections. The spatia camporum.*

perfect equality was secured. The original lots, being intermixed, were obliterated.

Acre lots. There was still another way in which the original lots were distributed. The cultivators met together and marked off on the ground a number of acres (small *agri*), one for each man. These were then distributed by lot and ploughed up, each man ploughing his own acre. Then, presumably the next day, for the acre was *The morgen,* regarded and described as a day's work (*morgen* *or iurnalis.* in the German, *iurnalis* in the Latin) ([12]), another set of acres was marked off, distributed, and ploughed up; then another, and another; and so on, until the original lots were all redistributed in acres. These lots, being intermixed, were *Intermixed* obliterated. Their boundaries were lost. *Nullus* *acres.* *certis terminis, sed iugera iacent ad iugeribus; quia iugera altrinsecus copulata adiacent; singulis iugeribus mixtim in communi rure huc illucque dispersis.* These are some of the phrases by which this arrangement of lands is described in the records ([13]).

Existing Vestiges of arable lots redistributed in this way *vestiges of* *ancient in-* have been found in almost every country occupied *termixed* *holdings.* by the Germans. The traveller in England, in France, or in Germany, cannot fail to notice that the arable land is still quite commonly cut up in very small pieces, usually narrow strips; and if he makes inquiry regarding the distribution of property, he will find that it is, and has been, from the remotest time, scattered and intermixed in the manner described. The sections (*spalia*) in which the lots were originally redistributed often remain (¹⁴).

When an acre lot extended along a slope of ground, the ploughman ploughed one furrow after another down the slope. In so doing he brought earth from the upper side of the lot to the lower side, so as to level it. After several ploughings the acre had the appearance of a terraced border. If there were several acres side by side, there was a series of terraces down the slope. Such terraced acres may be seen in many places in England and Germany (¹⁵). Some narrow, far-stretching terraces may be seen at Deisenhofen, between Munich and Holzkirchen. They are crossed by a Roman road, which must, it is said, have been built before A. D. 201. They differ, however, in many respects, from those we are here describing (¹⁶). *[margin: Terraced acres.]* *[margin: The Bavarian Hochäcker.]*

When the same lots — *agri pro numero cultorum occupati* — had been repeatedly cultivated, the soil became exhausted, and new lots had to be substituted for them. From time to time new lots were cultivated, and the old ones were allowed to lie fallow. This fact is recorded by Tacitus in the words, *arva per annos mutant et superest ager*. That the arable lots were shifted about over the meadow and pasture lands is known, not only from this statement of Tacitus, but from the testimony *[margin: Shifting about of arable fields.]*

8 EARLY HISTORY OF LAND-HOLDING

of later records. For example, in one of the St. Gall documents, a certain inheritance is described as embracing two tenements (*colonicas*), with the arable lots cultivated in successive years (*analies terris*), besides meadow, pasture, and other lands (*pratis, pascuis, etc.*) (¹⁷).

The field-grass system. This is the field-grass system of tillage, — *Feldgraswirthschaft*, the Germans call it. There was, in the first place, an indefinite tract of meadow and pasture land. Upon this land arable lots were marked off, ten, fifteen, twenty, more or not so many, according to the number of cultivators. Then these lots were shifted about from one position to another; every other year, or from time to time in the course of years, — *per annos*, as Tacitus says.

Ploughs and plough-lands. Each cultivator received from his lord a plough, besides a yoke of oxen; hence the arable lots were called plough-lands, — *terrae aratrorum* or *carrucatae* (¹⁸). They were called plough-lands whether they were intermixed or not. Each of the cultivators ploughed his land himself, with the aid of other members of his family; except in certain
Co-operative ploughing. cases, when the ploughing was done co-operatively. In such cases the cultivators were not all provided with ploughs. One plough was assigned to several cultivators. Then each man brought out his yoke of oxen, and all the yokes of oxen were hitched to the one plough, and the lots of the associate cultivators were ploughed in

turn ([19]); unless the plough was used in turn, which plan may have been preferred.

In the early time, and in some places long afterwards, the meadow land was not separated at all from the pasture land. We suppose, therefore, that the free-lord, or his people, cut the grass in certain places, here or there, and the herdsmen kept the animals away from these places until it had been cut ([20]). When there was plenty of grass, every man cut as much as he wanted; but when the amount of grass was limited, an allowance was made to each man. He was allowed to cut and carry off one, two, or more loads. Grass land was regularly estimated, according to the number of loads of hay (*carradue feni*) it was capable of producing ([21]). At a later time, the grass land was divided into lots, one lot for each tenant. Then most of what has been said regarding the arable land may be said of the grass land. When the grass produced upon the various lots was nearly equal in quantity and quality, one lot was assigned to each tenant; but when the lots were of unequal value, they were redistributed by sections, and so scattered and intermixed ([22]). When the lots of grass land were permanently located, they were often taken by the cultivators in rotation; the holder of lot 1, one year, taking lot 2 the next; the holder of lot 2 taking lot 3; and so on. Sometimes, when the lots were redistributed in sections, the shares

The grass land.

Enjoyment ad libitum.

Enjoyment limited.

Grass land divided into lots.

The rotation system.

in each section were taken in rotation, in the same way (²³).

Arable lots in rotation. So, in certain cases, when the arable lots had been located permanently, when the field grass system had been given up, and a system of permanent fields had taken its place, the shares were taken in rotation (²⁴). The rotation system was preferred to redistributions by lot, because of its perfect justice and equality. It was a compromise which the inequality of the lots made necessary.

The pasture land. In regard to the pasture land, so long as there was plenty of it, the enjoyment was *ad libitum*. *Enjoyment at first unregulated;* Every man turned out as many animals as he had: but when the pasture ground was limited, *afterwards limited.* each man was allowed to turn out a certain number of animals; five or ten, more or not so many. Pasture lands were quite regularly estimated according to the number of animals, of one kind or another, that could be maintained upon them. We have pastures for fifty, a hundred, more or not so many, cows, or sheep, or swine, to be shared between the free-lord and his tenants (²⁵).

The forest land. Enjoyment unregulated. The enjoyment of the forest land was usually unregulated in the early time of which we are speaking. The free lord allowed his tenants to cut all the wood that they wanted for building purposes, for the erection of enclosures, or for fuel, and he had all that he wanted for himself besides (²⁶).

Sometimes the free-lords took lots of the arable Domain lots.
land with their tenants. Then we have domain
lots (*hubae indominicatae*) as distinguished from lots
in tenure (²⁷). The free-lords seldom cultivated
these domain lots however. They obliged their The domain lots were
tenants to do this for them. Hence the agricul- cultivated by the tenants.
tural services upon domain land which were
exacted almost everywhere during the early and
middle ages.

The ploughing upon the domain land was Agricultural services on
done by the tenants. They sowed the seed in it, domain land.
gathered the harvest from it, and stored this in
the lord's barns. They cut grass for the lord,
and stored it. They cut wood in the forest, and
brought it to where it was needed for building or
for fuel. They went on errands, and performed
other services, as ordered: all this in addition
to cultivating their own lands and paying to
the lord a portion of the produce thereof. These
manifold dues and services were at first imposed Dues and services reg-
by the lord according to his will; but he always ulated by custom.
found it difficult to increase them afterwards.
The tenants were constantly referring to precedent, and were discontented, and sometimes
riotous, if it was not adhered to. The precedent
worked in both ways, however; for when the
tenant called for a reduction of his dues and
services, the lord referred to the precedent, and
usually persisted in adhering to it. The dues
and services became, in this way, fixed by

precedent, in other words by custom. There were different customs, of course, in different places, according to different precedents referred to ([28]).

The mansi vestiti and absi.

When the tenants of the houses and lots of land which we have been describing (the *mansi cum hubis*) died, and were not replaced by others, we have empty houses and unoccupied lots (*mansi absi* and *hubae absae*). The freeman, in describing his possessions, said he had a certain number of occupied tenements (*mansi vestiti*, or *possessi*), and a certain number of unoccupied tenements (*mansi absi*). The unoccupied tenements were filled up as soon as possible ([29]).

Terms used to describe the tenants.

The tenants are variously described as *familiae, manentes, mansionarii, mansores, casarii, cassati, servi, mancipia, tributarii, parscalchi, censuales, accolae, cultores, coloni, villani, rustici, rusticani, liti, inquilini, homines* ([30]).

No boundaries between the isolated domains.

There were no boundaries between the lands occupied by one free-lord and another, in the early period; in the time of Cæsar, for example. He says of the Germans, that no man had any definite amount of land, or any boundaries to what he occupied, — *necque quisquam agri modum certum aut fines habet proprios* ([31]). There were, probably, no boundaries between the holdings of the free-lords, in the time of Tacitus; for even after the wanderings, when settlements were permanent, and the population was increasing and spreading, the forest or waste was commonly regarded as a sufficient boundary. It was called the *confinium silvarum*, the *marca de silva*, or *marca silvatica* (³²). Then gradually it became customary to define boundaries more precisely, and the free-lord would go out, in company with his neighbors and friends as witnesses, and make a circuit of his domain, noting as he went, by means of marks on trees or stones, mounds of earth, or other signs, the limits to his property (³³). When this had been done, and he had occasion to refer to his estate, he usually mentioned the fact that boundaries had been marked, and he often described them briefly (³⁴).

The marca de silva.

How boundaries were first laid down.

Beyond the land which the free-lord occupied at first,—when he had built a house for himself, and houses for his people, when he had assigned arable lots to the cultivators, when he had cleared a sufficient tract of meadow and pasture land for the live-stock of his colony,—there was often a good deal of land still unoccupied, which he could appropriate, as he had occasion or need; and from time to time he extended his possessions in one direction or another (³⁵). When the free-lord described his possessions, he said that he had besides his own house (the *mansus indominicatus*) certain other houses (*mansi ingenuiles, letales, serviles*) (³⁶), a corresponding number of arable lots (*hubae*) (³⁷), and an indefinite extent of meadow, pasture, and forest land round about

Appropriation of unoccupied land.

Unoccupied land regarded as undivided property.

(*pratis, pascuis, silvis, etc.*) (³⁸); and he often added that he had also lands not yet occupied or appropriated, to be occupied or appropriated whenever occasion or need should arise, — *terras extirpandas, inquirendas, incullas, inquisitas* (³⁹). In a Middle-Rhine document a certain man alienates: *de proprisa silva jornales octo, et aliam communem silvam non proprisam*. In a document of the Regensburg collection: *has itaque res*, are alienated; *et quicquid in posterum· silvarum extirpatione omnique alia cultura amplificetur*. In another document of the same collection a certain man named Papo (*urbis praefectus*) alienates what he calls a *praedium silvaticum*, which, inasmuch as it lay within sight of his estate of Steninga, he appropriated, *in sylva communi Nordwald* (⁴⁰).

Establishment of tenant colonies.
If the free-lord had so many cultivators that he could not find lots for them all near his residence, he sent off a colony or colonies to distant places, where there was plenty of land (⁴¹). The leadership of such colonies was intrusted to a member of the family, or else to a faithful servant and agent, — a *prepositus, actor, major*, or *villicus* (⁴²).

It was the business of the agent to superintend the division of the land, and its cultivation; to collect the dues, and to keep the peace among the colonists. Sometimes the free-lord had in his possession several, or a great many such colonies (⁴³).

It was in order to make room for colonies that the freemen endeavored to enlarge the border land around their original settlements, as much as possible in every direction. It was thought very desirable that the state should have a wide border land. This was the object of many expeditions. Cæsar says of the Suevi, that they had extended their border land in one direction six hundred miles (⁴⁴). Upon such a tract of country a great many colonies might be planted, with dwelling-houses for the colonists, with arable lots, with clearings of meadow and pasture land, with the forest and waste, or mark-land, as it was called, spreading round about and in among them, as a boundary for each one and for all. *Conquered land reserved for tenant colonies.*

The freeman usually gave some name to his farmstead or colony, to distinguish it from others. Names ending in the syllables -*bach*, -*feld*, -*wald*, are very common in the early documents. They illustrate very well what Tacitus says of the Germans: *colunt discreti ac diversi ut fons ut campus ut nemus placuit.* The names given to farmsteads or colonies often refer to peculiarities of the soil or situation; its mountainous, hilly, rocky, flat, or swampy character. Sometimes they refer to certain kinds of trees growing in the neighborhood,— oaks, elms, lindens, pines; or to animals or birds, — wolves, bears, eagles, falcons (⁴⁵). The most interesting names, however, are the personal names. The freemen were very apt to name their farm- *Names given to the farmsteads and colonies.*

Personal names of places.

steads or colonies after themselves. Widerholt, for example, in one of the Fulda records, alienates his villa named Widerholtesleba, — *villam sui nominis Widerhollsleba.* In another record of the same collection, a certain man alienates a *villam sui nominis Rechendorf*. In one of the St. Gall records we have a *roncale, meo nuncupatum nomine* ([46]).

Local names of a personal or patronymic character abound in the records. They are probably more numerous than any other class; and they help to establish the fact, that in the earliest time individuals and families settled apart from one another, and not together in groups, — in isolated farmsteads, and not in villages.

<small>The isolated domain described.</small>

The holding of the freeman consisted, in the first place, of his homestead. Then there were houses of dependants, freedmen, or slaves. There were also outbuildings, — sheds for the animals, barns, and storehouses ([47]). Around all these buildings there was, usually, an enclosure, — a fence, hedge, ditch, rampart, or wall ([48]). Beyond this enclosure were the lots of arable land, — the *agri pro numero cultorum occupati*. Beyond and around the lots of arable land spread the open meadow and pasture. The mark of forest and waste land enclosed and surrounded the settlement ([49]).

<small>Absolute independence of the freeman on his domain.</small>

From an economic point of view, the freeman was completely independent. He had at his farmstead, and in the lands round about it, belonging to it, every means of living comfortably. From the wood of the forest he built his house, houses for his people, sheds for the animals, barns and storehouses. The wood of the forest served also for fuel. From the live-stock came meat, milk, and cheese. From the hides of the animals, warm clothing was made. There was pasture ground, upon which the animals grazed in summer, and grass land, which provided them with winter fodder. There was also land to plough, upon which the grain was planted. From this a supply of bread, and beer, which was brewed from barley or some other grain, was obtained. Out of flax or hemp, cloth was made by the women. Thus the freeman had at his farmstead, and round about it, every necessary means of subsistence. This independence of the house-father (*Selbstständigkeit des einzelnen Hausvaters*) in early German society, is a fact of great interest (⁵⁰).

It is often argued, that because there were no fixed limits, no boundaries, to individual holdings, the land must have been owned collectively or communistically. It is said that the statements of Cæsar go to prove the existence of community of land; *Feldgemeinschaft*, the Germans call it. The argument is inconclusive. The absence of fixed limits and boundaries proves simply that the land was undivided property; it does not prove that it was common property. From what Cæsar says it remains an open question whether the land was regarded as common property or not. Nor

No evidence of community of land from Cæsar.

18   EARLY HISTORY OF LAND-HOLDING

<small>No evidence of community of land from Tacitus.</small> do we gather anything from Tacitus in regard to the ownership of the land, — whether it was vested in the freemen collectively or distributively. We know from the statement *colunt discreti ac diversi*, that there was no association between the freemen in their stock farming and agriculture; no *wirthschaftlicher Verband*, as the Germans say. We know this, but we know nothing more. The question whether the ownership of the land was vested in the freemen collectively or distributively, remains to be settled by the testimony of the later records.

<small>No equality of holding in Cæsar's time.</small> It has been argued from the passage of Cæsar, *quum suas quisque opes cum potentissimis acquari videat* (⁵¹), that the holdings of land were all equal; and it has been argued, that this goes to prove the existence of community of land. It is not at all likely, however, that Cæsar meant to imply, by the words cited, that the holdings of the freemen were equal. If every man could appropriate as much land as he wanted, it could very well be said that there was an equality of rights in regard to the land. Cæsar can hardly have meant anything more than that. The existence of *potentissimi*, as distinguished from *humiliores* and *plebes*, points clearly to the existence of unequal holdings. If no man held more land than another, it is not likely, unless some men held a great deal more than they could use, that there would have been any *potentissimi*.

Then we must remember that equal holdings imply precise limits or boundaries; and Cæsar says that there were none, — *neque quisquam agri modum certum aut fines habet proprios:* so if he meant to say in one passage that the holdings of the freemen were all equal, he gives us to understand in another that they were not equal. He contradicts himself, and we may believe what we please.

According to the testimony of Tacitus the holdings of the freemen were unequal. He tells us that the freemen had slaves, who cultivated the land for them in the manner of Roman *coloni.* Then he tells us that the amount of land brought under cultivation at any time depended upon the number of cultivators. The amount of land which the freeman brought under cultivation depended, therefore, either upon the number of able-bodied persons in his family, or upon the number of his slaves, or both together. It was determined by the number of agricultural laborers he had in his household, or attached to it in houses of their own, near by or in distant colonies. The number was variable in every case. The holdings of the freemen were therefore unequal (52). _{No equality of holding in Tacitus's time.}

Let us suppose, however, for the sake of argument, that the holdings of the freemen were equal. Would that prove the existence of community of land among them, — collective or _{Community of land not to be inferred from equality of holdings.}

communistic ownership of it? Ten men go out with a net to catch fish, and catch some, and on their return divide them equally. Should we say that the fish were common property after they had been thus divided? Surely not. So in regard to land: when a body of men unite together and occupy, by appropriation or by conquest, a tract of land, and then divide it into equal shares, that is no evidence of collective ownership. This must be proved upon other grounds. Equality is found where there is collective ownership. It is also found where there is no collective ownership. In itself, therefore, equality is no evidence of collective ownership.

It was only for the sake of argument, however, that we allowed that the holdings of the freemen may have been equal. The statements of Cæsar and Tacitus, taken together, prove quite conclusively that no such equality existed. The concurrent testimony of the later records might be adduced if it were necessary.

The question as to the ownership of the land must be referred to later records. The question whether the ownership of the land was vested in the freemen collectively or distributively, still remains. There is nothing in the statements either of Cæsar or of Tacitus to enable us to answer it. We shall have to turn to the laws, formulæ, and documents of later times. From these we shall be able to reach a conclusion, without doubt.

In the law of the Bavarians ([53]), the holder

of a piece of land declares that he has witnesses to tell of the labor he has expended upon it; how his father left him in possession of it; how therefore it must be his. If, however, the claimant declared that this was not so, that the land belonged to him, there was no appeal except to the issue of battle. The litigants met and fought, and he who won the battle took the land. *The right of possession secured by force, among the Bavarians.*

So in the Saxon law (⁵⁴): when a man found his land occupied by another, he collected witnesses to say that the land was his. Nevertheless, if he who had possession of the land refused to accept this testimony, the matter was settled by battle, — *si occupator contradixerit campo dijudicetur*. *Among the Saxons.*

So also in the Ripuarian law (⁵⁵): if any one wished to fight for his inheritance, he first brought witnesses to say that it was his inheritance; then, unless the claimant withdrew, the matter was settled by a combat, before the king. — *cum armis suis se defensare studeat ante regem*. We find the same custom among the Alamanni, the Lombards, and other German peoples (⁵⁶). *Among the Franks.* *Among the Alamanni, Lombards, and other nations.*

If a man trespassed upon the land which a neighbor regarded as his, and persisted in doing so, and his neighbor persisted in resistance, they fought it out between themselves, and he who won took possession. There was no appeal except to the issue of battle. So when two or

This is true of families, as well as of individuals; of clans, as well as of families.

more groups of men, groups of kinsmen, co-heirs and neighbors, fell to quarrelling in regard to the extent of their respective possessions, they met in battle, or else, appointing representative champions, allowed the matter to be settled by a duel. This we know from a passage of the Alamannic law (⁵⁷).

When the Germans told Cæsar (⁵⁸) that they were afraid, if they settled anywhere permanently, the powerful would drive the weak from their possessions (*possessiones*), and so make great estates (*latos fines*) for themselves, they must have had this lawless condition of landholding in their minds.

Possession in the early time.

The word meaning *possession*, which occurs in mediæval records, *gewere*, is without doubt the same word as *gwerra* or *werra*, the French *guerre*, our *war;* which leads us to believe that a taking possession in early times amounted to a declaration of war against all possible claimants (⁵⁹). The word *seisin* in our modern law should be remembered in this connection. When a man brought suit for the recovery and possession of landed property he declared war, *gwerra* or *werra; invasionem fecit*, in the Latin (⁶⁰). The fact is recorded in certain quite early documents.

Seizures and conquests by individuals, families, and clans.

Landed possessions are constantly described as seizures or conquests, — *comprehensiones, proprisa, conquesta, capturae* (⁶¹). The phrase of the early formula, *ego et progenitores mei eam* [*villam*] *potes-*

tulive possedimus (⁶²), illustrates the same idea. The conclusion is, that the possession of land was, in the early time, secured by appropriation and maintained by force. Land, being appropriated or conquered by the nation, was subject to appropriation or conquest by the clans. The land appropriated or conquered by the clan was subject to appropriation or conquest by the family. The land appropriated by the family was subject to appropriation by the individual.

These conquests or appropriations were usually made in an orderly and peaceable manner. So long as there was plenty of land, it was not worth while to quarrel about it. The clans separated from one another, under their respective leaders, and each clan took a territory for itself. Then the families in each clan separated from one another, in the same way, and each family took a tract of land for itself. Within these family appropriations the individual established himself in the manner already described. He built a house wherever he pleased, and houses for his people. Arable lots were marked off for the cultivators. Some land was reserved for a hay crop, and some more was given over to the herds of animals, as pasture ground (⁶³). As long as there was plenty of land there was very little quarrelling about it.

There were no precise boundaries between the possessions of one free-lord and another. There was no need for any. The free-lords settled apart from one another, and there was more Absence of fixed boundaries.

than enough land for everybody, in the early time of which we are speaking.

Terms used to describe possessions of land.

Possessions of land are very commonly described as *occupationes, possessiones, conparata, elaborata, collaborata, exarta, stirpi, stirpationes, extirpationes, novalia, mastunga, runcales, cincludae, ambita, circuiti, circuitiones, septi, comprehensiones, proprisa, bifanga, conquesta, conquisitiones, capturae, concapta, dominationes* ([61]). The formula *praedia proprio labore meo libera manu acquisita* is not uncommon. We meet with the *villare meis propriis manibus acquisita*. The formula *carpere et possidere hereditatem* occurs ([65]).

The nature of the inheritance in primitive times.

In view of this we are not surprised to learn that the earliest idea in the word *erbe*, an inheritance, is of something worked out or elaborated. It is *arbi* in the Gothic; *erbi*, in the Old High German; and these words have the same root as *arbeit*, a piece of work ([66]). The inheritance, according to the primitive German idea, was something which a man acquired for himself, by his own labor.

The people spread over the country. They took possession of tracts of land, made clearings, built houses, and in that way established inheritances for themselves. They were no inheritances properly speaking, but as they came to be inheritances whenever settlements were permanent, they may be correctly enough described as inheritances ([67]).

In a document of the Chartularium Werthinense (^{68}), a certain man alienates his appropriation and inheritance, describing it by the words, *particulam haereditatis et proprii laboris mei; id est totam comprehensionem in sylva que dicitur Huissi.* <small>A case in illustration.</small>

It is not necessary to suppose that any divisions of land among descendants were thought of at first. They lived on in the father's or grandfather's house, and held their property in common. Grandsons and even great-grandsons often continued to dwell together in this way upon one inheritance, as a house community. <small>No division of inheritances in the early time.</small>

The time came after a while, however, in most cases, when the heirs were too numerous to live in one house together, as a house community. The pasture and grass lands were insufficient to maintain all the live-stock; or else the number of slaves or serfs had increased so much that lots (*hubae*) could not be found for them all. It was then necessary to migrate to a larger territory. The live-stock and slaves were divided, presumably in equal shares, and a new settlement was made. Each man appropriated in the new territory an inheritance for himself and his descendants. He made a clearing, and built a house for himself, houses for his people, and sheds for the animals. Arable lots were marked off for the cultivators, and the animals were turned out to pasture, as already described. We have many inheritances then instead of one. <small>How migrations were made, and new inheritances established.</small>

Multiplication of inheritances.

Sometimes the original settlement was permanent, and other settlements arose round about it, as offshoots from it. One heir remained in the original settlement. This was, perhaps, the eldest son, or the eldest male of the eldest line in the family. The other heirs went off with their movable property, their shares of live-stock and slaves, and established themselves here and there in the surrounding country. Thus out of one household others arose, from these still others, and the population spread away from the original settlement farther and farther. In this way individuals became families, families became clans, and clans became nations. The original appropriations and inheritances, instead of being divided and subdivided, were multiplied. It was only at a later time, when there was a lack of land, that inheritances were subdivided. In the early time they were multiplied, according to the increase of the population.

Ancient houses.

The original households, as the sources and centres of national life, were probably regarded with a certain veneration. The heads of these households were probably looked upon as representatives of the original stock of the nation,— the stock from which all its families and clans had been derived. They were consequently regarded as chiefs or kings of the clan or nation; and the heads of the other households were subordinate chiefs or kings, or noblemen, or simply freemen, according to the antiquity of their respective households. We have no evidence to offer in support of this theory, however.

At this time divisions of the land among descendants were very rare. Stock and slaves were divided, not the land. The people spread freely, taking their stock and slaves with them, and settling wherever they pleased. As soon, however, as the land became thickly populated everywhere, so that there was little or no room for new inheritances, the heirs in those already established were obliged to continue living together. It seldom happened, however, that the heirs could remain under one roof. New houses were built, in which the members of the family distributed themselves. Thus villages arose in the place of house communities. In the place of the *Einzelhof* we have a *Gehöferschaft* (⁶⁹). *The origin of clan villages.*

The Einzelhof becomes a Gehöferschaft.

When the time for cultivating the land arrived, arable lots were marked off for the slaves, as before, distributed among them, one apiece, ploughed up, and cultivated. The lots were no longer, however, embraced within one inheritance; they were distributed among several or many inheritances. Each householder in the village regarded the lots which were held by his slaves as his. As new lots were brought under cultivation (*per annos*), the householders in the village took, always, each one as many lots as he had slaves. If then the householder was

Arable lots assigned according to the number of cultivators.

The inheritance in the clan village. asked to describe his inheritance, he said, he owned a house which he occupied himself, and two or three, or more, other houses, occupied by dependants or slaves, a corresponding number of arable lots, and an indefinite amount of meadow, pasture, and forest land beyond.

How the undivided land was regarded. The meadow, pasture, and forest land, being subject to appropriation, was regarded as undivided property. It is so described in the early records (⁷⁰). If a householder in the village acquired so many slaves that he had no place for them in the village proper, he sent them out upon the undivided land. There they made a clearing, marked off arable lots, and built houses for themselves. The householder in the village counted these houses and arable lots with his other possessions, as part of his inheritance.

Enlargement of inheritances by appropriations of undivided land.

A case in illustration. In a Lower Rhine record of Lacomblet's Collection, Hembald the son of Heribald alienates an appropriation which he has made upon the common land of his kindred, — *in communione proximorum suorum,* — and he calls it a *comprehensio in propria hereditate.* Many similar examples might be adduced (⁷¹).

The shares in the undivided land are defined. As time went on, however, the question arose, how much of the undivided land (the *communio proximorum*) one man should have, — what was his rightful inheritance thereof. In answer to this question it was decided that, inasmuch as inheritances in the village, and of the arable land, were already defined, the inheritances of the undivided land ought to be determined accordingly. It was decided that every householder in the village should have as many shares of the undivided land as he had houses (*mansi*) in the village or outside of it, or arable lots (*hubae*); and if the land remained undivided, rights of enjoyment were to be proportioned to rights of property.

We read in the Burgundian law that forest, mountain, and pasture lands were to be enjoyed pro rata: *sylvarum, montium, et pascuorum, unicuique pro rata suppetit esse communionem.* At the same time they might be divided among the shareholders, if any one wished to have his share separated from other shares: *agri quoque communis, nullis terminis limitati, exaequationem inter consortes nullo tempore denegandam.* Then we read how the division, when it took place, was to be made with reference to the extent of land, or lots of land, held in severalty: *secundum terrarum modum vel possessionis suae ratam* ([72]).

Through the early time, live-stock and slaves alone were divided. The heirs spread freely over the land, with their respective shares of stock and slaves; but after a while it became necessary to divide the land also, and the rule of inheritance which governed the distribution of stock and slaves came to govern the distribution of land also. References to shares of land

Passages from the Burgundian law.

Inheritances of stock and slaves divided; inheritances of land multiplied, in the early time.

Afterwards the inheritances of land were divided also.

Divisions among brothers. received in divisions among brothers are very common in our early documents ([73]). We read in the early formulæ how brothers ought to divide their inheritance equally, and how they did so, — *ut inter se de res eorum dividere debuerunt, quod et ita et fecerunt.* We read how, in these divisions, each heir received his rightful portion, — *unicuique ex ipsis justi debita portionem terminetur* ([74]).

The rule of the Alamannic law is, that brothers must not alienate or otherwise scatter their inheritance until a just division has been made, — *ut fratres, post mortem patris eorum, hereditatem non dissipent, antequam dividant eam.* In the St. Gall records, containing alienations of Alamannic inheritances, we see that they consisted of land *Inheritances consist of land as well as movable property, at the time of the Folk-laws.* as well as movables ([75]). We find a similar rule of inheritance in the law of the Bavarians; and in the documents of the Historia Frisingensis we have descriptions of the inheritances which were divided, according to this rule ([76]). So in the other Folk-laws. The rule prescribing an equal division among sons and brothers obtained generally ([77]); and in the documents of various localities we see how the inheritances divided consisted, regularly, of land as well as movables. It became customary for brothers to divide the land of their inheritance soon after receiving it, and the portions which they received respectively passed to their respective descendants, to be divided and subdivided through the branches of the family and clan.

Still it often happened that an inheritance, or part of it, remained undivided for a generation or two; in certain cases, for many generations. We read in the Lombard law about property of different kinds (*de rebus seu de casis vel de terris*) not yet divided among the heirs (*inter fratres vel inter parentes*). Reference is also made to property which has been divided among grandsons (*quae divisae fuerint inter fratres seu nepotes*) (⁷⁸).

In a document of the Lower Rhine, we have a grant of hereditary land (*agrum hereditarii*) by a body of coheirs and kinsmen (*coheredes et conparticipes et consanguinei*). In another document of the same region we have a number of kinsmen described as coheirs and shareholders in an undivided inheritance (*coheredibus et conparticipibus in uno patrimonio*) (⁷⁹). In the year 855, a dispute arose between the Abbot of St. Gall and a group of heirs in regard to the right of ownership in certain lands. *Inter nos et Rihwinum et coheredes ejus [fratribus necnon ceteris coheredibus] fuit contentio.* The parties came to an agreement, and boundaries were fixed; and Rihwinus and his associates held their inheritances distinct from the property of St. Gall. *Rihwinus et coheredes ejus suas portiones per se habeant, excepto ut pascua communia in agris habeamus.* It is an interesting case (⁸⁰). In a document of Freising the members of the ducal family, the Agilofingi, joined together and alienated a tract of uncultivated and waste land, which was their undivided inheritance. They are described as *heredes, participes,* and *consortes* in it. The members of another family, the *genialogia* Fagana, did likewise (⁸¹). In a Westfalian document the shareholders in an undivided inheritance are described as *successores alodii.* In a document of the Middle Rhine they are called *alodiones* (⁸²).

<small>The heir could call for his share of the inheritance at any time.</small> The heir was always entitled, however, if he was of age, to call for a division of the inheritance. He could have his portion divided off and given to him at any time. This we know from the passage of the Burgundian law already cited,— *agri quoque communis, nullis terminis limitati, exaequationem inter consortes nullo tempore denegandam* (⁸³). Even a minor, provided his kinsmen had no objection, could have his portion of the common inheritance divided off and given to him. This we know from a passage of the Lombard law, beginning with the words, *si infans, dum intra aetatem est, res cum fratribus aut cum parentibus suis dividere voluerit* (⁸⁴).

<small>Divisions among co-heirs.</small> Such a division is described in the early formula as a *divisio vel exaequatio inter consortes de alode* (⁸⁵). We have a reference in a Middle Rhine document to such a division in the words, *quantumcunque mihi obvenit de genitore meo Pippino,*

quod contra allodiones meos recepi (⁸⁶). In the Codex S. Galli we meet with an *hereditatem, quam in Ludolteswilare in meam portionem a coheredibus accepi* (⁸⁷).

In the early time, whenever a division of the inheritance was called for, it was, probably, divided into equal shares, according to the number of heirs, one share being assigned to each of them. The division of the inheritance was *per capita*. But when the rule of equal division among sons had been generally adopted, it was naturally argued that a division in equal shares among grandsons or great-grandsons was not lawful, unless the sons and grandsons left the same number of heirs respectively and individually. The result was the institution of *per stirpes* divisions, instead of the *per capita* divisions. When an inheritance continued undivided for several generations, but came at last to be divided, the division was made according to descent and the law of inheritance prescribing equal division among sons. It was only when the knowledge of genealogical relationships was lost, or a subject of dispute, that the division was made *per capita*. The evidence of this lies in the Herold Text of the Lex Salica: *De alodis*, in the clause, *ubi inter nepotes ant pronepotes, post longum tempus, de alode terrae contentio suscitatur, non per stirpes sed per capita dividantur* (⁸⁸).

The distribution of an inheritance, whether

[margin:] Inheritances divided among the heirs *per capita*, at first;

afterwards *per stirpes*.

The passage *De alodis* of Lex Salica, according to the Herold Text.

Distributions per stirpes were often made by lot.

made *per capita* or *per stirpes*, was usually made by lot. It is sometimes assumed that a distribution *per stirpes*, according to descent and the law of inheritance prescribing equal division among sons, would not be a distribution by lot. The assumption is erroneous. The fact that there was a distribution by lot is no evidence to show that the distribution was not made *per stirpes*. Suppose A, the progenitor of a family, has five sons, B, C, D, E, F; and B has three sons, G, H, I; and G has four sons, J, K, L, M; and J has two sons, N, O. O's share of the family land would be, according to descent and the law of equal division among sons, one half of one fourth of one third of one fifth of the whole; that is, one one-hundred-and-twentieth of the whole (if we may assume that his brother and descendants of his uncles and great-uncles remain to take their shares). The division would be made by lot, in the following manner. The family land, all of it, or a section of it at a time, would be divided into five equal parts, which would be assigned, by lot, to the descendants of B, C, D, E, F, respectively. The descendants of B would divide their portion, thus received, into three equal parts, which would be assigned by lot to the descendants of G, H, I, respectively. The descendants of G would divide their land, one fifteenth of the family land, to be assigned by lot to the descendants of J, K, L, M, respectively.

Then the sons of J would divide their share, one sixtieth of the family land, into two parts, and take one apiece, by lot (⁸⁹).

Inheritances thus acquired were very properly described as lots, *sortes*. Already among the Latins the word *sors* had come to signify an inheritance, rather than an allotment simply. The reader will remember, perhaps, the definition of Festus: *sors patrimonium significat*. The word is constantly used in this sense in our early and mediæval records (⁹⁰).

Sors patrimonium significat.

The word *sors*, and the German word *alod*, signifying an inheritance, interchange meanings in the records. In the formula already cited, which dates before the end of the seventh century, we have the *divisio vel exaequatio inter consortes de alode*. The word *consortes* is regularly used for the word *coheredes*, the word *alodiones*, or the phrase *successores alodii*. In one of the St. Gall records a certain man alienates his inheritance (*hereditas*) with the exception of a certain part not yet divided between himself and the other heirs, — *quod cum consortibus meis adhuc in commune visu sum possidere*. Among the Burgundians, Visigoths, and Lombards, an inheritance of land was quite regularly described as a *sors*, or *terra sortis titulo acquisita* (⁹¹).

The *sors* and the *alod*.

In dividing an inheritance it was quite customary to divide the house lots and arable lots, the *mansi cum hubis*, and to leave the shares of the meadow, pasture, and forest undivided, to be held in common. We have then *prata communia* (⁹²), *pascua communia* (⁹³), and a *silva communis* (⁹⁴). Although the undivided land was thus described as common land, property rights in it were very exactly defined. He who owned an eighth part of the arable land of the village owned an eighth part of every other kind of land that there was, and he could have his eighth part divided off and assigned to him at any time; or, if he pleased, he could help himself to it. If he did this, however, he had to be very careful not to take any more than his rightful share. We know this from a passage of the Lex Ripuaria: *si quis consortem suum quantulumcunque superpriserit, cum quindecim solidis restituat* (⁹⁵).

Rights of enjoyment in the undivided and common lands, the *prata communia, pascua communia, silva communis,* were either unregulated, or else they were defined with reference to rights of property. They are described as *communes usus cum aliis, communia,* and *communiones* (⁹⁶).

So long as the right of enjoyment in the common land was unregulated, every man cut as much grass as he wanted for his animals, and wood for building or fuel, and he turned all the animals that he had into the village pasture. Such an unlimited enjoyment of the undivided land lasted, however, only so long as there was more than enough grass, wood, and pasture for everybody. We have seen how every man could have his share of the undivided land marked off and given to him at any time. When, therefore, disputes arose in regard to rights of enjoyment, the land was divided, or else the rights were defined. This was easily done. If there was grass land enough to produce eighty loads of hay, he who owned an eighth part of the land was allowed, he or his servants, to cut and carry off ten loads, and no more. In a document of Wirtemberg we meet with a *pratum carrorum quinque, quod cum consortibus meis adhuc in commune visa sum possidere* ([97]). If there was pasture land enough for one hundred and sixty animals, he who owned an eighth part of it was allowed to turn out twenty, — no more. In a Weissenburg record, for example, we meet with a pasture right for fifty hogs,— *pasturam ad* L *porcos*. In an early English record we have an LXX *porcis saginam in commone silvatica* ([98]). {Such rights were often defined, however, as time went on. Stinted meadows. Stinted pasture.}

The shares of the *silva communis*, being proportioned to shares of land held in severalty, could be determined at any time. He who owned an eighth part of the arable land owned an eighth part of the *silva communis*. Inheritances of arable land being divided and subdivided, inheritances of the *silva communis* were divided and subdivided also; and when inheritances of arable land came to be alienated, a *pro rata* share of the {The *silva communis* of the early records.}

silva communis went with every one. It is a great mistake, therefore, to speak of the *silva communis* of the early records as land owned collectively or communistically. The *silva communis* was simply undivided property, regularly an undivided inheritance. The ownership of it was not vested in the shareholders, the heirs, collectively, but distributively. This is evident, not only from the passages of the Burgundian law cited above, but from many passages in the documents. There is a good example in the Lauresham Codex, where we find an undivided share of the *silva communis* described in the following terms: *de illa silva communis quantum jure hereditario ad me pertinere videtur.* So in the Codex S. Galli, a certain man alienates *de communi silva, quantum ad portionem nostram pertinet.* In a Westfalian document we meet with a certain estate described as consisting of *mansos duos cum terris cultis et incultis, et silvis communibus ad eosdem mansos pertinentibus* ([99]). It is clear that the *silva communis* did not belong to the community. It belonged to the members of the community. They owned it in undivided shares; and these shares were hereditary and then alienable.

[marginal notes: It was owned distributively, not collectively, nor communistically. Cases in illustration. Alienation of shares in the silva communis, equivalents being unknown.]

Very often the land-owner did not know how much of the common forest belonged to him. It was not always easy to make the calculation. He knew, however, that a certain share was his, and at his disposal. In several of the Freising

AMONG THE GERMANS.

records we read how the shares of land held in common with those of other men could not be exactly estimated, nor particularly described, — *quod commune est cum aliis, numerum non possumus computare.* Nevertheless the shares were divisible by inheritance and alienable. One man alienates what he believes to be an ample share, — *de silva in commune cum aliis habundanter.* Another man alienates a *maximam partem de silva optima communem cum ceteris nobilibus viris* ([100]).

Holding in common and communistic holding must be carefully distinguished. They are very different things. We have plenty of holding in common described in the early records, but no communistic holding. Cases of this may, of course, be adduced from the later records; modern instances may be cited; but with these we are not at all concerned. No cases of communistic holding have as yet been adduced from records of the early period. *[Holding in common to be distinguished from communistic holding]*

Without doubt a great deal of undivided property was converted into common property during the middle ages. Rules and regulations had to be made in regard to rights of enjoyment in the undivided land. The rules and regulations were made in assemblies of the shareholders; and under this condition of things, when the claim of the individual was opposed to the interests of his associates, it was made null and void. The will of the best men in the assembly, or a *[How communistic holding was introduced in later times.]*

majority, was law. The rights of the individual shareholders were thus usurped by the shareholders as a body. The property of the individual became the property of the corporation. In the place of a voluntary association of landowners we have a land-owning corporation. The *universi* became a *universitas* ([101]). In this way collective, and even communistic, holding of land came into existence. Cases are rare, however, before the twelfth century. They are common only after the thirteenth.

The universi became a universitas.

These cases from the later centuries have been adduced, and modern instances have been cited ([102]), as evidence to support a theory of primitive communism; according to which, private property has been derived from the disentanglement of individual from collective rights; the rights of the family from those of the clan; the rights of the individual from those of the family. We hold a theory which is quite the reverse of this. We believe that private property existed first; that common property came into existence afterwards, in consequence of an entanglement of individual rights and gradual annihilation of them: and this theory is, we believe, supported by the concurrent testimony of the early records. From these it is evident that the principle of individual property was dominant everywhere. Those who hold to the theory of primitive communism cannot have read these

The theory of primitive communism.

The theory of individual property to be preferred.

records with sufficient care, if, indeed, they have read them at all.

Even the roads and ways, in which every man walked, were regarded rather as undivided than as common property, in the early time. The ownership therein was distributed among neighboring land-owners. It was transmitted by inheritance, and divided and subdivided. Then when inheritances came to be alienated, undivided shares in the roads and ways were alienated also. In one of the Lauresham records, two brothers alienate all their property, except a piece of newly cleared land (*stirpo*) and a road (*via*). When these brothers died, this road must have passed to their descendants as an undivided inheritance. In describing his property, the landowner very often mentioned the roads and ways of which he was part owner,—*viis et inviis, exitibus et reditibus* ([103]).

Ownership of the roads and ways.

At the time when the undivided land was subject to *ad libitum* appropriation, when the heirs in an undivided inheritance made *comprehensiones in communio proximorum*, they sometimes appropriated pieces of land out of the public roads or by-ways. We read, in the Burgundian law, that the possession or ownership of the roads in which wagons and carts were wont to pass could be lost or acquired by occupation during two years ([104]).

Appropriation of the roads and ways.

This condition of things did not, however,

How the roads and ways became the property of the community.

endure long. The appropriation of the public ways by individuals was an annoyance to everybody, and the question was raised whether it should be allowed or not; and in answer to this question it was decided, that he who appropriated the roadways and closed them up should withdraw at once and take away his enclosures. Fines were imposed as a penalty for the offence. If the land appropriated lay upon the highway, the fine was heavy. If it lay upon neighborhood roads, the fine was light (¹⁰⁵). Thus the ownership of the roads and ways was taken away from individuals, and vested in the various communities of which they were members.

Rights to water, — aquis aquarumve decursibus.

What has been said in regard to public roads and ways is true also of water, whether still or in running streams. Rights to water were not distributed by the community to its members, but passed with the land from father to sons, — *per stirpes et jure hereditario*. They were alienated with the land. With every inheritance or acquisition of land came a *pro rata* right of enjoyment *in aquis aquarumve decursibus*. The phrase occurs regularly in descriptions of property.

When there was plenty of water, the right of enjoyment was unregulated; but in certain cases, especially where the water was needed for irrigation, the supply must have been limited. An agreement was probably made in such cases, according to which the associate owners of the water took the flow of it during certain periods of time, determined by their respective rights of property. This is a practice not unknown in our own time ([106]).

We read in the Burgundian law ([107]), that the ownership of a running stream could be acquired by an exclusive enjoyment during two years, so that the previous owner would have no further right in it. *(Ownership of a running stream acquired by prescription.)*

A well was owned either in severalty or in common. *(Wells.)* When it was owned in severalty and was polluted, he who had polluted it had to pay a fine to the proprietor, besides clearing the well and making it clean and pure as before. When the well was owned in common (*si autem plurimorum in vicinia putens fuerit*) and it was polluted, he who polluted it had to make it clean and pure again, and pay the fine; and this fine was divided among the owners of the well, each one receiving his share (*compositionem inter se mutentur*). The well was owned in common, but not communistically. The ownership was vested distributively, not collectively ([108]). We have searched in vain through the early records for a reference to water rights being held by the community to be distributed among the members in usufruct. If a pond of water, a stream, or a well was not owned in severalty, it was owned in undivided shares, which were regarded as private property, and were hereditary and alienable.

Many indivisible things were held in this way, in shares. Dwelling-houses were constantly held in shares, and the shares were alienable. In one of the Lauresham records, for example, we have alienated a third part of a house: *tertia parte de illa curticella, quicquid nostra portio ibidem habere videamur.* Many other examples might be adduced ([109]).

Houses owned in shares.

The same thing is true of mills: they could not be divided without being destroyed, so they were owned in shares, which were transmissible and divisible by inheritance, and alienable. In one of the Salem records we meet with a *communitas vel patrimonium in molendino.* It is very interesting to observe here how the words *communitas* and *patrimonium* interchange meanings ([110]).

Mills owned in shares.

The communitas vel patrimonium.

So it was with churches, as soon as churches were built. They could not be divided among the descendants of the founder, so they were held in undivided shares, — *per stirpes et jure hereditario,* — and the shares were alienable. In one of the Fulda records half of a church is alienated, — *dimidiam partem ecclesiae quae mihi ibidem in hereditatem convenit.* In a document of Freising the coheirs in a certain church fell to quarrelling in regard to their several rights of property, — *coheredes contentionem inter se pro ipsam ecclesiam habuerunt.* In the Capitulary of Worms, of the year 829, we have a passage entitled, *De ecclesiis inter coheredes divisis* ([111]).

Churches owned in shares.

When two or more persons inherited a slave, they did not always sell him and divide the proceeds. They often kept him and held him in undivided shares, the shares being transmitted to descendants and alienable, as long as he lived. The owners had his services during periods of time proportionate with their several rights of property, or else they shared the proceeds of his labor ([112]). A slave owned in shares.

The right to hunt in the undivided and common forest was an hereditary right. It was divisible by inheritance, and alienable in fractions. We read in the Breves Notitiæ Salsburgenses that Madelhelm, a certain nobleman, alienated his portion of the hunting at Albina, which he held in common with his kinsmen and coheirs,— *portio venationis communis cum cohaeredibus* ([113]). The right to fish, the *piscatio* or *piscatura*, was hereditary in the same way, and alienable in fractions. In a Lauresham record, for example, we have an undivided share of the fishing in Edingero marca given to the church of St. Nazarius,— *portio nostra de piscatura* ([114]). Rights to hunt and fish were through the early period unregulated. Everybody hunted and fished *ad libitum*. But as the hunters and fishermen increased in numbers, and game or fish became scarce, quarrels arose, and it became necessary to define every man's right, or else to limit the season of hunting and fishing. Various rules were adopted by which conflicting rights were reconciled. We remember a case in Hunting.

Fishing.

How rights to hunt and fish were defined.

which a certain man was permitted to fish at a certain place for two weeks at Christmas (115). It might have been four weeks at Easter. In this way the right of the individual could be defined and limited, and inequalities maintained.

The family or clan defined.

The German family and the clan which grew out of it was not, properly speaking, a land-owning corporation. It was simply a group of heirs, with a partly divided, partly undivided inheritance in the land and the things on the land (116).

The family or clan village is commonly described as a *villa;* but this word is used to describe the isolated farmstead and the colony of serfs as well. The family or clan village is described specifically by the word *genealogia*. A man was said to live in a certain *genealogia*, — *in vico et genealogia ubi rivolus ille intrat in illum flumen,* for example (117).

The vicus et genealogia.

Looking over the modern map of England, we find many hundred names of places containing the syllable *ing*, — Basing in Hants, Cocking in Sussex, Dorking in Surrey, Gilling in Yorkshire, Reading in Berks, for examples. Most of these places must have been, in early times, family or clan villages; for the syllable *ing* in the early English language is patronymical, and signifies the son of, the descendant of, the issue of, the stock of. Thus the name Elfingas refers us to the sons or descendants of Elf, and the name

Evidences of the existence of family and clan villages in England.

Totingas refers us to the sons or descendants of Tot, whoever he was. A village was called Elfingas because the Elfings, the descendants of Elf, lived in it. It was called Totingas because the Totings, the descendants of Tot, lived in it. A great many such local names have been collected out of the early charters (¹¹⁸). Many of these family or clan villages are further described as *hams*, i. e. homes, or *tuns*, i. e. enclosed farmsteads, afterwards villages, then towns, — Buckingham in Bucks, for example, and Abington in Cambridgeshire. Buckingham was probably, in its origin, the home of the descendants of Buck, and Abington must have been the enclosed farmstead, then the village, then the town of the progeny of Ab. In regard to single examples it is easy to fall into error; but in general the argument is sound. We have mentioned, in the laws of Ethelbert, a man's *ham*. If his name was Aes, and he left sons, they would be described as Aesingas, and their residence would be Aesingham. In the same laws we have mentioned a man's *tun* (¹¹⁹). If the man's name was Aes, again, his sons would be Aesingas, and their place of residence would be Aesingtun or Aesington. The names of first proprietors were in this way perpetuated. We have first the isolated farmstead, and then the family or clan village growing out of it.

Many vestiges of these early settlements — first

Patronymical names of places.

The hams and tuns, isolated farmsteads at first, then clan villages.

Similar evidence for the existence of clan villages upon the Continent.

isolated farmsteads, then family or clan villages — may be found in Continental records and on Continental maps. Long lists of the names of places containing the patronymical syllable *ing*, or *inga*, have been collected from these sources ([120]).

A good deal of surprise has been expressed that the same patronymical name should be found in different places; as if, so it has been argued, branches of the same family were established in different places. It should be remembered, however, that the names to which the patronymical syllable is affixed are personal names, — names like John, James, and Henry; they are not family names: so we have no more right to argue that the Bassings of Bassingbourn, Bassingfield, Bassingham, Bassingthorpe, Bassington, were one family scattered in various localities, than we have to argue that the sons of men named John are all related to one another as a large and widely scattered family ([121]).

The so-called vicini right.

Among the Franks, from the time of the Lex Salica until the end of the sixth century, if a man died without sons, his land passed to his neighbors. The fact may be inferred from a passage of the edict of Chilperic, which dates between the years 573 and 575. According to this edict, the right of inheritance in land was conceded, — 1st, to sons (*sicut et Lex Salica habet*); 2d, to daughters; 3d, to brothers; 4th, to sisters; to the express exclusion of the neighbors, *vicini* (¹²²). That is to say, when there were no other heirs at law, the neighbors (*vicini*) took the inheritance.

The question arises, how did they take it, — collectively, as a body corporate, or distributively, as an assemblage of heirs. It is usually assumed that they took the land collectively. The assumption is an arbitrary one, and it is erroneous. The evidence goes to show that the *vicini* received the land as a body of heirs, that is distributively. They had it to divide among themselves. They took it and divided it, and each man received a share, which he added to his other property. When it was not divided at once, it was still divisible, when any one called for a division. The law regarding common land in which it is said to be divisible at any time among the shareholders has been already cited, but must be cited again in this connection: *Agri quoque communis nullis terminis limitati exaequationem inter consortes nullo tempore denegandum.* Nor must we forget the formula in which a division of this kind is described, the *divisio vel exaequatio inter consortes de alode ;* and how every man received his share, — *unicuique ex ipsis debita portionem terminetur* (¹²³). We have reference, in several passages of the Visigothic law, to the divisions of land which took place among the *vicini.* They are described as permanent divisions. No subsequent redistributions were thought of; — *quod a parentibus vel vicinis divisum est pos-*

teritas immutare non tenet. References to divisions of land among kinsmen and neighbors are common in the documents (¹²⁴). From such evidence we know that when a man died without heirs at law, and his property passed to his neighbors, they received it distributively, as a group of heirs. It was an inheritance to be divided among them, at once, or at some time or other, whenever a division was called for.

<small>The *De Migrantibus* of Lex Salica considered.</small>
Now we must consider the famous passage, *De Migrantibus,* of the Lex Salica (¹²⁵); which is quite conclusive evidence, in itself, to show that the *vicini* owned their lands distributively, as a group of proprietors, and not collectively, as a body corporate. We read, that if any one desired to settle in a village upon any man's land there (*super alterum*), he might do so, provided nobody objected.

<small>A curious feature of the law.</small>
The owner of the land upon which the *migrans* proposed to settle was of course likely to object, and if he did the *migrans* had to go away. But we read that if any one or another resident in the villa objected to the settlement of the *migrans,* he had to go away. The inquiry naturally suggests itself: Why should any one stand in the way of the *migrans,* except the owner of the land which he proposed to appropriate?

<small>The explanation.</small>
Referring to the principle of inheritance, already described, we find the explanation of this anomaly. If a man died, his land went to his

sons. If he had no sons, it passed to the neighbors. That is the reason why the neighbors had a right to prevent the entrance of the *migrans* into the village, even when he did not propose to settle on their lands. They objected to the settlement of the *migrans*, although it was *super alterum*, because they were potential proprietors of *alter's* land. The objection was admitted to be valid.

But the question arises, Why should one of the *vicini* (*unus vel aliqui*) have the right to prevent the settlement of the *migrans*? We read in the law that, though only one man objected, the *migrans* had to go away. We read that, if nobody (*nullus*) objected, he might remain. The explanation is, that every resident in the villa would, if the owner of the land which the *migrans* proposed to occupy died without sons, come in for a share of that land. The land would be divisible among all the *vicini*, and each one would come in for a share of it. The village landholder was not only proprietor of the lands in his possession, but potential proprietor of all other lands, and in virtue of this potential proprietorship he could control the action of the community in regard to the admission of strangers into the village. In this matter it was not the community which controlled the individual, it was the individual who controlled the community. Far from being evidence of community of land the passage *De*

[margin: Another curious feature of the law.]

[margin: Explanation.]

Migrantibus, in the Lex Salica, is very good evidence to show that the principle of individual property was pushed to the very last point.

<small>The principle of individual property pushed to the last point.</small>

An inquiry here suggests itself,—In what way did the neighbors (*vicini*) come into the right of succession which we have been describing? The question is easily answered. We have already learned how, when a territory was first occupied, the people did not settle in towns, nor even in villages, but in isolated farmsteads. When the first settlers died, their sons succeeded to their places, and, after the sons, the sons' sons and their descendants. New houses were built round the original farmsteads, and we have, instead of these farmsteads, clan villages (*vici vel genealogiae*); associations of heirs with partly divided, partly undivided inheritances of the land. The inhabitants of the clan village were kinsmen, descendants and heirs of the founder of the village. It was natural, therefore, that when any villager died without sons his land should pass to the other villagers. They were the surviving descendants and heirs. At any rate they found themselves in possession of the land, and nobody had any better title to it. It was an inheritance for them,—an undivided inheritance. There was no other description for undivided land. In the early time, as we have seen, the individual was at liberty to appropriate as much of the undivided inheritance as he pleased, provided he did not, in so doing,

<small>Origin of the *vicini* right.</small>

<small>The *vicini* were the surviving representatives and heirs of the founder of the village.</small>

<small>The undivided inheritance of the *vicini*.</small>

<small>It was subject to appropriation at first.</small>

trespass upon land already appropriated. The inheritance of the villager who died without sons was, at first, subject to appropriation by the other villagers. After a while, however, as we have also already seen, the question arose, how much of the undivided land could one man appropriate, and the rule was then adopted that the shares of meadow, forest, and pasture land should be in proportion to severalties of arable land already established. After that, when a man died without sons, his arable land was regularly divided among his neighbors, and with every share of this was associated a *pro rata* share of his other lands, meadow, pasture, and forest, — a *pro rata* share which the owner could have separated from the shares of his neighbors and assigned to him whenever he pleased. It was often, however, left in common (¹²⁶). *Systematic divisions introduced afterwards.*

The primitive rule of inheritance prescribed an equal division among sons; or, if there were no sons, a division among kinsmen and neighbors, without discrimination. Other rules of inheritance appear to have been derived from this one, by a substitution of kinsmen to the exclusion of neighbors, as such, and by a discrimination of different degrees of proximity; so that the inheritance passed to the nearest kinsmen to the exclusion of those who were more distant. In the law of the Angli and Werini, for example. the inheritance of the sons, the inheritance which *The rule of equal division among neighbors if there were no sons.* *Exclusion of the neighbors, as such.* *Adoption of the rule that the inheritance must go to the nearest kinsmen, to the exclusion of others.*

the sons would have received, had there been any sons, passed to the male relatives on the father's side, in the order of their proximity: *ad proximum paternae generationis consanguinium perlineal .... usque ad quintam generationem paterna generatio succedat* ([127]). As among the Angli and Werini, so among the Lombards the neighbors succeeded only when they were also kinsmen, and they succeeded by classes, *per gradum et parentelam* ([128]). Though we may not know precisely what is meant by this phrase, it indicates, of course, a classification of collateral heirs. When a man died without sons, the neighbors, as such, had no longer any right of inheritance from him. Only those persons who were kinsmen had this right; and these kinsmen no longer took the inheritance one and all indiscriminately. They were distributed in classes, and took the inheritance in order, one class after another, according to proximity. If there were no representatives of the first class, the inheritance passed to the second; if there were no representatives of the second, it passed to the third; and so on.

In this connection it is interesting to note the fact, that, when a proprietor in the clan village proposed to alienate his land to an outsider, he was obliged, until the right of alienation was established by general consent, to obtain the approval, not only of his sons, who were his direct heirs, but that of his kinsmen and neighbors also, who were only potential heirs, so to speak. In one of the Freising documents a certain man named Wolfer comes to alienate his homestead and lands, with a crowd of his relatives, *cum proximorum turma*. In another document the *proximi et vicini* appear. In another, the *conmar[cani] et coheredes*. In one of the records of the monastery of Scheftlar the grantor is asked, in the presence of all the kinsmen, *coram omnibus coheredibus; si aliquis eorum contradicere voluisset*. As no one objected, the grant was made, — *parentibus enim pari devotione consentientibus*. Other examples might be adduced (¹²⁹). It is often argued that, inasmuch as alienations required, in this way, the consent of the neighbors and kinsmen, there must have been community of land among them. This does not follow. The neighbors and kinsmen were heirs; that is the reason why their consent was required. They were not in any sense owners of the land alienated, when they were asked to give their consent to the alienation. They were only potential owners. It was as potential owners, not as joint owners, that they were referred to.

After the right of alienation had been established by general consent, or by law, it was customary to warn all heirs, kinsmen, and neighbors, that no claims on their part would be valid. This appears plainly in the following formula: *sive filii ex nobis nascantur aut non, supra dicta res in illa villa*

<small>Examples in illustration of this.</small>

<small>The custom is no evidence for community of land.</small>

<small>The consent of kinsmen was required, because they were potential owners of the land.</small>

<small>Establishment of the right of alienation. The claims of kinsmen and neighbors annihilated.</small>

et in omni marchia illius, absque contradictione ullius proximorum aut vicinorum meorum diebus vitae suae possideat. This is only one among many cases ([139]). The claims of heirs were no longer considered.

Qualification of preceding remarks. It must here be observed, however, that the objection to an alienation of land, in the early times, was not so much an objection to the alienation of the land, as it was to the admission of strangers into the clan villages, as proprietors. In most cases there must have been land enough for everybody; so a possible inheritance from a neighbor and kinsman would not receive very much consideration. The admission of a stranger, however, into the family or the clan was a serious matter, and objection would

Another explanation of the vicini right. be made in many cases. After all, it is upon this ground, more than upon any other, that the *vicini* right rests. If any man objected to the entrance of a stranger, as proprietor, into the family or clan of which he was a member, the stranger

Strangers admitted to the clan villages as dependants or slaves, not as proprietors. had to go away. If no one objected, he might come in. As a rule strangers were admitted into the family or clan as dependants, or slaves, not as proprietors.

No element of communism in the German clan system. The German clan system, to return to our main argument, was in no respect based upon community of land. We do not propose to enter here into any personal controversy with the advocates of a primitive communism. It will be worth while, however, to enumerate certain facts for the consideration of open-minded students. *Theses against the theory of a primitive communism.* Some of these facts have been already described; but it will be well to set them out together in order and array.

There is no evidence of community of land in the statements of Cæsar. We mean by community of land collective or communistic ownership of it, as distinguished from private or individual ownership ([131]). *Community of land not to be inferred from the statements of Cæsar;*

There is no evidence of community of land in the statements of Tacitus ([132]). *nor from the statements of Tacitus.*

As soon as the migrations were over, individual property existed everywhere. This fact is established beyond question by passages of the early laws, formulæ, and documents. There is no trace of community of land, i. e. collective or communistic ownership of it, discoverable in these records ([133]). Property was often held in common. Holding in common, however, is one thing, and communistic holding is another. Community of land is not to be inferred from a holding in common. *Individual property existed everywhere after the wanderings. Community of land nowhere discoverable. Holding in common no evidence of communism.*

Had the ownership of the land been vested in communities rather than in individuals, we should find some direct reference to the fact in our records. We should find laws and regulations regarding the use of common lands. The records abound in references to the rights of individuals in land held in common; but the rights of the community therein are nowhere

The land of the community was the land of its individual members. referred to. The conclusion is, that the community had no rights. The community did not exist as a land-owning corporation. The land of the community was the land of its individual members (¹³¹).

Disputes regarding land settled by battle. Disputes in regard to the possession and ownership of land were commonly settled by battle between the litigants, not by the community of which they were members, — which would certainly have been the case had the ownership of the land been vested in the community rather than in the members (¹³⁵).

When fighting for land was given up, disputes in regard to rights of property were referred neither to local assemblies nor to local magistrates, *Afterwards they were settled by the chief or king, or his agent.* but to the chief or king, or an agent of the chief or king. One of the earliest of our Frankish formulæ is entitled, *De relatione directa inter regem et pagenses.* When neighbors fell to quarrelling in regard to their respective rights of property, and could not agree, the chief or king sent his agent, or *missus*, to settle the matter, — to divide the property and to give each man his rightful share (*debita portio*). This we know from the formula entitled, *De divisione ubi rege accederit missus.* When fighting for land had been given up, disputes in regard to it were settled by the chief or king, or an agent of the chief or king (¹³⁶).

The land to be divided is described in the formula just cited by the word *alod*, which reminds us of the fact, that the land was everywhere held, from the time of the Folk-laws on, according to descent and laws of inheritance. The laws of inheritance may be read, and it can be seen, by reference to formulæ and documents, that they governed the distribution of land, as well as of movable property ([137]).

Land everywhere held, according to laws of inheritance.

In so far as neighbors were kinsmen, descendants of a common progenitor, the ownership of the land, whether divided or undivided, would, according to the law of inheritance, be vested distributively, and not collectively ([138]).

The ownership of land was, therefore, distributed among individuals.

Undivided lands were undivided inheritances. This follows, — 1st, from the existence of the laws of inheritance; 2d, from the fact that the individual was allowed to appropriate his share of the undivided land, or could have his share divided off and assigned to him at any time; 3d, from the fact that shares in the undivided land were regularly proportioned to inheritances held in severalty; the lands held in severalty being divided by inheritance, the shares in the undivided land were divided also; 4th, from the fact that, when severalty lands were alienated, *pro rata* shares of the undivided land were alienated with them; 5th, from the fact that shares of the undivided land are repeatedly described as inheritances ([139]).

This is true of undivided, as well as of divided land.

Now we must bring forth a fact which we have not yet considered, — the fact that any

How the individual could withdraw from his kinsmen with his inheritance.

man could, if he pleased, separate himself from his kinsmen and neighbors, and his inheritance from their inheritances, so that they had no longer any right of inheritance from him nor he any from them. This fact is contained in the passage of the Lex Salica, *De eum qui se de parentilla*

The bearing of this fact in regard to the vicini right.

tollere vult ([140]). It is a great argument of the advocates of a primitive communism, that, if a man had no sons, his inheritance passed to the kinsmen and neighbors, — " back to the community," we are told, " from which it was originally received." Inasmuch, however, as it lay in the power of the individual to cut off his neighbors and kinsmen from this right of succession, the argument is worthless.

The vicini right is no evidence for community of land.

The mere fact that when a man died without sons his land passed to his neighbors and kinsmen, is no argument, in any case, to prove the existence of community of land; because it remains an open question whether the land was received by the kinsmen and neighbors collectively or distributively. If they received it distributively, so that any one of them could, whenever he pleased, have his portion given to him as a permanent severalty (for himself and his descendants), community of land is out of the question. That the neighbors and kinsmen received the land distributively, in this way, has been established conclusively by testimony of the records ([141]).

In view of all this, the student will certainly

hesitate before he accepts the theory of a primitive communism; unless he prefers authority to facts.

The chief error of the advocates of a primitive communism is, that they argue community of land wherever they find undivided land, or land held in undivided shares. The argument is surely inconclusive. The *silva communis* of the early records, for example, which was simply undivided property, subject to appropriation or division among the owners, at any time, has been regularly described as their common property. It was not their common property, it was simply their undivided property. Given a case of undivided land, the following questions should be asked. Is it subject to appropriation or division? If not, is it a joint possession held in undivided shares? If so, how is the shareholding governed? Are the shares regarded as private property? Are they transmissible by inheritance? Are they divisible? Are they alienable? Perhaps the holding is communistic. If so, why? Are there any redistributions of the same land among the same persons, or their representatives? Upon what principle are the redistributions made? Are they made *per stirpes*, according to descent and the law of inheritance? If so, the ownership would not be communistic. Are the redistributions made according to rights of property vested in individuals? If so, the ownership would not

The advocates of a primitive communism have described undivided land as common land.

Questions to be asked in regard to a case of undivided land.

be communistic. Are the redistributions made according to the judgment of the community, or that of magistrates representing the community? In that case only would the ownership of the property be correctly described as communistic. The advocates of the communism theory are, therefore, bound to adduce from the early records cases in which the same land is subject to redistribution among the same persons, or their representatives, according to the judgment of the community, or of magistrates representing the community, irrespective of any claim or claims on the part of individuals. Can the advocates of a primitive communism do this? We think not. They will find a great many cases of undivided property, of property held in undivided shares, in the early records. They will hardly find a single case of communistic property.

What the advocates of a primitive communism have to show.

Suppose, however, they were to find, here or there, a few cases; would that be a sufficient basis for the theory, that the holding of land among the early Germans was generally communistic? Surely not. The conclusion would be, that, although the principle of individual property in land was generally recognized, communistic holding was not altogether unknown. The cases of communism would be exceptions to the general rule. They would be explained as the result of peculiar conditions or circumstances.

Suppose a few cases of communism are adduced.

No general conclusion could be drawn from them.

The first reason why the advocates of the communism theory are in error is, that they have regularly mistaken undivided property for common property, holding in common for communistic holding. Another reason is, that they have ignored the distinction between proprietorship and tenancy. Finding cases of communistic tenancy, they have brought them forward to prove the existence of communistic proprietorship; forgetting all the time, that with every case of tenancy there is a case of proprietorship concomitant with it, embracing it. When the case of tenancy is adduced to prove the existence of a primitive communism, it remains for those who do not believe in such communism to adduce the case of proprietorship under which the case of tenancy is included, to prove the existence of private property.

The advocates of a primitive communism have ignored the distinction between proprietorship and tenancy.

How they lay themselves open to attack, in citing a case of communistic tenancy.

It will be well to illustrate this with an example. The following passage occurs in the records: — *In hac silva nullus nostrum privatum habebat aliquid, communiter pertinebat ad omnes villae nostrae incolas.* This passage (¹⁴²) has been cited very frequently to show that forest land belonged originally to the community, that the individual members had only a usufruct.

Case in illustration.

It should be observed, in the first place, that the document dates from the year 1173, so that it is too late to prove anything in regard to the condition of things in primitive times. Then it should be noted, that the land-holders are tenants under landlordship. They are *nostri incolae in villa nostra*. They are not the owners of the land. The owner of the land is outside of the community. There exists a proprietorship or landlordship outside of the community, embracing it. The passage is therefore no evidence for a primitive communism, because it proves primitive landlordship as well. It is an open question whether we have in the communistic tenancy of land in the villa, or in the landlordship over it, the earlier form of landed property. Is it an open question? Hardly; for in the natural course of events landlordship or proprietorship antedates all forms of tenancy existing under it ([143]).

Is the tenancy, or the landlordship over it, the earlier form of landed property?

The landlordship, presumably.

The communism theory reversed by the chronology of the evidence.

It may be urged against the advocates of the communism theory, that the theory is reversed by the chronology of the evidence. It is said, that private property has arisen from the disentanglement of individual from collective rights; but the evidence adduced to prove the existence of collective rights is, all of it (the statements of Cæsar not being regarded as such evidence), very much later in date than that which is adduced to prove the early existence of private property. It will be found upon examination, that the theory of individual property rests upon testimony dating from the time of Tacitus. Then it will be found that the theory of communism rests entirely upon records of later mediæval and modern times. The advocates of the communism theory have adduced, we believe, no unquestionable cases of communism of earlier date than the twelfth or thirteenth century. We are warranted, therefore, in concluding that the advocates of the communism theory have disregarded the chronology of the evidence. This being considered, the conclusion must be, not that there was communism before there was individual property, but that there was individual property before there was communism (¹⁴⁴).

According to the chronology of the evidence, there was individual property before there was any communism.

Lastly, it may be urged against the advocates of the communism theory that they have put too much faith in the accuracy and judgment of certain eminent writers. A professes to have established certain facts; B, pleased with them, has accepted them, upon A's authority. C has accepted them upon the authority of A and B. D has accepted them upon the authority of A, B, and C; and so on. The result is a consensus of opinion based upon the judgment of one man,— an opinion of questionable value in many cases. What we want in science is a consensus of opinion based upon the results of independent investigations. This will not be disputed.

The advocates of the communism theory have deferred too much to authority.

We have answered the arguments of the advocates of a primitive communism, so far as this was possible without entering into any direct personal controversy. It will be well now to state once more the conclusion to which we have ourselves been led. We conclude, that the German clan system was based upon kinship, upon the principle of individual property, and upon the principle of inheritance. All lands held in severalty, even for a very short time, were regarded as inheritances, and all undivided lands were undivided inheritances, to be appropriated or divided among the heirs at any time. The clans were associations of heirs with partly divided, partly undivided inheritances of the land and the property placed upon it.

[margin: A brief statement of the conclusion to which we have been led.]

Now, having described the clan system of the Germans; having shown how it was based upon kinship, the principle of individual property, and the principle of inheritance; having shown that it was in no respect based upon community of property or communism; we may go on to describe the causes which led to the breaking up of the system, — to a dispersion of those groups of heirs with partly divided, partly undivided inheritances, which have been described.

The causes were, — 1st. The admission of daughters to the right of inheritance in clan land, when there were no sons; daughters who might marry men of alien clans. 2d. The custom of adopting strangers into rights of property and inheritance in the clan land. 3d. The custom of alienating clan land to strangers by gift or by sale. And 4th. The custom of admitting strangers to a pre-

[margin: Causes which led to the breaking up of the clan system.]

scriptive title in clan land. There were, without doubt, other causes which might be mentioned; but these were the principal causes, and we will confine our attention to them.

The German woman was not obliged, like a daughter of Zelophehad, to marry within the tribe of her father (¹⁴⁵); so, when she received an inheritance of the land, she often took this inheritance from the inheritance of her father's tribe and put it into the inheritance of the tribe of her husband. In other words, inheritances were removed from one tribe, or clan, to another. The inheritances of different clans became intermixed, and the clansmen with them. German women not obliged to marry within the father's clan.

Among the Angli and Werini, the right of inheritance was conceded to daughters only when there were no males left in the clan. The clan consisted of the male descendants of five successive generations. When no male was left within this limit, the clan was, properly speaking, extinct. The clan land might then go to the women if there were any, and with them into the clans wherein they were received as wives (¹⁴⁶). The admission of women to rights of inheritance in land, among the Angli and Werini. When there were no males left in the clan, the women took the land.

Among the Franks we have, instead of the descendants of five successive generations, simply the kinsmen and neighbors. The kinsmen and neighbors were not classified as they were among the Angli and Werini; so when a man died without sons, his inheritance passed to all How was it among the Franks, when there were no vicini?

of them, instead of to classes of them ([147]). Here we have probably a primitive condition of things. We do not know, however, whether, when there were no kinsmen, no neighbors, the women of the clan took the clan land or not. The law does not contemplate such a contingency. For some time, probably, there was no thought of women holding land; but we read in the Lex Salica: *De terra vero nulla in muliere hereditas;* so also in the Lex Ripuaria: *Femina in hereditatem aviaticam non succedat* ([148]); and it is evident, from the existence of such laws, that the question whether women should be allowed to hold land or not was coming under consideration. We see in some of the early formulæ that there was, in certain quarters, a sentiment and opinion opposed to the doctrine of the law. The exclusion of women from the right of inheriting land is described in one of these early formulæ as an impious custom: *Diuturna sed impia inter nos consuetudo tenetur, ut de terra paterna sorores cum fratribus portionem non habeant.* This is the reading of the Paris MSS. In the Vatican MS. a direct reference is made to the Lex Salica by the words *secundum Legem Salicam* ([149]). It was proposed that daughters should succeed to equal shares with their brothers. This was the radical as opposed to the conservative view. The result was a compromise. Daughters were allowed to take the inheritance when there were no sons, no brothers. This rule was adopted among the Salian Franks toward the end of the sixth century (¹⁵⁰). It was adopted at an early period by the Alamanni, the Bavarians, the Saxons, and the English (¹⁵¹). It was adopted afterwards by other nations.

As soon as women were admitted to inheritances of the land, to the exclusion of collateral kinsmen and neighbors, strangers came into the family or clan villages, as husbands of the female proprietors. They were the progenitors of new families, new clans, in the villages. *Result of this rule.*

Adoptions were not uncommon among the Germans. It appears, however, that the person adopted did not come under the authority of the person adopting. He did not become his son, did not take his name, did not perpetuate his family. The person adopted received gifts, goods or land, from the person adopting, and was expected, consequently, to behave like a faithful son and follower. That is all there was in the Teutonic adoption. The words *filius* and *heres* were usually employed in the procedure, and appear in descriptions of it, but they had no real significance, and were, probably, borrowed from the Roman law, thoughtlessly. The person adopted was little more than a receiver of gifts, — *equos, enses, clypeos, arma, terris, domibus*, etc., — who was consequently under a certain moral obligation towards the giver (¹⁵²). *Adoptions among the Germans.*

The person adopted was simply a receiver of gifts, obliged to the giver.

The passage De affatomie of the Lex Salica.

We have an elaborate account of the procedure of adoption in the Lex Salica, *De affatomie.* The clansman went into the assembly, and, throwing a rod into the lap of the person adopted, called him his heir, *heredem;* and then proceeded to describe what, as heir, he was to receive, — *de fortuna sua dicat verbum quantum voluerit, aut totam fortunam suam, cui voluerit dare.* The person adopted then proceeded to take possession of what had been given to him, in the presence of witnesses. *Ipse in cujus laisum fistucam jactavit in casa ipsius manere debet, et hospites tres suscipere debet, et de facultate sua de quantum ei datur in potestatem suam habere debet.* The fact of his having been adopted, of his having received a grant of property, of his having taken possession of this property, is afterwards proved by the testimony of the witnesses ([153]).

The adfatimi of the Lex Ripuaria.

According to the Lex Ripuaria, a person could be adopted into a right of property either by a *traditio testibus adhibitis,* as in the Lex Salica, or by means of a written document duly authenticated, — *per scripturarum seriem.* As in the Lex Salica, the act of adoption is described by the term *adfatimi,* — *cuicunque libet de proximis vel extraneis adoptare in hereditatem vel adfatimi* ([154]).

Was the *adfatimus* procedure employed to alienate land?

The question arises, Was the *adfatimus* procedure of the Lex Salica employed to alienate land? The question is readily answered by reference to an early formula, where we have an alienation described by the term *affatimum*, and the property alienated is supposed to consist of land besides other things, — *terris, domibus, et cetera* (¹⁵⁵). *Evidence to show that it was so employed.*

It has been argued that the *adfatimus* procedure of the Lex Salica was not employed for the alienation of land. It is said, in the first place, that the essential part of the procedure took place in-doors (*in casa*), where the movable possessions would be concentrated; that it was these movable possessions that were alienated, not the land, which would lie outside the house. *Argument upon the words in casa.*
The argument is invalid, because the house would naturally stand in the midst of the land, and would be as good a place as any other for the alienation of it. Unless the procedure of alienation took place here, there, and everywhere, the house (*casa*) would be the most convenient place for it. A complete refutation of the argument, however, is found in the formula where the alienation of *res illas vel villas illas* is made *per portas et per ostia de ipsas villas, vel de illas casas dominicatas*. There is another case equally conclusive in the Historia Frisingensis: *Ratoll, viriliter circumcinctus gladio suo, stabat in medio triclinio domûs suae, tradiditque quidquid ibidem habuit, et in alio loco, et in tertio loco, quicquid habuit, praeter unam colonicam* (¹⁵⁶). *The argument refuted.*

Another argument used to prove that the *adfatimus* procedure of the Lex Salica was not employed for the alienation of land is, that the *The word furtuna.*

word *fortuna*, which is used to describe the property alienated, would not be used to describe landed property. The argument is worth no consideration. The word *fortuna* is constantly used, even by the classical writers, usually in the plural, but sometimes in the singular, to signify what fortune gives, — possessions, property, wealth, riches of all kinds: so there is no reason why it should not have been used in this way by the writer of the *De affatomie*. It is surprising, however, to find a word correctly used by him. He is a very bad writer. It should be observed that the word *facultas* occurs in the passage in the place of the word *fortuna*. This word *facultas* is very frequently used in our records to describe landed property. In one of the Merovingian diplomata, for example, we read about the *facultatem vel villas illas de alode, cum terris, etc.* (¹⁵⁷). Landed property is frequently described by the word *pecunia*, and even by the word *numen*, in the records (¹⁵⁸). But it is wasting time to refute, in this elaborate way, the arguments against the *adfatimus* procedure being employed for the alienation of land. The arguments are quite without force. The procedure was used for the alienation of land, without doubt.

The evidence goes to show that the persons adopted by the *De affatomie* procedure were, as a rule, near kinsmen, as we should have sup-

The word facultas.

posed *a priori* (¹⁵⁹). Strangers were very rarely adopted into a right of property in clan land in the early time. Cases occurred, however. This we know from the Lex Ripuaria, from the words *de proximis vel extraneis adoptare;* also from the formula entitled *Si quis extraneo homine in loco filiorum adoptaverit.* It may be inferred, perhaps, from the words *hominem qui ei non pertineat,* in the *De affatomie* (¹⁶⁰). Of course, whenever strangers were adopted into rights of property in family or clan land, they came into the family or clan villages, and were the founders of new families, new clans, therein. In this way the villages came to have a heterogeneous population.

{Strangers rarely adopted at first.}

{The result of the adoption of strangers into rights of property in clan land.}

In some branches of the German race the right to alienate land was, without doubt, exercised in prehistoric time. The Franks alienated their lands in the time of Lex Salica, as we have seen. The right of alienation is described in a Frankish formula as a *lex et consuetudo longinqua* (¹⁶¹). We read in documents of the eighth century that the laws and customs of the Franks permitted a man to do what he pleased with his property: *Leges et jura sinunt et convenientia Francorum est, ut de facultatibus suis quisque quod facere voluerit liberam habeat potestatem.* In a document of the year 855 a certain man named Folker alienates his inheritance, consisting of houses, lands, and slaves: *coram testibus et nobilium virorum praesentia, secundum Legem Ripuariam et Salicam* (¹⁶²).

{Early alienations of land.}

{Right of alienation accorded by Lex Salica.}

Limitations to the right of alienation. Certain limitations were usually attached to the right of alienation, either by custom or by law; such, for example, as that which we find in the Lex Saxonum, where a man may alienate *A man must not disinherit his children.* his land provided he does not, in so doing, disinherit his children. A similar rule obtained among the Lombards: *nulli licet sine certa culpa filium suum exheredare, nec quod ei debetur per legem alii thingare* ([163]). Alienations of inheritances required, therefore, in many cases, the consent of the heirs. Their consent is often referred to in *He must not disinherit any of his heirs.* the documents ([164]). In some cases the consent of all the heirs, collateral as well as descendant, had to be obtained before an alienation could be made ([165]).

He must not alienate all of his land. A limitation imposed upon the right of alienation among the Burgundians was that a man could not alienate all of his land. He must reserve some of it for his descendants ([166]). Another limitation, which obtained among the Burgundians, and among the Bavarians also, was *After dividing the land with his sons, he might alienate his share.* that a man could not give away his land until he had shared it equally with his sons. After dividing the land equally with his sons, he could do what he pleased with his share ([167]). Although *The claim of heirs must be respected.* the principle of individual property was very fully recognized, the claims of heirs were admitted to be valid.

Another limitation to the right of alienation, the last of which we need here to speak, was imposed in many places during the middle ages. This was that a man should, before selling his land to a stranger, offer it to his neighbors (¹⁶⁸). A man was free to sell his land if he pleased, but he must offer it to his neighbors before offering it to any stranger. Properly speaking, this was no limitation to the right of alienation. The neighbors claimed a prior right of purchase, and this right was conceded to them. This is a better way of stating the case. Strangers being admitted to the family and clan villages, as grantees or purchasers of land, were founders of new families, new clans, therein. The villages lost their original character in this way. They might be described as *vici*. They could no longer be described as *genealogiæ*. {A prior right of purchase conceded to neighbors. The clan system broken up by these alienations.}

There was another mode by which a stranger gained access to land and an inheritance in the clan village; that was by undisputed occupation or prescription. {Prescription among the Germans.}

A prescriptive title to land was admitted among the Franks at the time of Lex Salica. If a stranger, *migrans*, settled on a piece of land in the clan village (*super alterum*), and no objection was made, either by the owner of the land or any of his neighbors (*unus vel alicui de ipsis qui in villa consistunt*), during the period of twelve months, the stranger acquired a right of property and inheritance in the land he had appropriated, and became a regular inhabitant of {A prescriptive title admitted by Lex Salica.}

the village, — *securus sicut et alii vicini* (^{169}). It will be remembered how, among the early Latins, the ownership of land was acquired by possession during two years instead of one (^{170}). It was agreed among the Burgundians that the right of property in land lying in byways, as distinguished from the highways, might be acquired by two years' occupation (^{171}). We may infer from this, perhaps, that the right of property in other lands could be acquired in a year, or less than a year.

A prescriptive title in the Lex Burgundionum.

Very soon after this we meet with the *præscriptio triginta annorum* of the Roman law. We find it among the Burgundians at the time of their permanent settlement in Gaul; also among the Visigoths. *Saepe proprium jus alterius longinqua possessio in jus transmittit alterius. Nam quod* XXX. *quisque annis expletis absque temporis interruptione possidet, nequaquam ulterius . . . . amittere potest* (^{172}).

The præscriptio triginta annorum among the Burgundians and Visigoths.

A prescriptive title was admitted among the Lombards in the time of King Rothar. We read, in his edict, that after five years the holder of a piece of land is not obliged to fight for it; provided he brings witnesses to say that he has had possession of the land during that time. In Grimoald's law, which comes after that of Rothar, we read that if any one possesses his house, slaves, and land, — *casam, familiam, vel terras,* — during thirty years, and the fact is generally known, he need not fight in order to maintain possession of them, — *ad pugnam non perveniat* (¹⁷³). It is interesting to observe here how the German custom of battle and the Roman prescription come in contact with one another.

Among the Germans generally, in the early period, the right of possession was in no way strengthened by the lapse of time. If the right was questioned, no matter when, it was referred to the issue of battle (¹⁷⁴). *No prescriptive title admitted among the Germans generally.*

As a rule, the stranger was admitted to a right of property in clan land only by a grant from the clansmen who were the owners of the land. A grant of this kind being made, the grantee took possession of the land and was permitted to enjoy it undisturbedly. His title was based upon the grant he had received, rather than upon any term of possession. *Strangers acquired titles by grant rather than by prescription.*

Whether the stranger acquired the right of property in clan land by grant of the clansmen or by prescription, he became, in virtue of this right of property, a member of the village. When he died his descendants were members of the village too, in virtue of the rights of property which they inherited severally. So we have a new family, a new clan, introduced into the village. Others were introduced in the same way. The village was no longer, after that, the home of one family, of one clan, descendants and heirs of an original proprietor. It was the home of several clans. It was no longer a group of *The result of admitting strangers to rights of property in clan lands.*

heirs with a partly divided, partly undivided inheritance. It was simply a group of proprietors with severalties of the land, or undivided shares thereof (¹⁷⁵).

The clan village becomes simply a group of proprietors.

Now having considered the clan system of the Germans, and the institution of the clan village, the *vicus et genealogia*, we will go on to consider the institution of free colonies. We have already spoken of the colonies of dependants and slaves, which existed in the earliest time; we have now to describe the origin, in a later period, of colonies of free proprietors.

The institution of free colonies.

People who have learned to live together in villages, who are accustomed to daily association with their fellows, do not, as a rule, care to give up this association in order to settle in isolated farmsteads. This was the case with the men who came out from the clan villages we have been describing, to seek new homes. As the population of these villages increased, and individual inheritances became small, the people went forth to seek new inheritances in the outside world. They did not, however, as a rule, settle in isolated farmsteads, each man by himself with his family, his dependants, slaves, and cattle, — like their ancestors in more primitive times. A life in villages was generally preferred. The colonists were mostly poor men, who had no means of cultivating extensive domains. They were usually satisfied with thirty acres of arable land, and a

Village life preferred to the life in isolated farmsteads.

The colonists mostly poor men.

moderate amount of meadow, pasture, and forest. The colonists had only a few slaves and a limited amount of stock, as a rule. Those persons who had many slaves, and large flocks and herds, continued to establish themselves in the old way, in isolated farmsteads. We are not speaking of this class of persons here, but of a poorer class, — the class of emigrants who were driven out of the clan villages by the pressure of the population, and the lack of land. These men looked about and found others to join them; and they went forth in companies, ten, fifteen, twenty, or more, together. When they had found a place where there was sufficient good land for them, they built houses in a row or cluster together, and then proceeded to divide the land among themselves. One man had no more right than another, of course, in the land which all had united to appropriate. The colonists had equal rights in the land. It was accordingly divided into equal shares, one for each man. In some cases, when the colonists brought slaves with them, shares of the land were assigned according to the number of householders, so that he who had five housed slaves, *servi cassati*, in the village received, in addition to one share of the land for himself, five other shares for his slaves. Thus he received six shares. Some of the proprietors may have received more, some not so many ([176]). We will suppose, however, that the

The rich men still settled in isolated farmsteads.

The emigrants from the clan villages united in companies.

Institution of free villages, — associations of proprietors.

They take equal shares of the land.

Not always, however.

colonists had no *cassati*, that the lands of the colony were divided into equal shares, one for each proprietor. In this way we may legitimately simplify our argument.

<small>The division was made in the same way as in the colonies of serfs.</small> If the land was level and nearly equally good in every part, which often happened in valleys between the hills, and in generally flat country, each man took one long, narrow strip of the land stretching from one side of the village territory to the other, or radiating away from the village in one direction or another. <small>Why strips of land were preferred to squares.</small> Strips of land were preferred to squares, because it was more convenient to plough a few long furrows than many short ones. The ploughs of the period were heavy and awkward, and not easily turned. Then again, if the lots assigned to the different proprietors had been equilateral in form, it would have been difficult to place them all at an equal and convenient distance from the village. When the lots consisted of long strips of land, they could be disposed so as to radiate from the village, and every proprietor had some of his land near the village, and the rest at a distance ([177]). <small>Division of the land by sections.</small> If the land was diversified and unequally fertile in different parts, however, such land as was fit for tillage was divided into spaces or sections, and the colonists took equal shares in every section. Or else <small>Acre lots.</small> they marked off upon the ground certain acre strips, one for each man, and repeated this process until as much arable land was marked off as was

needed. These modes of division had been previously adopted in the colonies of dependants and slaves (the colonies of serfs), as we have seen. Indeed, the system of colonization which we are describing originated in the first place among the serfs who were distributed in village communities upon the domains of the ancient free lords. Then when clan villages arose and the freemen went out of these villages to found colonies for themselves, the colonies of dependants and slaves served them as models for imitation ([178]).

The colony of serfs the model for the free colony.

In the earliest time, the portions of land which were marked off for distribution among the proprietors of the colony were probably distributed by appropriation. There is a tradition in England, and in certain parts of Germany also, that in early times, when a piece of land had been marked off into equal portions according to the number of shareholders, each man appropriated his portion. When the portions were of equal value, this was done without difficulty. There was no ground for preference, no cause for dispute. When the portions were of unequal value, however, disputes were inevitable. According to the tradition, the strong man of the crowd took the portion he preferred, and if any one else wanted that portion, he had to fight for it ([179]). Although this is merely a tradition, it agrees perfectly with all that we know regarding the hold-

The land being divided into equal shares, the shares were distributed among the shareholders.

Distributions by appropriation.

ing of land in the early times. We have already cited many passages of the records to show that primitive property was simply possession maintained, when necessary, by force (¹⁸⁰).

Distributions by lot. In order to prevent the disputes and the fighting which we have described, the distributions were often made by lot. In this way every proprietor had a chance of getting some of the best lands. It often happened, however, that disputes arose after the distribution by lot had been made. It was urged by those who had received the poorer lands, that the best lands ought not to be held by the same persons all the time. A redistribution was called for after a while; and, unless the holders of the best lands were able to resist the importunity of their neighbors, a redistribution was made. This was a precedent for others; and redistributions came to be made, every year, or from time to time in the course of years. They have been regarded as evidence of community of land. It is said that the land was owned by the community, that it was distributed by the community among its members, for temporary occupation, by lot. This was not the case. The land was owned in equal shares by proprietors. At the same time the land could not be divided into equal shares. The result was a redistribution of the shares every year, or from time to time in the course of years. By these redistributions,

Redistributions.

Community of land not to be inferred from redistributions by lot.

the claims of the different proprietors were reconciled and satisfied (¹⁸¹).

Another expedient suggested itself, which served the same purpose. The different lots of land were taken in rotation. This custom has also been regarded as evidence of communism,— erroneously. It was only an expedient to prevent disputes and fighting. The object was to reconcile rights to equal shares with shares which could not be equalized. The only way in which this object could be accomplished, satisfactorily, was by a rotation system; according to which the holders of the rights took the shares in turn. Far from being evidence of communism, it shows how completely the principle of individual property was established. Every proprietor had a certain right of property. Then, where the rights of the different proprietors came into conflict, they were so adjusted that no single right was at all diminished, but each one was preserved in its integrity (¹⁸²). The fields which were held in rotation or redistributed by lot were regarded as individual property. They have been very correctly described as "shifting severalties" and "movable fee-simples" (¹⁸³).

The rotation system.

The system explained.

Communism not to be inferred from the rotation system.

The arable land of the colony being divided, the question arose whether the grass land should be divided also, or held in common. Every man could, in the early time, have his share of the grass land divided off and assigned to him, if he pleased; but the colonists usually preferred to hold the land in common.

The grass land of the free colony.

When the grass was in a condition to be cut, the villagers, or their servants, went out and cut, each man as much as he wanted, unless the amount of the grass was limited. In that case each man took off a certain number of loads, one, two, three, or more ([184]). When the grass was better in some places than in others, the land was cut up into sections, and a portion of each section was assigned to each proprietor. The portions of the sections were usually assigned by lot. Such a division was not necessarily permanent. In many cases there were redistributions. We have then what have been described as "lot meadows." Before the grass was cut, the proprietors met together and there was a drawing of lots, by which means the portions of land in the different sections of the meadow were assigned to different persons ([185]).

Stinted meadows.

Lot meadows.

Common enclosures.

When the grass land was enclosed, the enclosure was built by the proprietors in equal shares, each man being responsible for the portion put up by him. The arable land was enclosed in the same way, unless the proprietors enclosed their portions severally ([186]). As soon as the crop either of grass or grain had been removed, the enclosures were usually thrown down, and the animals came in upon the close-cut turf or stubble, from the common pasture ([187]).

Most of what has been said of the grass land may be said also of the pasture and forest lands. Every proprietor could, in the early time at least, have his share divided off and assigned to him; but it was quite customary to leave the lands undivided, to be held in common. When there was plenty of pasture, every man turned out as many animals as he had; but when the pasture was limited in extent, and there was not quite enough of it for all the animals in the village, the number which each man might turn out was limited. He could turn out five, ten, or twenty, a number determined by his right of property in the pasture. When the rights were all equal, every man turned out the same number (¹⁸⁸). *The pasture and forest usually held in common. Stinted pastures.*

The enjoyment of the undivided forest was usually unregulated. Every man cut what wood he wanted, and had hunting and fishing *ad libitum* (¹⁸⁹). *The common forest.*

It is important, in this connection, to note the fact that in the clan villages, as well as in the colonies which were derived from them, the meadow, forest, and pasture lands were frequently divided into severalties, which, though they were severalties, were nevertheless held in common, from the fact of being unenclosed. Boundaries were fixed by corner stones, or marked trees; but they did not prevent, and were not intended to prevent, trespassing. Men and animals ranged freely over lands so divided; except over grass lands during the time before the grass was cut,—*in tempore*, or *ad tempus*, as they used to say (¹⁹⁰). Even in the time of Lex *Severalties often held in common, by being unenclosed.*

Grass lands divided into severalties in the time of Lex Salica.

Salica, the grass lands were often divided into severalties. This may be inferred from the passage, *si quis prato alieno seoaverit opera sua perdat* ([191]). Boundaries are often mentioned in connection with the grass lands in the documents.

Severalties of pasture land held in common.

In regard to the pasture land: when it was marked off into severalty holdings, it seldom happened that these holdings were enclosed so as to include the animals belonging to the proprietors. The extent of each man's land was considered, and its productive capacity estimated. He was then said to own a pasture for twenty, thirty, forty, more or not so many animals, of one sort or another; and he turned this number of animals out upon the open pasture. There they grazed at large over the land of their owner, and over the lands of other proprietors as well ([192]).

In regard to the forest land: when it was divided into severalties, limits were fixed by marks upon the trees. Then no man was allowed to cut live wood except within the limits of his own

Severalties of forest land in the time of Lex Salica.

land ([193]). Even in the time of Lex Salica, the forest land was often divided into severalties in this way. The *silva aliena* is mentioned in the passage *De furtis diversis*. The later laws and records abound in references to forest severalties. The references to undivided and common forests are, indeed, comparatively rare ([194]).

It is evident, from the frequent reference in the records to severalties of meadow, forest, and pasture land, that the formula *cum pratis, pascuis, silvis,* etc., which is regularly appended to descriptions of landed property, must refer to property held in severalty, as well as to property held in common. It is often assumed that this formula refers to lands belonging to the different communities, — lands in which individuals had merely rights of enjoyment. The assumption is perfectly arbitrary, and it is erroneous ([105]). In the first place, there is no evidence to show that any lands were owned by the communities in this way, and, in the second place, there is no evidence to show that individuals held rights in land from the communities, in the early time of which we are speaking. There is evidence, on the contrary, and plenty of evidence, to show that meadow, pasture, and forest lands were quite commonly held in severalties, as private property; that, when this was not the case, they were held as undivided property, to be divided or appropriated as occasion arose; or else in undivided shares proportioned to the number of house lots or arable lots, or to the extent of arable lands, held in severalty. As to rights of enjoyment upon unenclosed lands, they were either unregulated, or else they were determined with reference to rights of property vested in individuals ([106]).

Rights of enjoyment, both limited and unlimited, were sometimes alienated. In other cases they were acquired by prescription. Unless,

The so-called Allmend formula.

No lands owned by communities.

No rights in land acquired from communities, in the early time.

however, a right of property in the land was conveyed or acquired at the same time, upon which the right of enjoyment could rest, the right took the form of an easement or profit *in alieno solo*, — what is known as a "right of common," in the English law. As the proprietorship of the land was vested in the members of the community, and not in the community as a body (the evidence of this has been given), all easements and profits *à prendre* were acquired by grant of one or more of the land-owners, or else by prescription. It was only in later times — when rights of property belonging to individuals were usurped by the community, when rights of the *universi* were gathered into a right of the *universitas* — that rights of enjoyment in common lands could be acquired from the community ([197]). The community had no rights to grant, in the early time of which we are speaking; and the rights which it afterwards acquired were derived from individuals, — by concessions on their part, or by usurpations on the part of majorities. The origin of corporate rights is of comparatively recent date.

Rights of common.

This is perhaps a digression, however. We were describing the colonies which were derived from the clan villages; in which the ownership of the land was distributed in equal shares. This equality existed only for a short time. The first proprietors in the colonies died, and the

Equality of property in the free colonies prevented by the operation of the law of inheritance.

shares which they had severally owned passed to their descendants, to be divided and subdivided among them ([198]). *The original shares had to be divided.*

The original shares were usually preserved, however, as integral divisions of the village territory. They were very seldom confounded with one another ([199]). An inheritance in the village consisted regularly of one of the original shares, or a fraction of a share; or if an inheritance was increased by gift, or by purchase, or otherwise, it might consist of several of the original shares, or fractions of them. The number of proprietors in the village increased and diminished; but the original shares remained. They served as bonds to bind the proprietors into a number of groups, all the owners of a single share being classed together as co-proprietors therein. The proprietors of the village were thus distributed in little land companies, so to speak ([200]). Within these companies the rights of individuals were sometimes seriously invaded and confounded, and certain elements of communism introduced themselves here and there into the life of the village. They were in no case, however, so far as we know, a primitive feature. *The original shares preserved as integral divisions of the village territory. The heirs in each share were co-proprietors. How certain elements of communism introduced themselves into the village life, after a time.*

There was a very important difference between the original clan villages and the colonies of freemen which went out from them. The clan village was in all cases founded by an individual. It was a group of descendants and heirs upon *Difference between the clan villages and the free colonies.*

a partly divided, partly undivided domain. The village was essentially genealogical in its character. The colonies which were derived from the clan villages were not founded by individuals, but by groups of individuals; and they were not necessarily related to one another as kinsmen. The structure of these colonies was therefore not genealogical. Instead of having one group of heirs in the village, we have several or many groups, descendants of the associate founders of the village. The village was the home of several families, several clans.

Dionysius says of the Romans, under Servius Tullius, that they were distributed in φυλαὶ γενικαί and φυλαὶ τοπικαί, — genealogical and topical tribes ([201]). We might describe the German clan villages as genealogical tribes, to distinguish them from the colonies, in which the members were associated rather as neighbors than as kinsmen. In the clan villages the bond of union was blood, i. e. descent from a common progenitor. In the colonies, the bond of union was neighborhood. The colonists were associated topically, rather than genealogically.

There was another difference between the clan villages and the colonies. When the members of the clan villages went out to found colonies, they were very often joined by men of alien extraction. The inhabitants of the colonies were derived from many nations. They

[margin: φυλαὶ γενικαί and φυλαὶ τοπικαί.]

were a more or less mixed population. In the clan villages the descent from the progenitor of the nation was clear and unquestionable. The pure blood of the nation was to be found in the clan villages, rather than in the colonies. The members of the clan villages gained, from this fact, more or less prominence and influence.

The population of the colonies was more or less mixed.

There was another reason why the genealogical or clan villages gained a predominance over the colonies. In the clan village we have the increase of one family only. The inhabitants of the colony, however, represented the increase of several or many families, — the families of the original colonists. The colonies were apt, therefore, to be more populous than the clan villages. Property was distributed among a larger number of persons. The colonies were inhabited by a poorer class of people. The rich men of the nation would be looked for in the clan villages, rather than in the colonies sent out from them.

Another reason for the predominance of the clan villages.

The population in the colonies was a poor population, as a rule.

The state consisted, then, of many villages, centralized by the presence of certain chief villages, — the genealogical villages, in which the noble or dominant families resided (²⁰²).

The state of the early Germans.

The undivided forest or waste land which lay between the villages which we have been describing was, throughout the early period, subject to appropriation by the freemen of the nation. Colonies of slaves or serfs were set out upon this land. The villages of freemen were

Colonies of slaves and serfs.

usually surrounded by such colonies. The inheritance in the clan village was seldom very extensive. In the free colony it was often very limited. A few slaves attached to the household — *servi dominici* or *mancipia in domo* — were usually able to cultivate all the land. It often happened, however, especially in the early time, that there was unoccupied forest or waste land beyond the territory of the clan village or free colony. Upon such lands the clansmen and free colonists set out communities of slaves or serfs, — communities of tenants, as distinguished from the communities of proprietors. The freemen in the clan villages and other free villages were thus able to enlarge their inheritances. The slaves who were sent out into the tenant colonies are described as *mancipia in villis manentibus*, to distinguish them from the *mancipia in domo*, above referred to ([203]).

The free villages surrounded by villages of serfs.

Very often several freemen joined together to set out a tenant colony. In such cases, each one took shares in the colony, — *mansi*, *cum campis, pratis, pascuis, silvis*, etc., — according to the number of tenants he contributed to it. House lots and arable lots being occupied according to the number of tenants, one house lot with one arable lot being assigned to each one, he who sent out ten tenants had ten house lots with ten arable lots, while he who sent out five tenants had five house lots with five arable lots;

The serf village sometimes founded by several freemen.

and so on. The arable lots were cut out of the undivided meadow and pasture land, which was held by the cultivators in equal shares, by the lords according to their respective rights of property, determined in the manner described. He who owned ten house lots (*mansi*), or ten arable lots (*hubae*), owned also ten shares in all the other lands,—meadows, pastures, forests (*pratis, pascuis, silvis*). He who owned only five house lots or arable lots owned only five shares in the other lands (²⁰⁴).

The clan villages and free colonies were distinguished from the colonies of dependants and slaves—the tenant colonies—very much as the early Greek and Latin towns were distinguished from the communities of agricultural laborers which were established round about them. The free-lords in the free villages correspond, in many respects, with the γέροντες of the Greek town, the *patres* of the Latin town. In some of the free villages, where conditions and circumstances permitted a natural growth and development, there arose a civic life not at all unlike that of early Greece and Italy (²⁰⁵). In most cases, however, it was prevented. In the course of wars and conquests, most of the free villages were converted into villages of tenants, or ordinary agricultural communities. In many cases the distinction between these originally free villages and the villages of serfs was lost. Who can say, for

<small>Free villages and serf villages.

Tendency towards a civic life.

The tendency checked in most cases.

The distinction between the free villages and serf villages lost during the Middle Ages.</small>

instance, whether the *Gehöferschaften* along the Saar and the Mosel were, in their origin, free villages or dependent villages ([206])?

Origin of tenures in perpetuity.
It was customary, even in very early times, for the allodial lords to make grants of more or less extensive farms to dependants and slaves, — to them and to their descendants, upon condition of a regular annual payment of certain dues. In one of our earliest formulae, we have described the grant of land to a slave or dependant (*servo suo, gasindo suo*), — to him and to his descendants in perpetuity, upon condition, except when the *jus proprietarium* was conceded, of a regular payment of rent, from the increase of stock or from the produce of the fields, — *sub redditus terrae vel pascuario aut agrario* ([207]). It was, of course, merely a tenancy at will which a serf enjoyed. It was, however, a permanent and hereditary tenancy by custom. As long as

Tenants not evicted so long as they paid the customary dues or services.
the lord and his successors got their dues from the land, the tenants were rarely evicted. A law was passed in the reign of William the Conqueror to prevent evictions, — *nec licet dominis removere colonos a terris dummodo debita servicia persolvant* ([208]).

House communities of tenants.
The first tenant died. His sons and grandsons took the land and cultivated it, and paid the rent to the landlord or landlords, for there might be several landlords, heirs of the grantor of the tenure, or assignees. House communities fre-

quently arose, — associations of tenants living together in one house and holding the land in common, heirs with an undivided inheritance. Such communities existed in many parts of France and Germany during the Middle Ages ([209]).

When a family had so increased in numbers that it could not be contained in one house, new houses were built and the members of the family distributed themselves. The land was then divided among the heads of the different households, and each one received a share, — an inheritance for himself and his descendants. Then we have a clan village of tenants in place of a house community. We have examples of such villages upon the so-called *vavassoriae* in Normandy ([210]).

Clan villages of tenants.

These clan villages of tenants resemble very closely those of the ancient allodial proprietors, which have been described. The divisions and distributions of land were made upon a similar principle, and a good deal of land was held in undivided shares; but the clan villages of tenants must not be confounded with the clan villages of proprietors. In an investigation into the history of land-holding, it is of the utmost importance to keep tenancy and proprietorship clearly distinguished from one another. Though they be cast in the same mould, they are very different things. In regard to every holding of land the question should be asked: Is it a case

Clan villages of tenants not to be confounded with the clan villages of proprietors.

Tenancy to be carefully distinguished from proprietorship.

of proprietorship, or is it a case of tenancy? If it is a case of tenancy, it must not be used to illustrate the history of proprietorship. If it is a case of proprietorship, it must not be used to illustrate the history of tenancy. Many writers have been led into error by not observing this rule ([211]). We do not deny that landlordship was sometimes converted into tenancy, and tenancy into landlordship; but that is no reason why they should not be distinguished from one another. From the fact that one institution may be converted into another, we cannot argue identity between them.

Cases of tenancy not to be used to illustrate the history of proprietorship.

There are many cases, in the records, of landlordship being converted into tenancy. By war and conquest whole populations were made subject and tributary, and the land, with the owners upon it, was divided into estates for the conquerors. The owners of the land became tenants, the conquerors became owners ([212]). This was one way in which landlordship was converted into tenancy. There was another way This was by a voluntary action on the part of the landlords. It became customary in very early times for the allodial proprietors to surrender their lands to the king, the church, or one of the great lords, upon condition of receiving them again as tenures, to be held by them and their descendants, upon condition of a regular annual payment of certain dues ([213]). The origin of this custom must be explained.

How proprietorship was converted into tenancy.

By conquest.

By will of the proprietors, i. e. by a voluntary surrender of proprietorship.

In the early time, the land-owners were quite free from taxes. They held their property independently, and paid no dues of any kind on account of holding it. The property of the freeman was *alodialiter immunis*, as the phrase was ([214]). In the course of time, however, when governments were established, and when the authority of the people was intrusted to a chief or king, and a council of great men, and the kings and the great men could govern with the consent of the people taken for granted, the allodial proprietors found themselves taxed for one purpose or another; at first moderately, but more and more heavily as time went on. The chief, with the consent of the great men, a consent which was easily obtained by means of the special grants of immunity to be described presently, laid divers imposts and taxes upon the allodial proprietors, which, in most cases, they felt obliged to pay. The rule was adopted that every man should hold his property who paid his taxes, — *ut securus quicumque proprietatem suam possidens debita tributa solvat* ([215]).

The institution of state taxes.

No such taxes in early times.

Taxes imposed upon the people by the kings and great men.

In the early time it was customary for the allodial lords to make offerings of food, of cattle, and of grain, to their chiefs. The fact is recorded by Tacitus. He is careful to tell us, however, that these offerings, though customary, were voluntary; — *mos est civitatibus ultro ac viritim conferre principibus vel armentorum vel frugum* ([216]).

Voluntary offerings to the chiefs become obligatory by custom.

The offerings were voluntary. Still they were customary, and it is probable that a refusal to observe the custom was unusual. The minds of the people were by this means prepared for the imposition of a regular tax, and it is not likely that much objection was made to it when it was imposed, unless it happened to be particularly heavy or burdensome.

Taxation in the time of Chlothar I. and Chilperic, in the sixth century.

There was a regular tax levied upon the produce of the fields and upon the increase of stock (*agraria, pascuaria, vel decimas porcorum*) in the time of Chlothar I. The same tax was probably levied by Charibert: *promisit ut leges consuetudinesque novas populo non infligeret*. We read of new and burdensome taxes (*descriptiones novas et graves*) in the time of Chilperic. They were levied upon lands and slaves;—*functiones infligebantur multae, tam de terris quam de mancipiis*. Among other taxes was that of an *amphora* of wine upon every acre;—*unam amphoram vini per aripennem* (²¹⁷). State taxes were instituted and maintained generally during the Merovingian and Carolingian period.

The grants of immunity date from the time of Lex Salica.

While these taxes were being levied on the people at large, the chiefs and kings conferred grants of immunity upon the great men among their followers, laymen and ecclesiastics. Reference is made by Chlothar I., in a capitulary of the year 560, to the persons who had received grants of immunity from his grandfather, his father, and his brother. This takes the grant of immunity back to the time of the Lex Salica. Many early formulæ for grants of immunity have been preserved. In other cases we may read the grants themselves. A great many of them have been preserved from the seventh and eighth centuries. By these grants, allodial property of the ancient type (*alodialiter immunis*) was, as it were, re-created ([218]).

Sometimes the allodial land-owners who had been made subject to taxation purchased grants of immunity. Erfker, for example, in one of our records, sets aside eight acres of land with which to purchase an immunity, — *pro redemptione census, quem de prefata hereditate redere annis singulis debui*. In another case, a group of land-owners, apparently a clan village, unite to make up a sum of nine *plenos mansos cum mancipiis . . . . ut securi essent de illo censu, quod illorum antecessores nostris antecessoribus* [*Illudovici Regis*] *persolverunt* ([219]).

Immunities were, in some cases, purchased.

The effect of the immunity grants was very remarkable. On the one hand, there were certain great lords paying no tax upon their lands. On the other hand, there was the mass of the people paying an annual and often very burdensome tax. The result was that the estates held under immunity grants swallowed up all the rest. The property of the people at large was gathered into the hands of a few men. The holders of the immunity grants said to those who held them not, to those who had to pay taxes to

The effect of the immunity grants.

The estates held under immunity grants swallowed up all the rest.

the king or to the state: "Give us your lands, and we will give them back to you, and you shall pay for them a fixed rent, which shall be less than the state tax, and unchangeable." The argument was unanswerable. By it the mass of the people were led to convert their allodial estates into tenures, themselves into tenants. In this way the allodial landlordship, which through the early time had been distributed among the people at large, was gathered into the hands of a few great lords ([220]).

This was accomplished by substituting a low rent for a high tax.

In reading the monastic records, the student should observe how through the eighth and ninth centuries the number of acquisitions from private persons is very large, while after the beginning of the tenth century the kings and great nobles seem to be the only benefactors of the Church. The explanation of this is, that the class of small proprietors had almost entirely disappeared. They had become tenants under the great lords. They were no longer free proprietors. They had no longer any lands to give away.

The class of small proprietors disappears.

When the allodial proprietors gave up their inheritances, they gave them up, as a rule, upon condition that they should continue to hold the land, and their descendants after them, for a certain annual rent. The amount of this rent was determined for all time in the terms of the original contract. Let us take an example. In one of the St. Gall documents a man named

The origin of the free tenures.

Wolverat alienates his estate in the mark of Chezzinwilare, upon condition that he, and his sons legitimately born of his wife Engilsinda, and all their descendants (*legitima procreatio*) shall hold the land for a rent of one denarius every year. In case the heirs became incompetent to hold the inheritance (*si autem emmollierint heredes mei, ut proprietatem suam contineri non possint*), they were to be decently lodged, fed, and clothed, and the land reverted to the monastery ([221]). Almost any number of similar cases might be cited. In this way a class of free tenants came into existence. They were distinguished, on the one hand, from the class of free proprietors, the allodial lords, and on the other hand from the mass of serfs and common agricultural laborers. The rents which the free tenants paid were in many cases, as in the case cited, merely nominal.

An illustrative case.

The free tenants to be distinguished from the free proprietors and from the mass of serfs.

As soon as the allodial estates had been converted into hereditary tenures, in the manner described, and the first tenants died, and the heirs began to multiply upon the tenures, we have house communities and then clan villages coming into existence. They are house communities and clan villages of free tenants, to be distinguished from those of free proprietors and those of serfs. Free tenancy must be distinguished from free proprietorship, and also from servile tenancy ([222]).

House communities and clan villages of free tenants.

We have seen now how allodial landlordship was gathered away from the people at large into the hands of a few great lords, laymen and ecclesiastics, — in the course of wars and conquests, and in consequence of the distribution of immunity grants, which put the great lords into a position from which they could draw the mass of small proprietors into dependence under their over-lordship. We have now to consider, briefly, the manner in which the further distribution of such landlordship as remained to be distributed was prevented. We will speak of the adoption of the principle that landlordship must not be divided, and of the institution of a new rule of inheritance in accordance with this principle.

The division and subdivision of allodial property, and consequent impoverishment of the proprietors, — results of the law of inheritance which prescribed divisions among heirs, — were prevented in very early times by a practice which, in spite of its inconsistency with the common law, spread more or less everywhere. According to this practice, one heir took the family homestead with the lands attached to it, while the other heirs, if there were any, sought their fortunes elsewhere, or were maintained as dependants. The practice seems to have obtained among the Tencteri in Tacitus's time. We read, in the Germania, that among these people the household (*penates*) and the inheritance, including dependants and slaves (the *familia*), went to the boldest and best son, — *ferox bello et melior* (²²³). This curious exception to the general rule of inheritance (*heredes tamen successoresque sui cuique liberi*) established itself, probably, very much as a similar custom has established itself recently in the mountain country of Auvergne. Although according to the general law in France a man's land passes to all his children, it has come to be considered very undesirable, in the mountain region of Auvergne, that the farms should be divided. The result is, that one child usually takes the land, while the others go off to seek their fortunes in the cities, or else enter the Church. The heir who is best fitted for country life and farming is the one to whom the other heirs resign, voluntarily, their shares of the inheritance (²²⁴). So it was, probably, among the Tencteri; only the special fitness was not so much a fitness for farming as for fighting. Among the Germans, the farming was regularly intrusted to serfs. *A modern instance.*

We can imagine how, in many cases, it was difficult to decide which of a number of heirs should take the inheritance. They might all be equally competent to hold it, and they might all desire to do so. In such cases it is probable that the rule of equal division was reverted to until some other rule — the rule of primogeniture, for example — was introduced. According *Disputes among the heirs.* *Institution of primogeniture.*

to the rule of primogeniture, the eldest son took the inheritance, unless there was some very good reason for not giving it to him.

Primogeniture in Tacitus's time. We may infer from the words, *excipit filius, non ut cetera maximus natu, sed prout ferox bello et melior*, in the Germania, that the rule of primogeniture had already been adopted in some of the German clans, in the time of Tacitus ([225]).

The rule of primogeniture was introduced in most cases by family compacts, what the Germans call *Hausgesetze*. *The Hausgesetze.* The German nobles perceived, at an early time, that, unless some arrangement was made by which their estates and lordships would remain undivided, the power and influence of their families would depart. Agreements were therefore made among the heirs in the different households, that the family estates should not be divided. Various rules were then adopted to settle the question of succession. *Primogeniture and ultimogeniture.* Among them the rule of primogeniture was generally preferred. The right of inheritance was in some cases conceded to the youngest son, in which cases we have, instead of primogeniture, what has been called ultimogeniture, what is commonly called, in our law, Borough English; *Primogeniture generally adopted.* but the rule of primogeniture was generally adopted ([226]).

The eldest son was, usually, the best fitted to exercise the paternal authority. His brothers were commonly men of less experience, or young boys, and they did not object very much to resigning their inheritances; especially as they were promised a maintenance in honor and plenty under their brother's care. As they grew up, they often received grants of land in the place of their inheritances. These grants took the form of beneficiary holdings. *Disinherited heirs receive benefices.*

Thus again allodial landlordship was gathered away from the many, and given over to the few. The number of persons disinherited by the rule of primogeniture is of course enormous. We must remember that by disinheriting one man and one woman we may disinherit a family, a clan, and even a nation of descendants; and when several persons and all their descendants are disinherited in every generation, in every family, the aggregate of disinherited persons becomes, in the long run, inconceivably large. They are thrust down into dependence, and even into servitude. *The effect of primogeniture.*

It is not at all surprising that nearly the whole population of Western Europe was, during the Middle Ages, reduced to a condition of dependence or serfdom. It was reduced to this condition in the course of wars and conquests, in consequence of the introduction of general taxes, and special grants of immunity, concurrently with them; and in consequence of the adoption of the rule that property must not be divided. The holders of immunity grants were *The chief causes which brought the people at large into dependence and servitude.*

able to induce the people at large to convert their inheritances into tenures, by lowering rents below state taxes; and when the principle that property must not be divided was adopted, multitudes of people were cut off from the inheritances which they would otherwise have acquired. While allodial landlordship became in this way concentrated in a few hands, the mass of the people sank into positions of dependence, either as beneficiaries, free tenants, or serfs (²²⁷). These were the chief classes of tenants. The highest class was that of the beneficiaries.

The people distributed into three classes, — beneficiaries, free tenants, and serfs.

The beneficiary tenures were commonly held to be hereditary, according to the ancient law prescribing division among heirs, through the early period (²²⁸). By the division and subdivision of the tenures, however, the power of the tenants was very rapidly reduced, until it was evident that their importance and influence in the state could be maintained only by the adoption of the principle that a benefice was an indivisible estate, to be held by a succession of individuals. The rule of primogeniture was then introduced among the higher class of tenants, in the same way as it had been introduced among the allodial lords (²²⁹). Where it was not introduced, where the old rule prescribing division among heirs was in force, the beneficiaries sank down to a position of insignificance (²³⁰).

Primogeniture introduced among the beneficiaries.

The clan system tends naturally to pass into a

feudal system. The disadvantages of an indefinite subdivision of inheritances and the authority passing with them, and the evils of insubordination in the community, lead inevitably to a surrender of inheritances and lordships to certain individuals, and to a substitution of beneficiary tenures (for military service) in their place. Then the beneficiaries, in order to preserve the power and influence of their families, adopt the principle that their benefices must not be divided. Then the chief of the state, the person in whom the sovereignty is vested, adopts the principle that this sovereignty must not be divided. Unless he adopts this principle, the sovereignty is frittered away through the branches of the sovereign family, while the vassals remain rich and powerful upon their undivided estates. The process is often reversed. The chief of the state adopts the principle that the sovereignty must not be divided, hoping in this way, inasmuch as the estates of his vassals are divisible, to secure a predominance for his family. While the sovereignty remains undivided, the benefices are divided and subdivided, and the beneficiaries lose their wealth and their influence. Then the beneficiaries, to prevent this, have to adopt the rule that the benefice must not be divided. It is easy to see, that, if the sovereignty of the state remains indivisible, while the beneficiary holdings are divided, the beneficiaries soon sink down into

How the clan system is supplanted by a feudal system.

Need of subordination in the community.

Introduction of beneficiary holdings.

The struggle for power between the sovereign and his vassals.

The sovereignty not to be divided.

The benefices not to be divided.

the class of agricultural laborers or serfs. The
Conclusion. feudal system grows out of the clan system in consequence of a need of subordination and government, which leads the mass of free-lords to give up their independence; and in consequence of the desire on the part of the remaining free-lords to preserve their wealth, power, and influence. This desire leads them to adopt the rule that their free-lordships must not be divided. Secondly, the feudal system grows out of a desire on the part of the vassal lords to prevent the free-lords from acquiring an undue predominance. This desire leads the vassal lords to adopt the principle of indivisibility of fiefs. The sovereign lordship of the state and the benefices under it pass then to successions of individuals. The persons who are disinherited in successive generations sink down into a third or fourth order of tenants. If among these tenants inheritances continue to be divided, according to the primitive rule, the result is pauperism and servitude ([231]).

It is not our purpose, however, in this essay, to enter into the history of the feudal system, nor into the history of the agricultural communities which did not flourish under it. Having considered the primitive clan system of the Germans, its growth and its decay, and having learned how this system was based upon the principle of private property and the principle of inheritance, rather than upon any principle of collectivity or communism, we may properly bring our essay to an end. The history of land-holding under the feudal system is a very large and a very difficult subject, into which we will not now enter.

NOTES AND REFERENCES.

Convinci nemo potest judicio sine testibus aut scriptura.
CAPITULARIA, Lib. VII. 204.

WE give here a list of the original sources from which the conclusions presented in the preceding essay have been derived. The abbreviated titles are those which will be used in the notes which follow. They are arranged alphabetically, so that they may be easily referred to. The list does not pretend to be a list of all possible sources of information. There are many records bearing more or less upon the subject of our inquiry which are not included under the titles given. The Danish, Norwegian, and Icelandic records, for example, are not at all referred to. The list, though incomplete, will be found serviceable, and it may be regarded as a nucleus for something better.

ABINGDON CHRON.—Chronicon Monasterii de Abingdon. 2 vols. London, 1858. 8°. Record Commission.

ACTA MURENS.—Acta Fundationis Murensis Monasterii Vindicata. Opera P. F. Kopp. Typis Monasterii, 1750. 4°.

AISTULPH.—Aistulphi Leges. Lombard law of the 8th Cent. In Corp. Jur. Germ. and M. G. H. Leg. IV.

ALFRED.—The Laws of King Alfred. A. D. 871–901. In Thorpe and in Schmid.

ALSAT. DIPL.—Alsatia Diplomatica. J. D. Schoepflin, editor. 2 vols. 1772. Folio.

AMPL. COLL. — Martene et Durand: Veterum Scriptorum et Monumentorum . . . . Amplissima Collectio. 9 vols. Paris, 1724–1733. Folio.

ANGL.-SAX. CHRON. — The Anglo-Saxon Chronicle. A. D. 1–1154. In M. H. B. Thorpe's edition is perhaps the best. Vol. I. Texts; Vol. II. Translation. London, 1861. 8°. Record Commission.

ARNSB. URKB. — Urkundenbuch des Klosters Arnsburg in der Wetterau. Ludwig Baur, editor. Darmstadt, 1851. 8°.

ATHELSTAN. — The Laws of King Athelstan. 10th Cent. In Thorpe and in Schmid.

BAED. — Historiae Ecclesiasticae Gentis Anglorum. Autore Venerabili Baeda. A. D. 672–735. In M. H. B. For the Anglo-Saxon version, see Smith's edition. Cambridge, 1722. Folio. The Miscellaneous Works were edited by Dr. Giles. 6 vols. London, 1843. 8°.

BEYER URKB. — Urkundenbuch zur Geschichte der Mittelrheinischen Territorien. H. Beyer, editor. 3 vols. Coblenz, 1860–1874. 8°.

BODMANN. — Bodmann: Rheingauische Alterthümer. Mainz, 1819. 4°.

BOLDON BOOK. — Boldon Book. A Survey of the Palatinate of Durham. A. D. 1183. In Domesday, IV.

BRACTON. — Henrici de Bracton De Legibus et Consuetudinibus Angliae Libri Quinque. Edited by Sir Travers Twiss. 5 vols. London, 1878–1882. 8°.

BREV. NOT. SALZB. — Breves Notitiae Salzburgenses. F. Keinz, editor. 8°. 1869. In the Juvavia also.

BREV. RER. FISC. — Breviarium Rerum Fiscalium. A. D. 800? In Corp. Jur. Germ. (II. p. 141). In M. G. H. Leg. (I. p. 176).

BREV. UROLFI. — Breviarium Urolfi Abbatis de Altaha. A. D. 800? In M. B. XI.

BRITTON. — Britton: A. D. 1291? The French Text carefully revised, with an English translation, introduction, and notes. By F. M. Nichols. 2 vols. Oxford, 1865. 8°.

CAESAR. — Caesaris Commentarii de Bello Gallico. B. C. 50.

CAPIT. DE VILLIS. — Capitulare de Villis. A. D. 800? Among the Capitularia. See, however, the edition with notes by Guérard. Paris, 1853. 8°.

CAPITULARIA. — Capitularia Regum Francorum. In Baluzius. In the Corp. Jur. Germ. and in M. G. H. Leg. I.

CART. GLOUCEST. — Historia et Cartularium Monasterii Sancti Petri Gloucestriae. 3 vols. London, 1863–1867. 8°. Record Commission.

CASSIODORUS. — M. Aurel. Cassiodori Senatoris Opera. 6th Cent. The old edition of Nivellius is perhaps as good as any. Paris, 1579. Folio.

CHART. SITHIENSE. — Cartulaire de l'Abbaye de Saint-Bertin. M. Guérard, editor. Paris, 1841. 4°.

CHART. WERTH. — Chartularium Werthinense. In Leibnitz Scrip. I. p. 101. Cf. also Lacomblet Urkb. I.

CHRON. BENEDICTOB. — Meichelbeck; Chronicon Benedictoburanum. Sumptibus Monasterii, 1753. Folio.

CHRON. PETROB. — Chronicon Petroburgense. Curante Thoma Stapleton. London, 1849. 8°. By the Camden Society.

CNUT. — The Laws of King Cnut. 11th Cent. In Thorpe and in Schmid.

COD. DIPL. LUBEC. — Codex Diplomaticus Lubecensis. I. Urkundenbuch der Stadt Lübeck. Lübeck, 1843. 4°. II. Urkundenbuch des Bisthums Lübeck. Oldenburg, 1856. 4°.

COD. DIPL. MORAV. — Codex Diplomaticus Moraviae. A. Boczek, first editor. 10 vols. Olomucii and Brünn, 1836–1878. 4°.

COD. DIPL. RATISB. — Codex Diplomaticus Ratisbonensis. In Pez Thesaurus, I. Part III. Cf. Ried Cod. Dipl.; also the Liber Probationum. Ratisbon, 1752. 8°.

COD. DIPL. SILES. — Codex Diplomaticus Silesiae. 10 vols. Breslau, 1857–1881. 4°. See especially Vol. IV.: Urkunden Schlesischer Dörfer. Dr. August Meitzen, editor. 1863.

COD. PATAV. — Codices Traditionum Ecclesiae Pataviensis (Passau) olim Laureacensis. In M. B. XXVIII., XXIX.

COD. QUEDLINB. — Erath: Codex Diplomaticus Quedlinburgensis. Frankfurt, 1764. Folio.

COD. S. GALLI. — Urkundenbuch der Abtei Sanct Gallen. Dr. Hermann Wartmann, editor. 3 vols. Zürich, 1863–1882. 4°.

Cod. Trad. Lunaelac. — Codex Traditionum Monasterii Lunaelacensis. In Pez Thesaurus, VI. p. 10; also in Vol. I. of the Urkb. Land o. d. Enns.

Cod. Trad. Reichersberg. — Codex Traditionum Monasterii Reichersbergensis. In Vol. I. of the Urkb. Land o. d. Enns.

Cod. Trad. S. Emmeram. — Codex Traditionum Sanct. Emmerammensium. In Pez Thesaurus, I. Part III.

Cod. Trad. Westph. — Codex Traditionum Westphalicarum. I. Die Heberegister des Klosters Freuckenhorst. E. Friedländer, editor. Münster, 1872. 8°.

Corb. Trad. — Traditiones Corbeienses. Paul Wigand, editor. Leipzig, 1843. 8°. Cf. also the edition of Falke, Leipzig, 1752.

Corp. Jur. Germ. — Ferd. Walter: Corpus Juris Germanici Antiqui. 3 vols. Berlin, 1824. 8°. This is a very good and cheap edition of the early laws and formulae.

Coutum. de Nivernais. — Guy Coquille: La Coutume de Nivernais. Edited by Dupin. Paris, 1864. 8°.

Coutum. Gen. — Nouveau Coutumier Général. Coutumes Générales et Particulières de France. C. A. Bourdot de Richebourg, editor. 4 vols. Paris, 1724. Folio.

Diplomata. — Diplomata e Stirpe Merowingica. Dipl. e Stirpe Arnulforum. Dipl. Spuria. In M. G. H. Dipl. Hannover, 1872. Folio.

Domesday. — The Inquisitio Terrarum, or Survey of England, made by order of William the Conqueror. A. D. 1086. 4 vols. London, 1783. Folio.

Domesd. S. Paul. — The Domesday of Saint Pauls. A. D. 1222. Archdeacon Hale, editor. Published by the Camden Soc. London, 1858. 8°.

Du Cange. — Glossarium Mediae et Infimae Latinitatis. Du Cange, editor. The best edition is that of Henschel. 7 vols. Paris, 1840-1850. 4°. A new edition is now being published.

Dugdale Monast. — Monasticon Anglicanum. Sir William Dugdale, editor. New edition. 8 vols. 1817-1830. Folio.

Edgar. — The Laws of King Edgar. A. D. 959-975. In Thorpe and in Schmid.

NOTES AND REFERENCES. 115

EDWARD. — The Laws of King Edward the Elder. A. D. 901–924. In Thorpe and in Schmid.

EDW. CONF. — Laws of King Edward the Confessor. 11th Cent. In Thorpe and in Schmid.

ETHELBERT. — The Laws of King Ethelbert. Early 7th Cent.? In Thorpe and in Schmid.

EXON. DOMESDAY. — Exon. Domesday. A Survey of the Counties of Wilts, Dorset, Somerset, Devon, and Cornwall. A. D. 1086? In Domesday. IV.

FONT. RER. AUSTR. — Fontes Rerum Austriacarum. Oesterreichische Geschichts-Quellen. 42 vols. Wien, 1855. 8°.

FONT. RER. BERN. — Fontes Rerum Bernensium. Berns Geschichts-Quellen. 3 vols. Bern, 1877–1880. 4°.

FLETA. — Fleta: Commentarius Juris Anglicani sub Edw. I. A. D. 1272–1307. John Selden's edition is as good as any. London, 1647. 8°. Again in 1685.

FORMULAE. — E. de Rozière: Recueil Général des Formules usitées dans l'Empire des Francs du Ve au Xe Siècle. 3 vols. Paris, 1859–1871. 8°. Cf. M. G. H. Leg. V.: Formulae Merowingici et Karolini. Ed. K. Zeumer. 1882. But our references are to the Rozière Collection.

FREDEGAR. — Fredegarius Scholasticus: Greg. Turon. Hist. Epitomata. 7th Cent. Edited together with the Works of Greg. Turon. by Ruinart. Paris, 1699. Folio.

FULDA COD. — Codex Diplomaticus Fuldensis. E. F. J. Dronke, editor. Cassel, 1850. 4°.

FULDA TRAD. — Traditiones Fuldenses. Dronke, editor. Fulda, 1844. 4°.

GLANVILL. — Ranulfus de Glanvill: Tractatus de Legibus et Consuetudinibus Regni Angliae Tempore Regis Henrici Secundi. Edition of John Rayner. London, 1780. 12°. There is a Translation by J. Beames. London, 1812. 8°.

GREG. TURON. — Gregorii Episcopi Turonensis Opera Omnia. 6th Cent. The edition of Ruinart is a very good one. Paris, 1699. Folio. See also the edition of the Société de l'Histoire de France, with French translation. 4 vols. Paris, 1836–1838. 8°.

GRIMM RECHTSALT. — Rechtsalterthümer. Jacob Grimm, editor. Göttingen, 1828. 8°. A second edition in 1854.

GRIMM WEISTH. — Weisthümer. Jacob Grimm, editor. 6 vols. Göttingen, 1840. 8°.

GRIMOALD. — Grimoaldi Leges : Lombard Law of the 8th Cent. In Corp. Jur. Germ. and M. G. H. Leg. IV.

GUDENUS COD. DIPL. — Codex Diplomaticus Anecdotorum. V. F. de Gudenus, editor. 5 vols. Göttingen and Frankfurt, 1743–1768. 4°.

GÜNTHER COD. DIPL. — Codex Diplomaticus Rheno-Mosellanus. W. Günther, editor. 5 vols. Coblenz, 1822–1826. 8°.

HARDT WEISTH. — Luxemburger Weisthümer als nachlese zu Jacob Grimm's Weisthümern. Von Hardt, Regierungsarchivar in Luxemburg. Luxemburg, 1870. 8°.

HENNEB. URKB. — Hennebergisches Urkundenbuch. Karl Schöppach, first editor. 7 vols. Meiningen, 1842–1877. 4°.

HERREN-ALB. URK. — Urkunden Archiv des Klosters Herren-Alb. 12th and 13th Cent. Mone Zeits. I.

HIST. FRISING. — Meichelbeck : Historia Frisingensis. 2 vols. Augsburg, 1724. Folio.

HIST. FULD. — Schannat : Historia Fuldensis. With Codex Probationum. 2 vols. Frankfurt, 1729. Folio.

HIST. TREV. — Hontheim : Historia Trevirensis Diplomatica et Pragmatica. 3 vols. Augsburg, 1750. Folio.

HIST. WORMAT. — Schannat : Historia Episcopatus Wormatiensis. 2 vols. Frankfurt, 1734.

INDIC. ARNON. — Indiculus Arnonis (Bp. of Salzburg). 8th Cent. F. Keinz, editor. München, 1869. 8°. Also in the Juvavia.

INE. — The Laws of King Ine. 7th Cent.? In Thorpe and in Schmid.

INQUIS. ELI. — Inquisitio Eliensis. A. D. 1086? In Domesday, IV.

IORDANIS. — Iordanis de Getarum sive Gothorum Origine et Rebus Gestis. The edition of Closs is good. Stuttgart, 1861. 8°.

JUVAVIA. — Nachrichten vom Zustande der Gegenden und Stadt Juvavia, heutige Salzburg. Salzburg, 1784. Folio.

NOTES AND REFERENCES. 117

KELSO REG. — Liber S. Marie de Calchou : Registrum Cartarum Abbacie Tironensis de Kelso. A. D. 1113-1567. Published by the Bannatyne Club. 2 vols. 1846.

KEMBLE'S CODEX. — Codex Diplomaticus Aevi Saxonici. J. M. Kemble, editor. 6 vols. London, 1839-1848. 8°.

KENT CUSTUM. — The Custumal of Kent. Charles Sandys, editor. London, 1851. 8°.

KINDLINGER HÖRIGK. — Kindlinger's Geschichte der deutschen Hörigkeit insbesondere der sogenannten Leibeigenschaft. Mit Urkunden. Berlin, 1819. 8°.

LACOMBLET ARCHIV. — Archiv für die Geschichte des Niederrheins. T. J. Lacomblet, editor. 7 vols. Düsseldorf, 1832-1870. 8°.

LACOMBLET URKB. — Urkundenbuch für die Geschichte des Niederrheins. T. J. Lacomblet, editor. 4 vols. Düsseldorf, 1840-1858. 4°.

LAURESHAM COD. — Codex Laureshamensis Diplomaticus. 3 vols. Mannheim, 1768-1770. 8°.

LEIBNITZ SCRIP. — Scriptores Rerum Brunsvicensium. Leibnitz, editor. 3 vols. Hannover, 1707-1711. Folio.

LEX ALAM. — Lex Alamannorum. 7th Cent. In Corp. Jur. Germ. and M. G. H. Leg. III. Also in the Font. Rer. Bern. I.

LEX. ANGL. WERIN. — Lex Angliorum et Werinorum, hoc est Thuringorum. 7th Cent. In Corp. Jur. Germ. Separate editions, by Gaupp (1834), and Merkel (1851).

LEX BAIW. — Lex Baiwariorum. 7th Cent. In Corp. Jur. Germ. and M. G. H. Leg. III.

LEX BURG. — Lex Burgundionum. 6th Cent. In Corp. Jur. Germ., M. G. H. Leg. III., and in the Font. Rer. Bern. I.

LEX FRIS. — Lex Frisonum. 7th Cent. In Corp. Jur. Germ. and M. G. H. Leg. III.

LEX RIP. — Lex Ripuaria. 6th Cent. In Corp. Jur. Germ.

LEX SAL. — Lex Salica. A. D. 500? In Corp. Jur. Germ. In separate editions of Pardessus (Paris, 1843), Merkel (Berlin, 1850), Behrend (Berlin, 1874), Hessels and Kern (London, 1880), and Holder (Leipzig, 1879).

LEX. SAX. — Lex Saxonum. 8th Cent. In Corp. Jur. Germ. In separate editions of Gaupp (1837) and Merkel (1853).

Lex Wisig. — Lex Wisigothorum. 5th to 7th Cent. In Corp. Jur. Germ.

Lib. de Hyd. — Liber Monasterii de Hyda. — London, 1866. 8°. Record Commission.

Liber Eli. — Liber Eliensis ad Fidem Codicum Variorum, edited by D. J. Stewart. Only one vol. published. London, 1848. 8°. Compare Gale, Scriptores XV. p. 463. London, 1691. 4°.

Lisch. Urk. — Mecklenburgische Urkunden. G. C. F. Lisch, editor. 3 vols. Schwerin, 1837-1841. 8°.

Littleton. — Sir Thomas Littleton : Treatise of Tenures in French and English. To which are added the Ancient Treatise of the Old Tenures and Customs of Kent. By T. E. Tomlins. London, 1841. 8.°

Liutprand. — Liutprandi Leges. Lombard Law of the 8th Cent. In Corp. Jur. Germ. and M. G. H. Leg. IV.

Mauri. Chart. — Charta Bonorum Maurimonasterii. A. D. 1120? In Alsat. Dipl. I. p. 197. Cf. Polyp. Irminon. Introd. p. 930.

M. B. — Monumenta Boica. A Collection of Records for the History of Bavarian Lands. 51 vols. München, 1763-1877. 8° and 4°.

Meklenb. Urkb. — Mecklenburgisches Urkundenbuch. 11 vols. Schwerin, 1863-1878. 4°.

Melsa Chron. — Chronica Monasterii de Melsa. A. D. 1396. 3 vols. London, 1866. 8°. Record Commission.

M. G. H. — Monumenta Germaniae Historica. Edidit G. H. Pertz. Scriptores (Scrip.). Leges (Leg.). Diplomata (Dipl.). The publication was begun in 1826.

M. H. B. — Monumenta Historica Britannica ; or Materials for the History of Britain. Only one vol. published. London, 1848. Folio.

Mohr Cod. — Codex Diplomaticus. Urkunden zur Geschichte Cur-Rätiens und Granbünden. Th. von Mohr, editor. 3 vols. Chur, 1848-1852. 8°.

Mone Zeits. — Zeitschrift für die Geschichte des Oberrheins. L. J. Mone. first editor. 30 vols. 1850-1878. 8°.

Mon. Nideralt. — Monumenta Nideraltacensia. In M. B. XI.

Mon. Scheftl. — Monumenta Scheftlariensia. In M. B. VIII.

Mon. Schlehdorf. — Monumenta Schlehdorfensia. In M. B. IX.

Mon. Tegerns. — Monumenta Tegernseensia. — In M. B. VI.

Mon. Weihenstepii. — Monumenta Weihenstephanensia. In M. B. IX.

Moser. — Familien-Staatsrecht der deutschen Reichsstände. By J. J. Moser. 2 vols. Frankfurt. 1775. 4. See also his Persönliches Staatsrecht, and Deutsches Staatsrecht, for early Hausgesetze.

Münst. Beitr. — Kindlinger's Münsterische Beiträge zur Geschichte Deutschlands, hauptsächlich Westfalens. 3 vols. Münster, 1787–1793. 8°.

Neugart Cod. — Codex Diplomaticus Alemanniae et Burgundiae-Transjuranae. P. T. Neugart, editor. Typis San-Blasianis, 1791.

Niedersachs. Urkb. — Urkundenbuch des Historischen Vereins für Niedersachsen. 11 vols. Hannover, 1846–1875. 8°.

Oaths. — Oaths of the Early English Law. In Thorpe and in Schmid.

Oesterreich. Weisth. — Oesterreichische Weisthümer. I. Die Salzburgischen Taidinge. II., III., IV. Die Tirolischen Weisthümer. 4 vols. Wien, 1870–1880. 8°.

Orig. Nassoic. — Origines Nassoicae. With Codex Diplomaticus. J. M. Kremer, editor. Wiesbaden, 1779. 4°.

Osnabrk. Gesch. — J. Möser: Osnabrückische Geschichte. 3 vols. Berlin and Stettin, 1780–1824. 8°.

Pardessus. — J. M. Pardessus: Diplomata, Chartae, Epistolae, Leges, etc., ad Res Gallo-Francicas Spectantia. 2 vols. Paris, 1843–1849. Folio.

Perard. — Recueil de plusieurs Pièces curieuses servant à l'Histoire de Bourgogne. Par Estienne Perard. Paris, 1664. Folio.

Pez Thesaurus. — Pez: Thesaurus Anecdotorum Novissimus. 6 vols. Augsburg, 1721. Folio.

Polypt. Irminon. — Polyptique de l'Abbé Irminon. Dénombrement des Manses, &c. de l'Abbaye de Saint-Germain-des-Prés, sous le Règne de Charlemagne. Guérard, editor. 2 vols. Paris, 1844. 4°.

Polypt. de S. Remi. — Polyptique de l'Abbaye de Saint-Remi de Reims. Guérard, editor. Paris, 1853. 4°.

PROCOPIUS. — Procopius ex recensione Guilielmi Dindorfii. Greek and Latin. 3 vols. Bonn, 1833-1838. 8°. This is a good edition.

RACHIS. — Rachis Leges. Lombard Law of the 8th Cent. In Corp. Jur. Germ. and M. G. H. Leg. IV.

RANKS. — Ranks in Early English Society. In Thorpe and in Schmid.

RECT. SING. PERSON. — Rectitudines Singularum Personarum. Angl-Sax. and Lat. In Thorpe and in Schmid. In a separate edition by H. Leo. Halle, 1842. 8°.

RECUEIL. — Recueil des Historiens des Gaules et de la France. Rerum Gallicarum et Francicarum Scriptores. 19 vols. Paris, 1869-1880. Folio.

REG. WIGORN. — Registrum Prioratus Beate Mariae Wigorniensis. A. D. 1240. By the Camden Society. London, 1865. 8°.

REG. HIST. WESTF. — Regesta Historiae Westfaliae. Accedit Codex Diplomaticus. H. A. Erhard and Roger Wilmans, editors. 4 vols. Münster, 1847-1880. 4°.

REG. PRÜM. — Registrum Prumiense. A. D. 893. With the Glossae Caesarii Heisterbacensis. A. D. 1222. In Beyer Urkb. and in the Hist. Trev. CCCCLIX.

RIED COD. DIPL. — Codex Chronologico Diplomaticus Episcopatus Ratisbonensis. Studio Thomae Ried. 2 vols. Ratisbon, 1816. 8°.

RITZ URK. — Urkunden und Abhandlungen zur Geschichte des Niederrheins und der Niedermaas. By Wilhelm Ritz. Aachen, 1824. 8°.

ROTHAR. — Edictum Rotharis. Lombard Law of the 7th Cent. In Corp. Jur. Germ. and M. G. H. Leg. IV.

ROTUL. HUNDRED. — Rotuli Hundredorum. Temp. Hen. III. et Edw. I. 1812. 2 vols. Folio.

SACHS. GESCHICHTSQ. — Geschichtsquellen der Prov. Sachsen und angrenzender Gebiete. Halle. 8°.

SACHSENSPIEGEL. — Der Sachsenspiegel. Edited by Dr. C. G. Homeyer. Erster Theil (3d ed.) : Berlin, 1861. Zweiter Theil: Berlin, 1842, 1844. 3 vols. 8°.

SALEM REG. — Der Aelteste Güterbesitz des ehemaligen Reichsstiftes Salem. In Mone Zeits. I.

SALOMO FORM. — Formelbuch des Bishops Salomo III. von Constanz. 9th Cent. Ernst Dümmler, editor. Leipzig, 1857. 8°.

SCHMID. — Die Gesetze der Angelsachsen, mit Uebersetzung. Glossar, etc. Dr. Reinhold Schmid, editor. Leipzig, 1858. 8°.

SCHULZE. — Hausgesetze der regierenden deutschen Fürstenhäuser. Hermann Schulze, editor. Jena, 1862. 8°.

SPELMAN GLOSS. — Glossarium Archaeologicum. Authore Henrico Spelmano. 3d edition. London, 1687. Folio.

STENZEL URKB. — Tzschoppe und Stenzel: Urkundensammlung zur Geshichte des Ursprungs der Städte in Schlesien und Ober-Lansitz. Hamburg, 1832. 4°.

TACITUS. — Tacitus: De Origine, Situ, Moribus, ac Populis Germaniae (Germ.); Annales (An.). A. D. 100.

THEODORIC. — Edictum Theodorici: Ostrogothic Law of the 6th Cent. In Corp. Jur. Germ. Also in Nivellius's edition of Cassiodorus.

THORPE. — Ancient Laws and Institutes of England. Benjamin Thorpe, editor. London, 1840. Folio, or 2 vols. 8°.

TRAD. WIZ. — Traditiones Possessionesque Wizenburgenses. C. Zeuss, editor. Spier, 1842. 4°.

URKB. LAND. O. D. ENNS. — Urkundenbuch des Landes ob. der Enns. 7 vols. Wien, 1852-1876. 8°.

VAISSETTE. — Vaissette et de Vic: Histoire Général de Languedoc. 5 vols. 1730-1745. Folio. Another edition. 10 vols. 1840. 8°. New edition. 14 vols. Toulouse, 1872-1876. 4°.

VICTOR VITENSIS. — Historia Persecutionis Vandalicae in Duas Partes. Prior Complectitur Libros Quinque Victoris Vitensis Episcopi. Ruinart, editor. Venice, 1732. 4°. New edition in Vol. VII. of the Corp. Script. Eccles. Lat. Wien, 1881.

WENCK. — Wenck's Hessische Landes-Geschichte, mit Urkunden. 3 vols. Frankfurt, 1785-1803.

WERGILDS. — Early English Wergilds. In Thorpe and in Schmid.

WESTF. URKB. — Urkundenbuch zur Landes und Rechtsgeschichte des Herzogthums Westfalen. J. S. Seibertz, editor. 3 vols. Arnsberg, 1839-1854. 8°.

Whitby Cart. — Cartularium Abbatiae de Whiteby. Fund. An. MLXXVIII. Christopher Atkinson, editor. Published by the Surtees Society. London, 1881. 8°.

Winslow Manor. — Extracta Rotulorum de Halimotis tentis apud Manirum de Wynselowe. Tempore Edwardi Tertii a Conquestu. MS. in the University Library, Cambridge, England.

Winton Domesday. — Winton Domesday. A. D. 1107–1128. In Domesday IV.

Wirtemb. Urkb. — Wirtembergisches Urkundenbuch. 3 vols. Stuttgart, 1849–1871. 4°.

Wm. Conq. — Laws of William the Conqueror. 11th Cent. In Thorpe and in Schmid.

Zahn Urkb. — Urkundenbuch des Herzogthums Steiermark. J. Zahn, editor. 2 vols. Gratz, 1875. 8°.

The following notes are arranged according to the numbers given in the text. In referring to sources of information, we shall use the abbreviated titles in the preceding list.

Note 1. — Page 1.

Cæsar VI. 22: Agriculturae non student; majorque pars victus eorum in lacte, caseo, carne, consistit. Cf. IV. 1: neque multum frumento sed maximam partem lacte atque pecore vivunt, multumque sunt in venationibus. In the first passage Cæsar speaks of the Germans in general; in the second passage he is speaking of the Suevi. Then read Germ. 5: ne armentis quidem suus honor aut gloria frontis; numero gaudent, eaeque solae et gratissimae opes sunt. This is said of the Germans in general. Cf. Cap. 27. Then read Cap. 15, 21, 12. The chiefs received presents of live-stock. It was used for the pacification of feuds, and for the payment of fines. It served various purposes instead of money. See Lex Rip. XXXVI. 11, and Lex Sax. XIX; also Kemble's Codex, CXLVII: ager hoc pretio emptus est; c oues, xxx boues et vaccas, xxx equos indomitos dedit.

We find descriptions of stock owned by individuals in the documents. Vid. Cod. S. Galli 13, 352, 701; Lauresham Cod. MMMDCCXXXIII; Fulda Cod. 110, 202, 240, 306, 309, 355, 384, 473, 508, 520, 539, 540, 612; Hist. Frising. I. p. 126, and Num. CCXCV; also Num. DCLXXVII; Trad. Wiz. LIV; Wirtemb. Urkb. I. Num. XCIV; Cod. Patav. XIV. Vid. also the Formulae CCXXVI, CCXXXV, CCXXXVIII, CCXXXIX, CCXLIII, and CCCLXVII.

The passages of the Folk-Laws regarding live-stock should be read. See, for example, Lex. Sal. II, de furtis porcorum; III, de furtis animalium; IV, de furtis ovium; V, de furtis caprarum. Lex Rip. XVIII, de sonesti. Also XLVII. Lex Alam. LXXII: de eo qui in troppo de jumentis ductricem involaverit. Also LXXIII, LXXIV, LXXV: de eo qui taurum, gregem regentem, involaverit aut occiderit. LXXVIII: de preccio bovis. LXXIX: de eo qui pastores [porcorum vel ovium] occiderit. XCVII: silva tam porcorum quam pecorum. XCVIII: de eo qui gregem animalium in pignus tulerit. XCIX: de eo qui bisontem vel cetera animalia aut furaverit aut occiderit. CIII: de jumento quod hominem occidit. Lex Baiw. III. 10: de porcis dispersis [de sono ubi septuaginta fuerint porci]. VIII. 3: si majorem pecuniam furaverit . . . aut equum totidem pretii, vel mancipium, et negare voluerit, cum duodecim sacramentalibus juret de lite sua, vel duo campiones propter hoc pugnent. Ibid. 8: aurum, argentum, jumenta, vel pecora. Ibid. 11; XII. 4, 5; XIII. Lex Burg. XLIX: de animalibus damnum facientibus in clausura missis. Add. I. 2, 18, 20. Lex Fris. IV: de servo aut jumento alieno occiso . . . equi et boves, oves, caprae, porci, et quicquid mobile in animalibus ad usum hominum pertinet, usque ad canem. Many more references might be given.

From the time of the Folk-Laws on, however, the life of the people was agricultural rather than pastoral; that is to say, they depended rather upon the produce of the fields than upon the increase of stock for their means of subsistence. A great deal of the land was then brought under cultivation. But this was not the case during the migrations.

Note 2. — Page 1.

Tacitus Germ. 16: Nullas Germanorum populis urbes habitari satis notum est, ne pati quidem inter se iunctas sedes: colunt discreti ac diversi, ut fons, ut campus, ut nemus placuit, vicos locant non in nostrum morem conexis et cohaerentibus aedificiis; suam quisque domum spatio circumdat, sive adversus casus ignis remedium sive inscitia aedificandi.

There seems to be a contradiction here. The people settled apart from one another, and yet they had villages.

Compare, however, Germ. 25: Ceteris servis non in nostrum morem descriptis per familiam ministeriis utuntur: suam quisque sedem, suos penates regit, frumenti modum dominus aut pecoris aut vestis ut colono iniungit, et servus hactenus paret.

The *vici locati* of Germ. 16 must have been manorial villages, or villages of dependants and slaves; such, for example, as Chrodinus founded and gave to the Church. Vid. Greg. Turon. VI. 20: nam saepe a novo fundans villas, aedificans domos, culturas erigens . . . ipsas domos, cum cultoribus et culturis, benigne distribuebat.

Cf. Chart. Sithiense Folq. Lib. I. xxix: omnes villas meas cum adjacentiis. Lib. II. lxv: Hildincurtem cum villulis ad eandem pertinentibus. Lacomblet Urkb. 105: curtem dominicatam cum quadquaginta sex mansis. 169: curtim cum omni integritate mansorum. Fulda Trad. Cap. 4. 85: xxx villas et mancipia sine numero. Cap. 41. 4: Odiltag et uxor tradid. bona sua in pago Liergewe, xx villulis. Trad. Wiz. XVII: villas juris nostri. Orig. Nassoic. VII: villam juris nostri, habentem plus minus mansos decem et septem. Indic Arnon I. 7: villulam cum mansos x. Kemble's Codex CXL: dabo terram septies quinos tributariorum jugera continentem. Est autem rus prefatum in iiii villulis separatum . . . quartus viculus, hoc est Nordtun, x manentium. Ibid. CLI: omnes villulas et possessiones. CCCXXXVI: fundum cum suo hundredo, habens centum cassatos. CCCXLVIII: terram v cassatorum, id est vicus qui nominatur Eatun. Here we have the *vicus locatus* of Tacitus, with (Germ. 26) *agri pro quinque cultoribus*.

We shall see, as we go on in our argument, how in the early time property consisted regularly of isolated farmsteads with villages of serfs attached to them. It could very well be said of the freemen that they lived apart from one another and founded villages. The villages which they founded were villages of dependants and slaves, or serfs.

Note 3. — Page 1.

Cicero, De Republica II. 9 : quod tum erat res in pecore et locorum possessionibus, ex quo pecuniosi et locupletes vocabantur.

Note 4. — Page 2.

Rothar CXXXVI : De illis vero pastoribus dicimus qui ad liberos homines servierunt et de sala propria exeunt. Lex Alam. LXXIX: pastores porcorum vel ovium. XCVIII: gregem animalium. Lex Sal. Septem Causas, II (Merkel, p. 95): pecora qui pastore non habent. Beyer. Urkb. I. 32, 34: greges cum pastoribus. Trad. Wiz. LIV: vaccas et illo pastore, porcos cum pastore, berbices cum pastore. Formulae CCXXXVIII, CCXXXIX, CCXLIII: gregem agnorum, gregem armentorum, gregem porcorum, gregem ovium. Wirtemb. Urkb. XVIII: gregis cum pastoribus. So in XIX and XXIII. Hist. Trev. XLVII: pastoribus, gregis pecudum. Rothar CXXIX Form.: porcarius, pecorarius, caprarius, armentarius. Cf. Dipl. Spuria 56: pastoribus, vaccariis, porcariis, bervicariis, cum gregibus vel omni peculio promiscuo. Land was occupied, in the first place, by the flocks and herds. One tract of land was occupied by A's animals; another tract was occupied by B's animals. The position of a man's home was then determined by the position of his pasture ground. Each man settled himself among his flocks and herds, in the midst of the land which they occupied.

A settlement in isolated farmsteads is an almost inevitable feature of the pastoral life. We see how it is in our own country. In the cattle-breeding regions of the West we have isolated farms or ranches, instead of villages and towns.

Note 5. — Page 2.

Cæsar IV. 1: Sueborum gens est longe maxima et bellicosissima Germanorum omnium. Hi centum pagos habere dicuntur, ex quibus quotannis singula milia armatorum bellandi causa ex finibus educunt; reliqui qui domi manserint se atque illos alunt. Hi rursus invicem anno post in armis sunt illi domi remanent. Sic neque agricultura, nec ratio atque usus belli intermittitur.

Tacitus Germ. 26: Agri pro numero cultorum ab universis in vices [*or* invicem] occupantur. Then Germ. 27: Haec in commune de omnium Germanorum origine ac moribus accepimus. We read in the Angl. Sax. Chron., at the year 894, that King Alfred had his forces so divided that half of his men were at home while the other half were in the field.

Note 6. — Page 3.

Tacitus Germ. 4, 11, 13: Nihil autem neque publicae neque privatae rei nisi armati agunt. 14, 15: delegata domus et penatium et agrorum cura feminis senilusque et infirmissimo cuique ex familia. By the word *cura*, management, administration, or superintendence is meant. The actual work in the fields was done by slaves. Read also Germ. 17, 21, 22, 24. Agriculture was seldom resorted to, unless there were slaves to do the work. Even as late as the year 789 agricultural labor was regarded as servile labor. See the description of the *opera servilia* in the Capitulare Aquisgranense, LXXIX (Corp. Jur. Germ. II. p. 97); and in Lex Baiw. VI. Cap. II.

Note 7. — Page 3.

Slaves are first mentioned by Tacitus, Germ. 20, 24, 25, 38, 44. References to them are common in the early laws. See, for example, Lex Sal. X. XII, XXV, XXVI, XXVII, XXXV, XXXIX, XL, XLVII. Lex Rip. VIII. Slaves are referred to in all the fourteen sections XVII–XXX, in LVIII, LXI, LXII, and LXXIV. Lex Alam. III, V, VII, VIII, XX, XXI, XXII, XXXVII, XXXVIII, XXXIX, LXXXV, LXXXVI, CV. Lex Baiw. I, II, III, V, VI, VII, VIII, IX, XI, XII, XV, XVII. Lex Burg. II, III, IV, V, VI, VII, X, XV, XVI, XVII, XX, XXI, XXVI, XXVII, XXXII, XXXIII, XXXV, XXXVIII, XXXIX, XL, XLVII, L, LIV, LVI, LXIII, LXX, LXXIII, LXXVII; Add. (I), IV, V, VII, VIII, XII; Add. (II), I, II, III, IV, VIII. Lex Fris. I, II, III, IV, IX, XII, XVIII, XX; Add. VIII, IX. Lex Angl. Werin. I, VI, IX, X. Lex Sax. II, XI,

XV. So in the other Folk-Laws. Slavery and dependence upon slave labor were universal.

In order, however, to be completely convinced of this, the student should turn over the volumes of formulæ and documents to see how, in almost every grant of land, slaves are included as cultivators of it. The regular formula is: cum domibus, ædificiis, accolabus, mancipiis, campis, pratis, pascuis, aquis, aquarumve decursibus. Slaves were regarded, like cattle, as a regular and proper means of subsistence.

In the course of wars and conquests they were accumulated in vast numbers; so that the members of victorious nations, clans, and families were, as a rule, well provided with them. With plenty of slaves the freemen had no occasion to work in the fields. We shall see, as we go on in our argument, how property consisted regularly of houses occupied by slaves, and lands cultivated by slaves. Vid. Formula CXVIII: mansis cum mancipiis commanentibus. The number of slaves owned by the free-lords was often very large. Gerard and his wife, in Ritz Urk. 12, owned as many as three hundred and sixty. This is not an isolated case. One tract of land was cultivated by A's slaves. Another tract was cultivated by B's slaves. The position of a man's home was determined by the position of his colony or colonies of slaves. The free-lords lived as a rule among their slaves, in the midst of the land which they cultivated. Cf. Germ. 20: Dominum ac servum nullis educationis deliciis dignoscas; inter eadem pecora, in eadem humo degunt, donec aetas separat ingenuos, virtus adgnoscat. The settlement in isolated farmsteads was almost inevitable. We know how it has been in our own country. A system of isolated farms obtained in Maryland, Virginia, and other Southern States, up to the time of the Civil War, because agricultural labor was performed by colonies of slaves. The township system was almost unknown at the South. Villages of small proprietors existed mostly in the North, where the land was cultivated by freemen. Whenever men have great herds of cattle, or herds of slaves, they settle, as a rule, apart from one another upon isolated farms, — *Einzelhöfe*.

NOTE 8. — PAGE 4.

Freedmen, as distinguished from slaves, are mentioned in Tacitus Germ. 25. Their condition was not much better than that of slaves. Cf. Rothar CCXXIX. They were doubtless employed in agricultural labor, as in later times. In the later records they are called *liti*. Cf. Reg. Hist. Westf. XXVIII: de litis quam de ingenuis hominibus terram ejus incolentibus. In descriptions of landed property free tenants are frequently mentioned, as in the case just cited. If the land was alienated the free tenants were alienated with it, unless they gave up their tenures. Vid. Cod. S. Galli 42: Ego Duto dono quidquid in Chisineas habeo, hoc est casa curtile et terra salica, et servos tuos . . . ingenui tuo commanent terram illam, et si vultum manire post obitum meum, qualum servicium mihi fecerunt, talem faciant vobis. Cf. Capitularia, A. D. 812, I. Cap. 1: liber homo qui mansos vestitos de alicujus beneficio habet. Alsat. Dipl. XCVIII: ingenuos commanentes in villa E. They are alienated to Lucerne monastery. Formula LII: qui se in servitio alterius obnoxiat. Vid. Lex Baiw. VI. Cap. III: liberi, qui justis legibus deserviunt. Hist. Frising. 1. p. 52: mancipias, servos, liberos tributales. We find these various classes of tenants settled upon the inheritance of Suarzoth at Toolpach. They are given with the land to the church at Frising. Vid. Ibid. Num. XII: quicquid nobis in portionem evenerat tam liberis quam colonis et servibus. Indic. Arnonis VII. 8: similiter tradidit tributarios Romanos. Ibid. 10: mansos inter servos et liberos. Cod. Trad. Lunaelac. XIII: liberos ad ipsum locum detentos. Diplomata Merow. 15: ingenuis in eorum agris commanentibus. Vid. also Ibid. 58, 62, 95. Dipl. Arnulf. 23: pro susceptione pauperum et peregrinorum ipsas [res] reddidimus. Dipl. Spuria 1, 22. Cf. Baed IV. 13: terram octoginta septem familiarum, ubi suos homines qui exules vagabantur recipere posset.

The freemen who were in the position of dependants were often obliged to engage in agricultural labor. In the Reg. Baden. 3, for example, we have mentioned the tributa ac servitia, quae liberi homines persolvant. Cf. Hist. Frising. CDLXXXI: isti sunt liberi homines . . . arant dies III, tribus temporibus in anno, et secant tres dies, illud collegunt et ducunt in horrea et reddant modios xv . . . Hrodfrid arat pleniter sicut alii servi. The position of the dependent freeman was often little better than that of a slave. Only he could leave his lord, if he pleased. Vid. Lex Wisig. V. Tit. III. 1 : habeat licentiam cui se voluerit commendare. Quoniam ingenuo homini non potest prohiberi, quia in sua potestate consistit. Cf. Aistulph XIV. Then Rothar CLXXVII. Before leaving his lord, however, as we see in this passage of Rothar's edict, the freeman had to pay back to him, or to his heirs, all that he had received : res ad donatorem, vel heredem ejus revertantur. So in Lex Wisig. V. Tit. III. 1 ; cf. also Ibid. 2, 3, 4. According to a Frankish Capitulary (A. D. 813, II. Cap. 16), the vassal could not leave his lord after he had received the equivalent of one solidus : excepto si eum vult occidere, aut cum baculo caedere, vel uxorem aut filiam maculare, seu hereditatem ei tollere. According to Alsat. Dipl. LXXXII, the dependants were distributed into three classes, — familia tota, sive militaris sive censualis vel et servilis. The members of the first class, the *familia militaris*, did no servile work. It was all left to the members of the other classes. The *familia censualis* consisted mainly of free tenants The *familia servilis* consisted mainly of slaves. In the course of time, the condition of the slaves being raised, and the condition of the free tenants being lowered, the two classes came to be nearly or completely merged into one class, — the class of serfs, as we have said. The class of free tenants will be considered more particularly in another connection.

Note 9. — Page 5.

Germ. 26 : Agri pro numero cultorum ab universis in vices [*or* invicem] occupantur, quos mox inter se secundum dignationem partiuntur; facilitatem partiendi camporum spatia praebent, arva per annos mutant, et superest ager, nec enim cum ubertate et amplitudine soli labore contendunt, ut pomaria conserant et prata separent et hortos rigent : sola terrae seges imperatur.

The *agri* were small arable farms. One was assigned to each cultivator, in the time of Tacitus, as in later times. Hist. Frising. DCCXIX : mancipia et xii agros. Mon. Weihensteph. p. 487 : duos agros terre arate. Trad. Wiz. CXXVII : agros non modicos ad arandum. Reg. Hist. Westf. XXXIV: agris, familiis. Osnabrk. Gesch. LI: agros x in Threle; x in Bist, impari quidem magnitudine. Cf. also LXXXII, LXXXX. Stenzel Urkb. XXXVII: omnibus autem, qui in agris habitant extirpatis . . . hii vero qui agros occupant extirpandos. This illustrates what Tacitus says very well.

The *agri* of Germ. 26 are the *mansi* or *hubae* of the later records. Cf. Cod. Dipl. Lubec II. clx (p. 155): in B. non sunt agri sive mansi distincte mensurati, unde ignoramus quot sint ibi mansi . . . fecimus agros mensurari, et inventi sunt [x?] mansi. Ibid. cccvii: agri villæ cum colonis ibidem commorantibus . . . agri sicut nunc mensurati. These are the *agri pro numero cultorum occupati* of Tacitus, without doubt. See Cod. Trad. Reichersberg III: prediis [agri?] eidem curti appendiciis usque ad xxx, ut dicitur mansos. Also CXXII (p. 341): agris ad sedecim mansos et medietatem unius mansi. Henneb. Urkb. LXIII: sex agros in campis villæ [*agros in arvis* in Tacitus?]. Cf. CXXIII: sex mansus cum dimidio, sitos in campis Viselbreche. Beyer Urkb. 135, Glossa 1 (p. 144): mansis indominicatis qui sunt agri curie.

The *mansus* is often described as a *colonia* or *colonica*. The *agri* of Germ. 26 are the *coloniae* of the later records. See Mone Zeits. I. p. 395: tres coloniae seu agri. Cf. Lex Burg. XXXVIII. 7: in agro vel colonica. In the English records we have, instead of the *mansus*, the *hida*. The words have the same signification. Vid. Kemble's Codex CCCXCVIII: bis denas mansas, quod Anglice dicitur twentig hida. So also in DCXXI.

King Wulfher gave to St. Chad fifty hides of land at Barrow (?). Baed describes these hides as the land of fifty families: terram quinquaginta familiarum. This would be, in the phrase of Tacitus: *agri pro quinquaginta cultoribus occupati*. Vid. Hist. Eccl. IV. 3. The English estimated their lands according to the number of families (i. e. *cultores*) that could be set out upon it. Vid. Baed I. 25: Tanatos insula non modica, id est, magnitudinis juxta consuetudinem aestimationis Anglorum familiarum sexcentarum. So in II. 9: III. 4; and other passages. The land-owners divided the land into family allotments, which they distributed among their dependants and slaves, or serfs. This was the case among the Germans generally, from the time of Tacitus on.

The family allotments are described as *agri* by Tacitus, and by some of the later writers, as we have seen. They are called hides by the English. Vid. the Anglo-Saxon version of Baed's History, in which the Latin *terra familiae* is rendered by the Anglo-Saxon *hida*. Vid. also Angl. Sax. Chron. A. D. 565 and 648. Kemble's Codex CCXXX, CCXCVII, CCCCXLII : terrae meae portionem xx videlicet hidas secundum aestimationem. Ine 24, 32, 51, 64, 65, 66, 70. Wergilds 7, 8, 9. Ranks 2, 3. Lib. Eli. (Gale's edition) II. Cap. 40. Ibid. (Stewart's edition) II. Cap. 4, 7, 8 : xii hydas, scilicet manerium quod Lindune dicitur. Cap. 11 (p. 129) : hydam per sexies xx acras. Ibid. (p. 130) : hidas integras. Cap. 14, 17, 23 : collectis terris inventae sunt hidae sexaginta. Cap. 31, 32, 33. The hides appear to have consisted quite regularly of a hundred and twenty acres; not always, however; and the acre may have varied in different places. It is quite useless to try to arrive at equivalents in modern measures. The acre was in many cases a small field simply, i. e. an *ager;* and a hundred and twenty small fields were called a hide. A standard acre was hardly established until the thirteenth century. Vid. Statutum de Admensuratione Terre. Statutes of the Realm, I. p. 206. The extent of the acre was at first defined as the amount of land which one man could plough in one day. Under this definition there was room for considerable variations, and it was a long time before standards were instituted.

The word *cassatus* is often used instead of the word *hida*. Vid. Kemble's Codex XIX, XLVIII, LXXXIX, XC, CV, CXXXVIII, CXLIII, CCXXXII, CCCXXXV, CCCXLVIII, DCXXII : v cassatos . . . fif hida. So in Abingdon Chron. I. pp. 29, 30 : xii cassatorum . . . xii hida. Cf. p. 192. There are many other similar records. The word *mansus* is also common. Vid. Abingdon Chron. I. p. 201 : xx mansos . . . xx hida. Cf. pp. 205, 232-233, 240, 304. The word *mansus* is the word most commonly used upon the Continent to describe the family allotment. The word *huba* occurs very frequently, however. We shall consider the *mansi* and *hubae* more particularly in notes to come. We must now describe the manner in which the lots were measured off. According to certain traditions they were measured off with a cord made from the hide of an ox or some other animal. The hide was cut up in slender strips. These were then fastened together, and the cord thus made was used as a diameter for the length and breadth of the allotment. This is, perhaps, the reason why the allotment was called a *hide*.

See Grimm Rechtsalterthümer, 2d ed., pp. 89–91. We know from the records that a cord of some sort was used in measuring off the allotments. It is described by the Latin word *funis*, or *funiculus;* and by the German words *hofslach, repmate, schedemate.* See Cod. Dipl. Lubec. II. cccxix: trium mansorum debitam mensuram per distributinis funiculam, quod vulgo dicitur hofslach. Then Lisch. Urkb. II. p. 102: dimensionem funiculi [repmate efte schedemate]. Cf. also Ibid. p. 143.

Prof. Hanssen cites the following passage from A. Suneson's Schonisches Gesetzbuch (IV. 1): cujus (funiculi) dimensione tota villa in aequales redigitur portiones, quas materna lingua vulgaritur Boll appellant et nos in latino sermone mansos possumus appellare, earum fundis inter se praediisque inter se fundis ipsis adjacentibus adaequandis. See Hanssen's Abhandlungen, p. 8.

The length of the *funiculus* was in later times determined by the landlords. It was not necessarily made from a hide, and its length could be varied indefinitely. It differed in different localities, according to different standards which were introduced. Sometimes, when a landlord had more tenants than land, he would shorten the *funiculus*, and make a redistribution of lots. In that way, he could sometimes increase the number of lots. Cod. Dipl. Lubec II. cxcviii: quicquid super sedecim mansos, pro quibus nunctemporis villa jacet per funiculum dimensionis excreverit. Then read Ibid. clx (p. 154): hujus ville mansi et termini quando capitulo placuerit possunt mensurari: hereditas enim est ecclesie. One or two extra lots were sometimes eked out. As no reduction of dues and services was made in consequence of this reduction of the lots, complaints arose. So it became customary for the landlords to promise that the lots should not be measured again, or that, if measured again, the diameter-cord should not be altered. Lisch Bd. I. xcv.: exemptam et liberam ab omni mensuracionis et funiculacionis genere pro quatuor mansis perpetuo donavimus et posuimus. Cf. also Bd. II. viii, xxii, xxiv, xxv, xxvi, xxvii, xliv, xlix; Bd. III. xviii. When the Vandals came into Africa, in the fifth century, the *funiculus* was used in dividing the land. Vid. Victor Vitensis I. 4. Dudo tells us that the lands of Normandy were divided at first by the *funiculus*. Vid. passage cited by Lappenberg, in his " England under the Norman Kings" (Thorpe's translation, p. 18, note). Cf. also Helmold Chron. Slav. I. 91 (M. G.

II. Scrip. XXI. p. 83), and Mon. Nideralt, p. 33; ut maximus campus per funiculos mensuraretur, et cuilibet hube XII. jugera deputarentur.

The *funiculus* was given up after a time for the rod, *virga* or *pertica*. Different rods were used in different places (vid. Du Cange sub. voc. *pertica*), until standards were established by authority. Cf. Capitularia. A. D. 803, III. Cap. 8: De mensuris ut secundum jussionem nostram aequales fiant.

After a while we meet with the *virga teutonicalis*. Vid. Stenzel Urkb. XXIX: mensuram Teutonicalem, videlicet ducentas et septuaginta virgas Teutonicales. Was this *mensura Teutonicalis* the regular diameter for the *mansi* or *hubae*? When rods were used in measuring out the arable lots (the *agri*), a certain number were taken for the length, a certain number for the breadth. of each lot.

When the *agri* had been measured off, they were distributed by lot. Cf. Stenzel Urkb. VII: divisio mansorum per sortem, more Theutonico. The *mansi* were often called *sortes*, from this fact. Capitula ad Leg. Sal. LXXXVIII. (Merkel, p. 40): mansionem aut sortem. Lauresham Codex CCCCXLI: manso et sorte. So in DXXXVII, DCCCXII. DCCCCXLVII, MMDCCLX, MMMDLIX, MMMDCLXII, MMMDCLXXXIV. Beyer Urkb. 134: sortes ingenuiles. Alsat. Dipl. LXXXIX. Trad. Wiz. CC. Münst. Beitr. II. Urkb. p. 24: in villa O. sortes XXX.

Note 10. — Page 5.

The first step towards the payment of rent was probably taken by the tenant. It was understood that he was to bring to his lord some of the produce of his labor; but the amount was not necessarily described. The tenant came with a certain portion of his produce, and offered it to his lord. If the lord accepted it and was satisfied, and did not ask for anything more, a precedent was established. The tenants brought no more produce to the lord than he had received in the first place, and the lord was not satisfied with less, if less was offered. The rent was in this way fixed by precedent. But it was argued that the slaves ought to pay more rent than the freemen: and this they were obliged to do. The freemen paid rent according to one precedent; the slaves paid it according to another. New precedents were then introduced for every class of tenants, and new classes of tenants were formed by the institution of new precedents; until at last there were almost as many precedents as there were tenants. When this stage was reached, rents were fixed by contract rather than by precedent. The introduction of written documents, whereby the contracts made with individuals could be recorded, helped very much to bring about this result. When agriculture ceased to be the sole occupation of the laboring classes, when new occupations arose, these occupations served as a basis for the classification of society. Some men were fighters; some were farmers; others were artisans, mechanics, or tradesmen. The old classification according to dues and services was given up as soon as dues and services came to be fixed by contracts between individuals. The classification according to occupation was then introduced. Where the occupations became hereditary, a system of castes arose. This system has never been rigid in Western Europe, however, as it has been in India, and other countries of the East.

Note 11. — Page 5.

This interpretation will perhaps surprise the reader. It has not, so far as we know, been offered before. That, however, can be no ground of objection to it. The words used by Tacitus bear the interpretation; and it is consistent with the testimony of the later records, and with all that we know regarding the divisions and distributions of land in later times. The *spatia camporum* of Germ. 26 are, accordingly, the *quarentenae*, *furlangs*, *wannen* or *gewannen*, *wanden* or *gewenden*, of the open-field system. The *quarentenae* were, properly speaking, lengths of forty rods, as in Kemble's Codex CCXIII and CCXXI (see also Spelman sub. voc. *quarentena*); but the spaces or sections in which the original lots were redistributed being quite regularly forty rods long or wide, these spaces or sections came to be called *quarentenae*. The *quarentena* is of course the English *furlong* (the furrow-long). This word was used to describe the acre because it was always a furrow long. See Lib. de Hyd. p. 81 : tres acrae quod lingua Anglorum dicitur thry furlang. Cf. Lacomblet Urkb. 48 : dedit Gerfridus xx furlangas. See also Corb. Trad. 341. The word *furlong* was used in the same way to describe any piece of land which was a furrow long. In this way fields containing many acres came to be called furlongs. So, in the Winslow Manor Rolls, a MS. in the library of Cambridge, England. See the passage cited in Mr. Seebohm's book (pp. 27–29): ½ acre in Clayforlong, ½ acre in Brereforlong. There were several or many half-acres in each *furlong*. The German words which are used to describe the spaces or sections in which the original lots were redistributed, — the words *gewannen* or *gewenden*, — refer us, not to the length of the furrow, but to the turning of the plough at the end of it. The spaces or sections were called *gewannen* or *gewenden*, because the ploughs turned back and forth within them. The nature of the *furlangs* or *gewannen* may be studied upon the maps of old villages. Mr. Seebohm publishes a map of Hitchin fields, in Herts. See others in Prof. Meitzen's Introduction to Cod. Dipl. Siles. Bd. IV. See also his other work, Der Boden des Preussischen Staates, Bd. I. pp. 353, 362, 363; and the article entitled " Die Ausbreitung der Deutschen in Deutschland," in the Jahrbücher für Nationalökonomie und Statistik, Jahrg. XVII. Bd. I. The plan of Saarhoelzbach, in the district of Merzig on the Saar, a typical example, is given in another article in the same periodical. Neue Folge, 2 Bd. 1 Heft, p. 38.

It is possible that the *agri pro numero cultorum occupati* were redistributed in *gewannen* among the Suevi, in the time of Cæsar. He says, IV. 1: privati ac separati agri apud eos nihil est. Cf. Kemble's Codex DCXLVIII: cassatos segetibus mixtis.

NOTE 12. — PAGE 6.

See Diplomata Spuria Arnulf. 6: terris aratoriis ad dies plus minus 22 et quartariis 2. Then Fulda Trad. Cap. 42, No. 104: xx diurnales, hoc est quod tot diebus arari poterit. We meet with the *Tagwerch* (a day's work) as a measure of land at M. B. XXXIV. 2, p. 376, and also in Hist. Frising. Bd. II. Instr. CCCXVIII, CCCXCII, CCCCXXIII. The German word commonly used is *Morgen*.

NOTE 13. — PAGE 6.

Kemble's Codex DXIII: quinque cassatos . . . nullus certis terminis sed jugera jacent ad jugeribus. Abingdon Chron. I. p.

384 : ruris particulam, v videlicet cassatos . . . rus namque praetaxatum manifestis undique terminis minus dividitur, quia jugera altrinsecus copulata adjacent. Kemble's Codex DIII : tres cassatos, singulis jugeribus mixtim in communi rure huc illucque dispersis. Cf. DCXLVIII : xvii cassatos segetibus mixtis. The *cassati* were hides. Vid. DCXXII : v cassatos . . . fif hida. The phrase *aecer under aecer*, which occurs several times in the Abingdon Chron. (vid. I. pp. 248, 330, 350, 353), seems to be the equivalent of the *jugera ad jugeribus* in Kemble's Codex DXIII. The *mansi* or *cassati* were redistributed in acre lots. In the Codex, CXXVIII, we have mentioned the acres of a *mansus:* mansionis jugera. Vid. Abingdon Chron. I. p. 283 : unam mansam cum xii agrorum quantitate. The *agri* here were acres. Vid. p. 285. So in the Codex CCLXIV : dimidium agrum . . . healve aker.

In its origin the acre was simply a field to plough. The size of it varied indefinitely ; but it was usually oblong, and approximately rectangular. The furrows being of the same length, and side by side, made it rectangular ; and it was oblong for convenience' sake, — to avoid turning the plough too frequently. The furrows were long, and there were few of them as a rule. Cf. Lex Baiw. XII. 6.

It is probable that the length of the acres was at first determined by a cord, and the width by rods; but a certain number of rods was afterwards substituted for the cord as the measure of length. See Mon. Nideralt. p. 33 : ut maximus campus per funiculos mensuraretur, et cuilibet hube xii jugera deputarentur. The length of the acre (i. e. the length of its furrows) was determined by the cord. If the acre was less in width than in length, the cord, if used for the length, would not serve for the width. Something else must have been used. That was without doubt the rod. The acre of Lex Baiw. I. xiv is forty rods long by four wide. Our English acre is similarly proportioned. See Statutes of the Realm, I. p. 206. The Bavarian rod, however, is ten feet long, while the English rod is sixteen and a half feet long. The acre of the Bavarian law is therefore smaller than the English acre.

Note 14. — Page 7.

See Prof. Hanssen's writings, — his "Abhandlungen," and the recent essays in the Zeitschrift für Gesammte Staatswissenschaft; 3 Heft, 1880; 3, 4 Heft, 1882. These writings are the most valuable we have upon the remains of the open-field system in Germany. Prof. Meitzen's writings are also of great value. See titles in Note 11. See also Dr. Achenbach's essay on the "Haubergs-Genossenschaften" (Bonn, 1863, 8). The Reports from her Majesty's representatives on the Tenure of Land in the several countries of Europe, presented to the Houses of Parliament in 1869-70, contain some interesting matter upon the open-field system. For England, see the Report on the Agriculture in the several Counties of England, published by the Board of Agriculture, or the Reviews of these Reports by Mr. Marshall (York, 1815-17). The Report on Commons' Inclosure (ordered by the House of Commons to be printed, August 5, 1844) is of great interest. Prof. Nasse's book upon the Agricultural Community of the Middle Ages, translated for the Cobden Club in 1871, is well known. Mr. Seebohm's book, which has just been published, or will be published very soon, contains a detailed account of the open fields in England. Other references might be given, but these will be found sufficient. In consequence of the Inclosure Acts in England, the *Verkoppelungen* in Germany, the vestiges of the open-field system are fast disappearing.

Note 15. — Page 7.

Very good examples may be seen in the neighborhood of Hitchin, in Herts, and of Luton, in Bedford. Mr. Seebohm describes them in his "English Village Community," Chap. I. Similar acres may be seen in many parts of Germany, and in the Austrian dominions. They may be seen also in Engadine.

Note 16. — Page 7.

There is quite a little literature upon this subject. See Meitzen's article entitled, "Der älteste Anbau der Deutschen," in the Jahrb. für Nationalökonomie und Statistik, Neue Folge, 2 Bd. 1 Heft, pp.

31, 32. It will not be worth our while to go into the subject; but it should be observed that it is by no means certain that these *Hochäcker* were the work of Germans. They may have been made by the Kelts, who lived in the Bavarian Highlands before the Germans. They may have been the work of the Romans. Nor is it to be inferred that they were tilled by freemen. It must not be inferred that they were the common fields of a free village community. They may have been the fields of a manorial village, a village of tenants, serfs, or slaves. The question as to the ownership of land in early times, the question as to whether the land was first private property or common property, cannot possibly be solved by reference to the *Hochäcker*.

NOTE 17. — PAGE 8.

See Germania 26, and the Codex S. Galli 214: trado quicquid genitor meus W. genetrice mea K. ad dodidem egisset, id sunt II calonicas, Gerboldo et Heilboldo, et analies terris, mancipiis, pratis, pascuis, etc. In Abingdon Chron. I. p. 304, we have nine hides lying in among other partible lands, meadows in common, and other lands in common: thas nigon hida lieggead on gemang othran gedallande feldlaes gemane, and maeda gemane, and yrthland gemaene. Cf. Ine 42.

During the migrations the arable lots were shifted from place to place, and the number of them varied according to the number of cultivators. Afterwards, when the people settled down permanently, the lots belonging to the free-lord were shifted from one position to another round about his farmstead. The number of them was increased or diminished, as he had more or not so many cultivators at the farmstead, or attached to it in houses of their own. The land upon which the arable lots were thus shifted about was called the partible or common land, as in the passages above cited from Abingdon Chron. and Ine.

During the Middle Ages the word *almend* came into use. It was used to describe the land which was not under the plough, which served to supply the animals with grass and winter fodder. The word appears to be derived from the Keltic *al*, meaning fodder, and *main*, *maine*, an estate, property, or *min*, meaning land, a field or plain. The original meaning of the word was therefore *fodder-land*, not common land, as has been supposed. But, as the word was used constantly to describe undivided and common lands, it is natural that it should acquire a new signification. See Mone Zeits. I. p. 385 *et seq*. In the year 1270 Count Otto v. Eberstein alludes to his fodder-lands as *almendis nostris per totum dominium nostrum constitutis*. Ibid. p. 371. From Count Otto's point of view the *almendae* were private property. The tenants, however, regarded them as common lands. In the course of the Middle Ages the tenant's point of view prevailed over that of the landlord, and the *almend* was regarded simply as the common land. With this idea of it, it is not surprising that the etymologists have been trying to connect the word *almend* with the word *allgemein* (i. e. universal, general, common), making the etymology conform with the meaning. They forget that words often change their meanings by getting new ones.

NOTE 18. — PAGE 8.

The hide and the plough-land are the same thing. See Hen. Hunt. Hist. Angl., at the year 1008 (M. H. B. p. 753) : hida autem Anglice vocatur terra unius aratri culturae sufficiens per annum. The hides here mentioned are called *cassati* in Flor. Wig. Chron. (M. H. B. p. 585). Plough lands are frequently mentioned in the records. See Kemble's Cod. XXVII, XLIII, LXXVII, LXXXV : partem terrae, id est decem aratrorum. CXIV, CXXI, CXXXII, CXXXV, CLII, CLIII, CLVII, CLX : terram juris mei decem aratrorum, CLXXIX, CLXXXVII, CXC, CXCIX. The plough-land was called a *sulung* in Kent. See Domesday for that county. The word *carrucata* is used frequently in Domesday to describe the plough-land, the plough being described by the word *carruca*. It is doubtful whether the *carrucata* is mentioned before the Conquest. It occurs in Kemble's Codex CCXIII ; but the document is of doubtful authenticity. In Diplomata Spuria 82, we have the terra unius carrucae. See Fulda Trad. Cap. 40. 4 : CCXL jugera ad III aratra ; and Fulda Codex 744 : territorio duobus aratris sufficiente. Pez Thesaurus VI. Part III. p. 63 : quatuor araturae. Vid. also Cod. Morav. CXXX : unam araturam cum serviente. So in CLXII and CXCIV : terram unius aratri cum ministeriali. CXCVII : aratra cum rusticis. So in CXCVIII, CCX : terram ad duo aratra. CCXIX: terram ad duo aratra cum cultore arante. Cf. CCXXXI and CCLIII. The word *plough* occurs in Rothar CCXCIII: plouum aut aratrum. The German word *pflug* is used to describe the plough-land as well as the plough.

NOTE 19. — PAGE 9.

At Alvertune, for example, in Yorkshire, the land was estimated at forty-four plough-lands, but thirty ploughs were found to be sufficient for the work. At Walesgrif the land was estimated at fifteen plough-lands, but eight ploughs were found to be sufficient for the work. See Domesday I. p. 299. Any number of similar examples might be given. It follows that the holders of the plough-lands must have done the ploughing co-operatively, unless they used the ploughs in turn. At Walesgrif five tenants used two ploughs. At Picheringa (also on p. 299) the land was estimated at thirty-seven plough-lands; but the work could be done with twenty ploughs. Twenty of the tenants used six ploughs. Any number of similar examples might be given. It should be remembered that at this time the plough-lands were usually divided into fractions, and there were often several tenants on each plough-land. It appears to have been quite customary to put four tenants on each plough-land. The quarter-plough-lands were called yard-lands, or *virgates*. The holder of the virgate had one rod (*virga*) in the width of each acre, and the width of the acre was four rods. Compare Chron. Petrob. (Liber Niger) p. 157: et de istis x hidis tenant XL villani XL virgas terrae. It will be remembered that the plough-land and hide are the same thing. Vid. Hen. Hunt. Hist. Angl. A. D. 1008: hida Anglice vocatur terra unius aratri. Hen. Hunt. wrote this about the year 1135. The date of Liber Niger is between the years 1125 and 1128.

The fact that there were often not so many ploughs as plough-lands led to confusion. Sometimes we hear of plough-lands consisting of plough-lands. We have seen how the word *sulung* was used in Kent to describe the plough-land; and yet Coke tells us that seven solins were equal to seventeen plough-lands. He cites a passage from Domesday, which we have not been able to verify: septem solina terrae sunt 17 carucat. Coke Litt. 5 a. The explanation of the difficulty is that there were seven ploughs used upon seventeen plough-lands; there were plough-lands within plough-lands. See Domesday S. Paul, p. 58: vi hidis trium solandorum. Here there were three ploughs to six plough-lands. The hide was the plough-land, yet it contained plough-lands!

Note 20. — Page 9.

Capit. de Vil. XXXVII: prata nostra ad tempus custodiant. Compare Lex Wisig. Lib. VIII. Tit. III. 12: qui in pratum eo tempore quo defenditur pecora miserit.

Note 21. — Page 9.

Ritz Urkb. 15: prata ad fenum colligendum carradas LX. Alsat. Dipl. XXXVII: de prata unde potest secare de feno carradas centum triginta. Wirtemb. Urkb. CXX: de pratis carradas c. Mon. Nideralt. p. 108: de pratis ubi possunt colligi de feno carrade quadringente. Trad. Wiz. II, V: prato ubi potest annis singulis plus minus v carra de feno colligere. Cf. also XXI, XXV, XLII, and Fulda Cod. 42. 96. Hist. Frising. CCCXIV: xii carradas de pratis. Ibid. CCCXLVIII: de pratis carradas L. So in CDLX, DLXII, DCCXXXI: de pratis carradas ccc. Read also DCCXXXIX, DCCXLI, DCCCLXXVI. So elsewhere. It is useless to multiply examples. In certain cases the grass land was estimated according to the number of animals that could be maintained by the fodder produced upon it. See, for example, Fulda Trad. Cap. 7. 51; terram videlicet pascualem pecoribus xvi, idem tantum prati quantum sufficiat xv bubus, vel xv animalibus, per hiemem cum feno pasci; quod potest computari ad xv carradas. This supports the statements made on the second page of our text; that the amount of grass land that the freeman occupied depended upon the number of animals he had to maintain through the winter. It is possible that the tenants were sometimes allowed to take from the land as much grass as could be cut in one or more days. The measure of the meadow land was in certain places the day's work, *Tagwerch*. References were given in Note 12. The word *Tagwerch* may, however refer to the work of measuring off the ground, and not to that of cutting the grass. See Fulda Trad. Cap 7. 91: pratorum quantum una die a x viris meti poterit.

NOTE 22. — PAGE 9.

We read of *ceorls* with common or partible meadows in Inc 42. We do not know, however, how these meadows were divided. We have to come down to quite recent times to get any information upon this point. The records take little note of the internal affairs of the tenant communities. The modes of dividing and distributing the land are, therefore, known to us only in cases where old customs have been preserved to modern times. Fortunately these cases are quite numerous, and they have been described more or less satisfactorily by modern writers. See references in Note 14. The following passage from Giles's "History of Bampton" gives us a very good account of a lot-meadow. We give the passage at second hand, from Mr. Charles Elton's Observations on the Commons Bill, 1876 (London, Wildy and Sons).

"The common meadow is laid out by boundary stones into thirteen large divisions technically called layings-out; these always remain the same, and each is divided into four sets. As the meadow is not equally fertile in every part, it is desirable to adopt some mode of giving all an equal chance of obtaining the best cuts for their cattle. From time immemorial there have been sixteen marks established in the village, each of which corresponds with four yard-lands (allotments in the lands of the village). A certain number of the tenants consequently have the same mark, which they always keep, the use of these marks enabling the tenants every year to draw lots for their portions of the meadow. When the grass is fit to cut, the grass stewards and sixteens summon the tenants to a general meeting, and the following ceremony takes place. Four of the tenants come forward, each bearing his mark cut on a piece of wood, — as the frying-pan, the hern's foot, &c. The first drawn entitles its owner to have his portion in Set 1, the second in Set 2, and so on; and thus four tenants having obtained their allotments, four others came forward, and the process is repeated. When the lots are all drawn, each man cuts out his mark upon his piece of ground, which in many cases is so narrow a strip that he has not width enough for a full sweep of the scythe . . . and another peculiarity of the system is that a single farmer may have to cut his portion of the grass from twenty different places."

NOTES AND REFERENCES. 143

See also Joshua Williams's Rights of Common and other Prescriptive Rights (London, 1880, 8º). Some drawings of the "marks" are given in this work, facing p. 90. By the kindness of Mr. Williams the writer was permitted to see some of the originals, — little notched sticks about two inches long. Similar marks were used in Germany. See Otto Beck, Beschreibung des Regierungsbezirks Trier (3 vols., 1868-1871, 4°). Vol. I. p. 426, and the Appendix. A great many drawings of marks are given. Compare Germ. 10 : sortium consuetudo simplex. virgam frugiferae arbori decisam in surculos amputant, eosque notis quibusdam discretos super candidam vestem temere ac fortuito spargunt.

NOTE 23. — PAGE 10.

The rotation system was adopted to prevent quarrelling in regard to the distribution of lots. The lots were seldom equal in value, so those who got the poorer ones were apt to complain. Redistributions were called for; but the redistributions served merely to substitute one body of discontents for another. Then it was suggested that the lots might be taken in turn, in rotation. By this means all reasonable cause of dispute was removed.

NOTE 24. — PAGE 10.

See references under Note 14. It is not our purpose to enter much into the internal history of the tenant communities of the Middle Ages. It is a subject which stands apart, by itself. Our object is to explain how these communities came into existence. It is their origin and place in history which we are here considering. For this reason, we shall not take up the open-field system in its details; nor shall we describe at all the various systems of tillage which were adopted or introduced in different places. The history of the three-field system, the system which was so generally introduced during the Middle Ages, is an extremely interesting subject, but it lies beyond the limits of our investigation. It was not introduced much before the tenth century. It is nowhere referred to before the eighth.

Note 25. — Page 10.

Münst. Beitr. II. No. III: terra xxx animalium. Fulda Trad. Cap 7. 14: pascua xiiii pecudum. Ibid. 18: terram pascualem quatuor boum. Ibid. 20: x pecudum pascua. Cf. also 22, 49, 52, 53, 60, 61, 72, 110, 113, 121, etc. Trad. Wizenb. IV: silva mihi aspicientem ad porcos crassare plus minus xv. See also CXLVI. CCLXXII. Lacomblet Urkb. 61: terram xx animalium et dimidiam unius. Also Ibid. 56: x porcorum pascuam. These few examples may be sufficient to show that property in pasture land was quite commonly estimated according to the number of animals of one kind or another that could be supported upon it. When the free-lord had a pasture for a large number of animals, he allowed his tenants to turn out each a certain small number, five or ten, more or not so many. In the Lauresham Cod. XXXIII, Ansfrid has a pasture for a thousand hogs. Three free tenants turn out ten apiece, while the slaves turn out five apiece: unusquisque autem de servis ipsis de sua huba debet mittere in sylvam porcos v. The tenants had what are called in the English law "rights of common," that is to say, rights to enjoy the product of land not their own. Their rights were stinted, as the phrase is, because their enjoyment of the land was defined and limited. The free tenant, for example, had only so much of the herbage, nuts, and so on, as ten hogs could consume during the year. Where there was plenty of land, more than enough for all the animals, the rights of common were usually unstinted. Mr. Charles Elton's Law of Commons and Waste Lands (London, 1868, 8°) will be found instructive in this connection.

Note 26. — Page 10.

We know that the tenants required wood for building purposes and for fuel; and inasmuch as we have no records, of early date, to show that the amount which one man could take was limited, we may infer that, in early times, the wood was cut *ad libitum*. There was probably plenty of forest land, and no occasion, therefore, to limit rights of enjoyment in it. In later times, when boundaries were fixed, and forest lands came to be held in severalties, no man could cut wood except upon his own land; and the tenants, of course, could not cut wood beyond the territory of their lord.

Sometimes the tenants received severalties of forest land. See
Fulda Trad. Cap. 41. 16 : xxx jugera et unum lidum nomine Cuteo,
et silvam, sicut alii lidi habere videntur, xl jugerum. In such
cases, of course, the tenants could not cut any wood outside the
limits of their respective allotments. As a rule, however, the tenants had no allotments, but simply rights of common in the forest
of their lord. These rights of common (*common of estovers*, as it
is called in the English law, in Bracton IV. 41) were usually unstinted, in the early time of which we are speaking.

Note 27. — Page 11.

Fulda Trad. Cap. 42. 305: hubam unam dominicale, serviles vero hubas xiiii. So in Lauresham Cod. XXXIV. See
also XXXVII, LXXXIII, CXII, MMDCXXI, MMDCXXII,
MMDCLXXXII, MMMDCLI. Alsat. Dipl. XCV: hobas septem excepto terra dominicata. Cod. S. Galli 38 and 143:
hobas v, excepto ea que in usus proprios collere videtur quod
dicitur hoba siliga [salica]. Cf. Beyer Urkb. II. Add. 21 and
40: dominicalem terram, legali verbo selegnt. Lauresham Cod.
MMCCLVII: selhuben. Cod. S. Galli 331: unum agrum salicam. 372: casa salica cum terra sua salica. Münst. Beitr. II.
Num. V: selihova. Num. VIII: dominicatos mansos quod vulgo
dicitur selehouva. Num. III: mansus dominicales. Günther Cod.
Dipl. I. Num. 20: mansum indominicatum cum aliis mansis servilibus. Trad. Corb. 237. Ritz Urk. 15: mansum indominicatum
cum aliis mansis xi. See also Ibid. 12. Reg. Westfal. XV and
XXIII: casas dominicatas cum territorio dominicali, necnon et
mansos triginta. So in XXV. Hist. Trev. LXXVIII, CXXXIX,
CLI: mansum indominicatum et alios mansos. Also CLII, CLIII,
CLXVII: mansum indominicatum cum xi subjugalibus. See the
Registrum Prumiense, especially the first of the Caesarius-Glossae
where the *mansi indominicati* are defined as *agri curiae*. See also
Beyer Urkb. Nos. 173, 273: casa dominicali cum xii mansis ingenuilibus et xx servilibus. Then Cod. S. Galli 357: mansum
dominicatum cum aliis exterius inde pertinentibus. The domain
land is called *in-land* in the English records; and the land occupied by the tenants is called *gesettes-land*. The distinction between
lord's land and tenant's land is clearly drawn in Domesday and in
the Chartularies.

Note 28. — Page 12.

The student who desires to go into the subject of rents, dues, and services, will find the following list of references useful, and approximately complete. The subject is one of great interest. See Germ. 25. Lex Alam. XXII, XXIII. Lex Baiw. I. Cap. 14; VI. Cap. 2. Capitulare Aquisgranense A. D. 789. LXXIX; Capit. de Villis; Brev. Rer. Fisc. Alsat. Dipl. CCXLIX (Mauri. Chart.). Formula CL. Wirtemb. Urkb. VIII, XXVI, XXXIV, LXXIX. Polyp. Irminon. Polyp. S. Remi. Chart. Sithiense, pp. 67 and 97 to 106. Reg. Prumiense. Beyer Urkb. 120, 256, 332, 343, 400, 462. Nachtrag I. 34; Nachtrag II. 10, 11, 13, 14, 15. 16. Lauresham Codex CXL. DCCCLXVIII, DCCCCXXXVI, MDCCCLXXVII, and MMMDCLI–MMMDCLXXXIII inclusive. Trad. Wiz. p. 269 et seq. Cod. S. Galli 24, 39, 63, 89, 91, 93, 113, 117, 128. Mohr Cod. Dipl. 193. Hist. Frising. I. Part I. p. 126. Also Num. CDLXXXI. M. B. III. p. 454. M. B. XXII, p. 15, and p. 131 et seq. Lacomblet Urkb. 88, 290, 341, 351; also Nachlese (Bd. 4) 608. Lacomblet Archiv I. p. 309 et seq. Fulda Trad. Cap. 4. 133; Cap. 6. 99; Cap. 7. 31 et seq. Read also chapters 13, 36, 37, 43, 44 (Nos. 26, 37, 50), 45, 65. Fulda Codex 225, 361, 754, 804, 839. Günther Cod. Dipl. 44 and 76. Münster Beitr. II. Num. I. III, XIX, XX, XXXVI, XXXVII. Osnabrk. Gesch. Num. LXXXX. Lisch Urkb. II. Num. CLXXVIII et seq. Arnsb. Urkb. 43. Henneb. Urkb. CVIII, CXX, CXL. Reg. Westf. XXVI. Reg. Bad. 5, 6, 15. M. B. XXVIII, p. 158 et seq.; also p. 455 et seq. M.B. XXIX (2), p. 214 et seq, and p. 381 et seq. M. B. XXXIV (2), p. 348 et seq. M. B. XXXVI. Ennen: Quellen zur Geschichte der Stadt Köln. Bd. II. Num. 201. Dipl. Merow. 54, 96. Inc 67. Rect. Sing. Pers. (Thorpe, p. 431 et seq.). Domesday. Abingdon Chron. (II. App. III.) Chron. Petrob., the Liber Niger in the Appendix. Cart. Gloucest. (the Extenta in Vol. III.) Then Domesday S. Paul. Passages of interest may be found in the other Cartularies. The Rotul. Hundred. is also one of the most important sources of information regarding rents, dues, and services; and there are passages in Fleta upon this subject.

Note 29.—Page 12.

Registrum Prumiense, Glossa 1: mansi absi sunt qui non habent cultores, sed dominus eos habet in sua potestate. See examples in the Reg. Prum. See Hist. Trev. CLI: mansos ix absolutos absque ullo homine. Also Indic. Arnonis I: mansos x inter vestitos et absos. Hist. Frising. CCVI: mansos vestitos viiii, cum terrio cultum et incultum. Westf. Urkb. 8: hobas x possessas. Fulda Cod. 806: mancipiis hubas possidentibus et incolentibus. Cod. S. Galli 372: hobas tres vestitas. Ried Cod. Dipl. Ratisb. LXXV: hobas duas absas. Ibid. LXXVI and CXX: hobas possessas.

Note 30.—Page 12.

The tenants are described as *familiae* in Baed I. 25; II. 9; III. 4, 24, 25; IV. 3, 13, 16, 23; V. 19. So in Trad. Corb. 1, 2. 3, 4, 6, 30, 45, 65, 93, 114, 133, 147, 350, 414, 438: inter omnia sint familie xii cum territoriis [id est fundos. See Lacomblet Urkb. Bd. 1, No. 170]. This would be, according to Germ. 26, *agri pro* xii *cultoribus*. The tenants are described as *familiae* in Fulda Trad. Cap. 3. 196; in Brev. Not. Salzb. XVII. 2; in Wirtemb. Urkb. VIII, Reg. Westf. XIX, and in many other places. See, lastly, Osnabrk. Gesch. XXI: septem familias id est septem hobas. That would be *agri pro* vii *cultoribus*. The tenants are described as *manentes* in Kemble's Codex XIX, XXXV, CIII, CXIX: terram duarum manentium juris mei. Many other examples might be cited. In DCLV the land of five *manentes* is described as five hides. That would be *agri pro* v *cultoribus occupati*. *Manentes* are mentioned in Fulda Codex 188. Brev. Not. Salzb. II. 9; IX. 2, 4; XI and XII; in Hist. Trev. LXVI: and in many other passages. For *mansionarii* see Wirtemb. Urkb. VIII; Ried Cod. Dipl. Ratisb. No. CIII. In CVII we have a *mansum cum mansore*. Then see Du Cange sub. voc. *casarii*. *Cassati* are referred to very frequently in Kemble's Codex. The passage DCXXII: v cassatos . . . lif hida, has been already cited. This would be *agri pro* v *cultoribus occupati*. Cf. also Dipl. Arnulf. 13; Fulda Codex 113: servi cassati; and 364: cassatum servum cum elaboratu. References for *servi* and *mancipia* were given in Note 7.

Tributarii are often referred to in Kemble's Codex. See XXXVI. CXVIII. CXL. for examples. See also Mon. Scheftl., Traditiones III. VI, VII, IX. Also Ried Cod. Dipl. Ratisb. CXX: hobas possessas cum *parscalchis vel tributariis*. In Reg. Bad. 12 we have *censuales homines sive familiae*; in 43: viri censuales. *Rusticani* are mentioned in Rothar CCLXXXV, *villani* also. The latter word occurs all through Domesday. *Rustici* are referred to in Stenzel Urkb. X; and in Cod. Morav. CCCLXXVIII. *Accolae* are repeatedly referred to in the formula *accolabus mancipiis*, in alienations. *Coloni* are mentioned in innumerable records. See, for examples, Mohr Cod. Dipl. 9: Reg. Westf. XXXV: colonos et mansos xvi. Hist. Trev. LXIII. Westf. Urkb. 4. Cod. Dipl. Lubec. II. DXLIV. Stenzel Urkb. XLVII, CXIX. Lastly, Cod. Dipl. Siles. Bd. IV. XXVII. p. 21. *Inquilini* also are mentioned in this passage. *Liti* are mentioned in most of the Folk-Laws, and in many of the documents. Reg. Westf. XXIV. Lauresham Codex MMMDCLXXVIII: hubae lidorum. Fulda Trad. Cap. 43: lidi pleni . . . lidi dimidii. The student should observe, in verifying these examples, how the great mass of the people were settled as tenants upon comparatively few large estates, and he should observe too how these great estates consisted regularly of tenant allotments; i. e. *agri pro numero cultorum occupati*. The student will find that this phrase of Tacitus has an almost universal application.

Note 81. — Page 12.

Caesar VI. 22. It is usually assumed that, according to Cæsar, nobody had any land which he called his own. The assumption is not legitimate. There were no boundaries between one man's land and another's, so no man could say where his possessions came to an end, or where his neighbor's possessions had their beginning. In spite of that, however, there was a great deal of land which the free-lords regarded as their private and exclusive property, — the home lots, the arable lots which were cultivated by the serfs, the grass land which was reserved for a hay crop, and the land occupied by the animals as pasture ground. Beyond the grass lands and pasture lands lay the waste and forest land. There one man's estate was confounded with another's. So it could very well be said, that nobody held any definite amount of land, — that nobody had any boundaries to his possessions. Still he had possessions, as Cæsar himself tells us. See the words *ne latos fines parare studeant potentioresque humiliores possessionibus expellant.*

The persons whose estates extended one into another were called *co-marcani.* They were men who had a boundary in common. The common boundary was called a *co-marca.* We should describe it as a *confine.* See Münst. Beitr. II. Num. III : termini communes. Arnsb. Urkb. 27 : communi marchia. Dipl. Arnulf. 3 : communis terminatio. Fulda Codex 392 : in marca illarum villarum. When a dispute arose between neighbors in regard to the border land between their respective possessions, and they could not come to an agreement, the matter was usually settled by battle. See Lex. Baiw. XI. Cap. v : quotiens de commarchanis contentio nascitur ... The passage will be cited in full in Note 53. The nature of the *co-marca* appears clearly in some of the Regensburg records. See Ried. Cod. Dipl. Ratisb. XV, XX. See also Beyer Urkb. 108.

Note 32. — Page 13.

See Cod. S. Galli 631 : confinia silvarum. Cf. Hist. Frising. DCI. Mon. Schlehdorf. Dipl. XIII. Ried Cod. Dipl. XXXVI : confinia de venatione et piscatione. Salem Reg. p. 320 : per confinium terrarum ecclesiae. Lauresham Codex DCCCCXLVI : illam marcam de silva. Trad. Wiz. LXIX : marca silvatica. Cod. S. Galli 576 : silvaticis marchis. Lauresham Codex XXXII : waltmarca. Fulda Trad. Cap. 6. 67 : holzmarcham. So in Cap. 38, 201. Fulda Codex 317 : in ambitu id est in holzmarcu. Günther Cod. Dipl. 13 : confinium nemorum. Dipl. Arnulf. 3 : terminationes silvae.

Note 33. — Page 13.

See Kemble's Codex LXXXIII : terminos ab antiquis possessoribus constitutos. Abingdon Chron. I. p. 321 : rus sibi pertinens suis giratum terminis. Wirtemb. Urkb. CXLIII : vester minister et vestri servi, et nos ipsi et nostri servi de ambos partes finem fecerunt de illos arbores. Ried Cod. Dipl. CXIX : circumeundo praedium in silva communi captivaverat. Wirtemb.

Urkb. CXIX: concaptum legitimisque securarum adnotationibus habeo circumdatum. Cf. Hist. Frising. DXL: Memmo et filius ejus circumduxerunt missos Episcopi omnem rem. So in DXXVIII, DLXXXVII, and DCCCCLXXXI. In later times boundaries were fixed by the chief men and the common people assembled together. Cf. Formula CCCCII: factus est conventus principum et vulgarium ad dividendam marcham inter fiscum regis et populares possessiones in illo et in illo pago. We have a case in illustration in Cod. Trad. Lunaelae LXII. Compare Lex. Wisig. X. Tit. I. 3: si plures fuerint in divisione consortes, quod a multis vel a melioribus juste constitutum est a paucis vel deterioribus non convenit aliquantenus immutari. Then Ibid. I. 1: valeat semel facta divisio justa, ut nulla in postmodum immutandi admittatur occasio. Then Ibid. I. 8: sed quod a parentibus vel vicinis divisum est posteritas immutare non tentet. The result is we have, Ibid. Tit. III. 1: antiquos terminos et limites; and Ibid. 3: signa antiquitus constituta. Cf. Rothar CCXL et seq. Lex. Baiw. Tit. XI: de terminis. Also Lex Rip. LX. 5: quod si extra marcham in sortem alterius fuerit ingressus . . . The word *marcha* here is evidently used instead of the word *terminatio*, which occurs in the preceding passage, LX. 4: infra terminationem. Boundaries were designated by marks on trees. Lex. Baiw. XI. Cap. III. 2: in arboribus notas quas decoreas [decorticatas] vocant. So in Lex. Wisig. X. Tit. III. 3. Here we have also *lapides sculptos*, and *aggeres terrae*, *sive arcas*. Compare Lisch. Urkb. I. Num. VII: tres lapides terre affixos . . . arbores cruce notatas . . . per cruce signatas arbores. But upon this subject the reader may be referred to Grimm Rechtsalt. p. 541 et seq.

Note 34. — Page 13.

The boundaries are often given. The student will find a great quantity of them in Kemble's Codex. Some good examples are translated into English in Appendix D. of the Lib. de Hyd. For a few other examples, see Diplomata Merowig. 2. Lauresham X. Lisch Urkb. I. Nos. VII, X, XVI. Orig. Nassoic. LXXVIII. The student will easily find other examples if he wishes them.

Note 35. — Page 13.

Lex Baiw. IX. 12: amplicandum secundum morem antiquum. Wirtemb. Urkb. CVII: quidquid in confinio conprehensum vel elaboratum habuit. Ried Cod. Dipl. XXXIX: quod circumcapiebat. Cod. S. Galli 643: silvulam circa ipsum locum sitam ab aliorum potestate segregatam. Hist. Frising. DCI: quicquid ad colendum conprehensum habuissent. DCXVIII: quicquid deinceps elaborare potuissem. Lauresham Codex CCCCX: occupationem ad decem hubas [*agri pro x cultoribus occupati*]. DCXXVIII: proprisum quem pater meus proprisit. DCCCCXCVI: quicquid in ipsa marca laboratum habeo. Fulda Cod. 501: elaboratum in pago. Trad. Wiz. LXXVI: quicquid ibidem laboratum habeo aut inceps laborare potuero. Cod. S. Galli 25: quod ego adquesivi vel laboravi. Lacomblet Urkb. 27: quicquid habuimus per conprehensionem. Cod. S. Galli 547: quicquid in illo saltu conprehensum habuit. Then read Lex Baiw. XVI. 2: ego habeo testes qui hoc sciunt, quod labores de isto campo semper tuli, nemine contradicente exartavi, mundavi, possedi usque hodie . . .

Note 36. — Page 13.

Vid. Reg. Prum. Gloss. 1. *Mansi ingenuiles* are mentioned in Lauresham Cod. MMMDCLXXV; in Beyer Urkb. 273, 274; Hist. Trev. CLII: and elsewhere, but not very frequently. *Mansi litales* or *ledilia* are mentioned in Beyer Urkb. 135: Nachlese, 23; Münst. Beitr. II. Num. III: litus noster habet mansum: XIX; XXX: mansi et dimidius possessi a latis Teutonicis: Reg. Westf. XXIV: and elsewhere. They are not very common. *Mansi serviles* are mentioned in Lauresham Cod. CLXXXXIX; Wirtemb. Urkb. LXXXV: mansos xx cum servis super eos habitantibus [*agri pro xx cultoribus occupati*]; Beyer Urkb. 58, 173, 273: Indic. Arnon. VI; Brev. Not. Salzb. IV. 8; and elsewhere. The *mansi* which are not particularly described may be regarded as *mansi serviles*. When, for example, we read, in Formula CXL: mansum dominicum et alios mansos lx ad eum pertinentibus, we may assume that the latter were *mansi serviles*. The phrase *cum mancipiis* is frequently introduced, or else the phrase *et mancipia super comma-*

nentes. The *mansi* are regularly *mansi serviles.* If they are *mansi indominicati, mansi ingenuiles,* or *mansi litales,* they are described as such.

Note 37. — Page 13.

Beyer Urkb. 139 : hobas xcvii inter ingenuiles et serviles [*agri pro xcvii cultoribus occupati*]. Cod. S. Galli 576 : v hobas de terra arabili ; 643 : hobas legitime dimensas. Lauresham Cod. MMMDCLXXXI : hubas plenae lidorum. Hist. Frising. I. p. 214 : decem houbas censuales quae vulgariter parscalhes-hoba dicuntur. Num. DLXII : hobas servorum plenas vi [*agri pro vi cultoribus occupati*]. DCCCXLIX : de terra arabili hobas iiii. Alsat. Dipl. XCV : hobas octo excepto terra dominicata. Formula CCCLXVII : hobis possessis. Fulda Trad. Cap. 3. 12 : homines xii cum hubis suis [*agri cum cultoribus*] ; Cap. 7. 24 : terram x hubarum ; Cap. 42. 305 : hubam unam dominicale, serviles vero hubas xiiii. Osnabrk. Gesch. XXI : septem familias, id est septem hobas possessas ac censum solventes. Wirtemb. Urkb. CXXXII : hobas pleniter emensas. Lauresham Cod. XXXVII : hubas serviles vestitas x. These examples might be multiplied indefinitely.

Note 38. — Page 14.

Instead of describing the meadow, pasture, and forest lands in detail, the owner used this formula. It occurs in almost all the documents in which land is alienated and described. It may be observed that severalties of meadow and forest land existed, even in the time of Lex Salica, everywhere, so it cannot be maintained that the formula has reference to rights of enjoyment in common lands, rights in lands belonging to the community. In many cases, without doubt, it is used to describe lands held in common (undivided property, or property held in undivided shares) : but that is another matter. That severalties of meadow and forest land existed in the time of Lex Salica is proved by Lex Sal. XXVII. 10 : prato alieno ; and Ibid. 18 : silva aliena. Compare also the Capitulary of A. D. 615 : sylvas Ecclesiarum aut privatorum. Some more references will be given in other connections.

Note 39. — Page 14.

Cod. S. Galli 674: quaesitis et inquirendis, cultis et incultis. Ibid. 766: silvam quantum mihi necesse est extirpanda. Hist. Frising. DCLVI: terras aratorias extirpatas sive extirpandas, res quesitas et inquesitas. Wirtemb. Urkb. LXVIII: cultis et incultis, seu omne quod adquirere debeo, vel adquirens augere potuero. Ibid. CX: quesitis vel adhuc inquisitis. So in Reg. Hist. Westf. XXXVI. Mon. Weihensteph. p. 467: predium quesitum et inquisitum, cultum et incultum tradidit. Henneb. Urkb. I: quaesitis et inquirendis, omnibusque appendiciis et adjacentiis. Osnabrk. Gesch. XXVI: saltibus cultis et incultis, acquisitis et acquirendis. The records abound in examples.

Note 40. — Page 14.

Beyer Urkb. 63. Ried Cod. Dipl. CXIII and CXIX. Compare Cod. Morav. XLVI: proprietatem in omnibus marchis. So in Fulda Trad. Cap. 6. 98: bona sua et marca silve. See also Fulda Cod. 21: marcas vel fines. They are alienated as belonging to a certain estate. Then read Beyer Urkb. 108: in comarca ipsius ville bifangum unum ubi possunt edificari mansa centum necnon insaginari porci mille. The word *bifang* is used to describe appropriations. The Latin equivalent is *captura* or *novalis*. Cf. Beyer 465 (b): terram novalium circumjacentium ad xx mansos vel amplius. Ibid. 513: novalia de nemore. Other examples will be given in other connections. The freemen were constantly extending their possessions by appropriating unoccupied lands. No fact is more fully illustrated in the records than this.

Note 41. — Page 14.

Greg. Turon. VI. 20. See the passage cited in Note 2. Chrodinus founded a great many villages, and put tenants into them to cultivate the land. The case of Chrodinus was not an isolated case. All the rich lords were founding villages and putting their dependants and slaves into them. It was very profitable; for the tenants paid rents and dues for their lands. The more tenants a man had, the richer he became. Captives in war were divided, and then distributed in tenant colonies over the land. The owners of the colonists were the owners of the lands which they cultivated. In some cases many villages were under one lord. In Beyer Urkb. 19, Egid gives to the Abbey Prüm thirty or more villages: cum omni integritate, tam terris, domibus, edificiis, accolabus, mancipiis, vineis, silvis, campis, pratis, pascuis, aquis aquarumque decursibus, farinariis, cum pastoribus, gregis pecundum utriusque sexus, mobilibus et immobilibus. These villages were probably founded by Egid, or by his ancestors. Of course very few persons in private life were so wealthy as Egid: still the number of persons who owned two or three villages was large, as may be seen by any one who will read through some of the collections of early documents. The villages are often described, as in Hist. Trev. XXIX: villa nuncupata Waderlo . . . id est tam terras aratorias, campis, pratis, pascuis, aquis aquarumque decursibus, mobilibus et immobilibus, et silvam ad eundem locum pertinentem, et VIII casatas cum hominibus et mancipiis et cum omni peculio suo. Compare Formula CLIX: aliquam rem meam, in pago illo; hoc est mansos tantos cum hominibus ibidem commanentibus vel aspicientibus, cum terris arabilibus, silvis, campis, pratis, pascuis, vel quicquid in ipso loco mea fuit possessio vel dominatio. This is a common formula. Cf. CLXXII, CC, CCXXVIII, CCLI, CCC. We have a slightly different formula in CCXII: villam juris mei nuncupatam illam, sitam in pago illo cum terris aedificiis, accolabus, mancipiis, libertis, vineis, silvis, pratis, pascuis, aquis, aquarumve decursibus, mobilibus et immobilibus; cum omnibus appendiciis suisque adiacentiis, sicut a me presenti tempore videtur esse possessum; totum et ad integrum. Cf. the passage cited above from Hist. Trev. We see, in Formula CXXIV, that it was assumed that an inheritance consisted of villages of this character. The heirs are supposed to take one or two apiece: Accepit itaque ille villas nuncupatas illas, sitas ibi, cum mancipia tanta illa. Similiter et ille accepit e contra [contra germanum suum] in conpensatione alias villas, nuncupantes illas, sitas ibi, cum mancipia tanta illa. Property consisted quite regularly of villages of serfs, or portions of villages, for when a man died, and the sum of his villages was not a multiple of the number of his heirs, one or more of the villages were divided. Also when the villages were of unequal size they were usually divided. Then we have, instead of whole villages, shares or portions of villages: portiones in villis. So in Formula CCXIII. The *villa* was regularly a village of serfs, that is to say, a colony of dependants or slaves. It is evident from the records that the freeman was supposed to own one or more such colonies. See Lex Rip. LX: si quis villam aut vineam, vel quamlibet possessiunculam ab alio comparavit . . . See also Lex Baiw. I. Cap. 1: et quidquid donaverit, villas, terram, mancipia, vel aliquam pecuniam. These *villae* of the free-lords appear to be the *vici locati* of Germ. 16. See Note 2, and the citations there given. It will be remembered how in India, among the Hindus, and in Russia, among the Slaves, landed property has consisted quite regularly of village communities, — villages occupied by tenants or serfs, and owned by the members of an aristocracy. That this was the case in Western Europe during the Middle Ages is well known. It is our object to show that it was the case also in the earliest period of recorded history, — even in the time of Tacitus. Read once more Germ. 16, 25, and 26.

Note 42. — Page 14.

Athelstan II (Thorpe I. p. 217): si tunc sit aliquis qui tot homines habeat quod non sufficiat omnes custodire, praeponat sibi singulis villis praepositum unum, qui credibilis sit ei, et qui concredat hominibus. The *villae* here are the *vici locati* of Germ. 16. Why not? The *praepositi* are often described as *villici*, i. e. head-men of villages. See Lacomblet Urkb. 186: si villicus vel de edificiis vel de agricultura placitum ibidem habuerit . . . Cf. Beyer Urkb. 343. The duties of *villici* are described in Capitularia A. D. 813. II. 19. In Cap. de Villis the *villici* are called *judices*, and their duties are clearly set forth. Then read Alsat. Dipl. XXVIII: ipsos qui dicuntur schoffele aut villici, aut mansorum possessores qui dicuntur habere. Lex Burg. L. 3: actor patrimonii nostri, vel cujuslibet alterius. He is sometimes called *major*, as in Cod. S. Galli 13. Cf. Greg. Turon. IX. 36. Rothar CCLXXVI: gastaldius aut actor. See also CCCLXXVII: sculdasium aut actorem. See Wirtemb. Urkb. VIII: magister tributariorum. Stenzel Urkb. XLVIII: schultetus. This is a very interesting document, and others might be cited from the same collection. There are other passages bearing upon the position and duties of the *schulte-*

tus (*Schuldheiss*) in Cod. Dipl. Siles. IV. See Index. Lastly, read what Fleta says (Lib. II) about the officers of the manor, and their duties.

Note 43.— Page 14.

The evidence of this has been already given. See Notes 2, 41, 42. Property consisted regularly of lands occupied and cultivated by serfs, and as a rule the serfs were distributed in villages. We find that this was the case among the Germans generally at the time of the Folk-Laws, and the inference is that it was the case also in the time of Tacitus and Caesar. It will be urged that in the time of Tacitus and Caesar the life of the people was unsettled, nomadic; that the modes of life must have changed in many respects as soon as the migrations were over and settlements were permanent. This is true without doubt. The objection does not, however, touch our argument. Dependants and slaves were accumulated quite as easily during the migratory life as during that which was settled, — more easily, perhaps. Then whenever settlements were made the dependants and slaves were distributed in villages. The dwelling-places of the free-lords were surrounded by these villages. This was the case whether settlements were permanent or merely temporary. In other words, the conditions of the migratory life were not inconsistent with the growth and development of the manorial system. Perhaps, indeed, they were favorable to it. If this was not the case, how are we to explain the fact, that immediately after the migrations we have a fully developed manorial system, — free-lords dwelling apart from one another, with bands of dependants and slaves settled in villages round about them, rendering dues and services to them, or to their agents, *villici* or *praepositi*? It must be that this system was, to a certain extent at least, developed during the period of migrations.

Note 44. — Page 15.

Caesar IV. 3 : Publice maximam putant esse laudem, quam latissime a suis finibus vacare agros: hac re significari, magnum numerum civitatium suam vim sustinere non posse. Itaque una ex parte a Suevis circiter milia passum DC agri vacare dicuntur. So in VI. 23: Civitatibus maxima laus est, quam latissimas circum se vastatis finibus solitudines habere. Hoc proprium virtutis existimant, expulsos agris finitimos cedere, neque quemquam prope audere consistere: simul hoc se fore tutiores arbitrantur, repentinae incursionis timore sublato.

The object of the state in extending its border land in every direction as far as possible was not merely to display its power and secure itself against sudden attack. The chief object was to secure a territory upon which the people could increase and spread, and have as much land as they needed for their agriculture and stock-farming. The object was to make room for the herds of slaves and cattle. By these means states grew rich and powerful; by these means they were able to command the supplies which were needed in time of war. The more plentiful the supplies, the longer they were able to fight their enemies, the surer they were to triumph over them at last. The Germans were not slow to learn that success in war, in the long run, depends upon economic conditions at home, — upon the extent of lands, the number of cultivators, and the increase and supply of live-stock. We have seen (Note 5) how, in order to keep on fighting, the people took turns in going to war and in staying at home to look after their estates.

Note 45.—Page 15.

See lists of local names in the Altdeutsches Namenbuch, by Dr. Ernst Förstemann, Zweiter Band: Ortsnamen (2d edition, Nordhausen, 1872, 4°). See also Die Deutschen Ortsnamen, by the same author (Nordhausen, 1863, 8°). A very complete Bibliography is given in Section II (p. 9). See also Dr. Wilhelm Arnold's valuable treatise entitled: Ansiedelungen und Wanderungen Deutscher Stämme, zumeist nach Hessischen Ortsnamen. Long lists of local names are given. Most of the collections of early records have indices of local names. It is easy to glance over them. It is surprising to see how much of the early life of the people is contained in them. Isaac Taylor's Words and Places (2d edition, London, 1865, 8°) is deservedly well known.

Note 46. — Page 16.

Fulda Trad. Cap. 38. 265. Ibid. Cap. 5. 150. Cod. S. Galli 239. See also Fulda Trad. Cap. 6. 6: unum biuane sui nominis, Adoltesbiuane. The *biuane* was an appropriation of land. Cap. 38. 168: capturam id est biuane. Then read Fulda Cod. 115: quicquid in Perahtleibeshusom germanus meus Perahtleib manu potestativa mihi tradiderat. Also Mon. Scheftlar. p. 367: in villa nuncupata Reginprehteshusen, quicquid genitores illorum Werinpreht et Reginpreht relinquerunt. A great many personal names of this type occur. They may be easily found by reference to the indices of local names appended to the different collections of early documents. See for example the Orts-Register of the Cod. S. Galli. Twelve or fifteen personal names of places occur on the first half-page (Bd. II. p. 475), — Adaghiliniswillare, Adaldrudowilare, Adalgozzeshusa, Adalholteshoba, Adalrammiswilare, and so on. In many cases corresponding names may be found in the Personen-Register. The name Adalcozzus, or Adalgoz, occurs; also the name Adalramnus or Adalhram. An enormous proportion of the early names of places contain the names of persons. This is evidence, of course, in support of the *Einzelhof-system*.

Note 47. — Page 16.

Regarding houses, farm-buildings, sheds, yards, enclosed gardens, and so on, the student may read Germ. 16. Then Lex Sal. XVI, XXXIV, XXVII. 6, 7, and Novella 73 (Merkel, p. 62). Cf. Germ. 26. Gardens and orchards were planted in the time of Lex Salica, and afterwards (see espec. the Capit. de Vil.); but not at all in the time of Tacitus. Various farm-buildings are mentioned in Lex Alam. LXXXI. and in Lex Baiw. IX, X. See also Alsat. Dipl. XV, LXXXVII. Formulae CCXXXVIII, CCCLXV. Cod. S. Galli, 373. Mohr. Cod. Dipl. 9. Günther Cod. Dipl. 49: una curte cum lapidea domo. The date of this record is 1017–1047. Stone houses were probably rare, even at that date. Lastly, read Henneb. Urkb. CXL: curiam nostram, dictam fronhof.

Note 48.—Page 16.

The farmstead is quite commonly described by the Latin word *curtis*, which means an enclosed court or yard. The Teutonic equivalent is *tun*. It is used to describe an enclosure. It is the Dutch *tuin*, a fence or hedge, the Old High German *zun*, the German *zaun*. Cf. Lex Baiw. IX. 10, 11, and Rothar CCXC. The primitive farmstead appears to have been a courtyard surrounded by buildings of various kinds, dwelling-houses, barns, sheds, and so on. The type is probably preserved in existing farmhouses in the Rhineland of the Franks. See a plan in Heinrich Otto's Geschichte der Romanischen Baukunst in Deutschland (Leipzig, 1874, 4 . p. 45). We find in Lex Sal. Nov. 285 (Merkel, p. 74) reference to the interior of the courtyard and apple trees growing there: pomario domestico intus curte.

The *curtis* is referred to very frequently in the Folk-Laws and documents. See also Capit. de Vil. XLI : ut aedificia intra curtes nostras, vel sepes in circuitu, bene sint custoditae. We read in the Brev. Rer. Fisc. that the king's villa Asnapio consisted of a *sala* built of stone, and seventeen other houses built of wood, all enclosed in a courtyard; *infra curtem*. Further on we read of a *curtem sepe circumdatam*, of a *curtem sepe bene munitam*, of a *curticulam interclusam, cum tunimo strenue munitam*, and of a *curtem tunimo circumdatum et desuper sepe munitam*. Then we have the *curtem muro circumdatam cum porta ex lapide facta*. We have here the germ of the feudal castle. The Gaelic word *dun*, which is the cognate of *tun*, means a fortress. The Welsh word *din* means a hillfort. The arrangement of the feudal castle, a courtyard enclosed by walls and buildings, is without doubt derived from the arrangement of the primitive farmstead.

Note 49.—Page 16.

It must be remembered that the *mark*, at this time, was simply the border land which separated one settlement from another. Wirtemb. Urkb. LX : conquesitum meum cum marca sua. Fulda Trad. Cap. 6. 98 : bona sua et marca silve. Lex Rip. LX. 5 : extra marcham in sortem alterius. Fulda Codex 21 : marcas vel fines. Ibid. 317 : in ambitu id est in holzmarcu. Laureshan

Codex VI: villa cum omnibus adjacentiis vel appenditiis cum omnibus terminis et marchis. Ibid. XII: in fine vel marcha. DCCCCXLVI: marcam de silva ad illos mansos pertinentem. Codex S. Galli 576: silvaticis marchis ad hobas pertinentibus. The *mark* was at first the enclosure of uncultivated land. Then the word was used to describe the lands within this enclosure. The *villa* was described by the word *marca*. Trad. Wiz. XXIV: in villa vel in marca. The words *villa* and *marca* interchange meanings. Fulda Trad. Cap. 38. 201: tradidit holzmarcham ad x hubas. Read also Fulda Cod. 84: locum nuncupatum Biberbah, cujus marca sunt xxx hube. This was a mark of land containing thirty arable lots. We should describe the tenants of these lots as a *Markgenossenschaft*. The lord of the mark was Warinus. If, instead of giving his mark to Saint Boniface of Fulda, he had kept it, it would have passed to his descendants, to be divided and subdivided among them. As they multiplied upon the mark, we should have had another *Markgenossenschaft* coming into existence, a *Markgenossenschaft* of landlords, as distinguished from the *Markgenossenschaft* of the tenants. There were two kinds of *Markgenossenschaft*, one the association of tenants, the other the association of landlords. They must be very carefully distinguished the one from the other.

We hear of common marks in the earliest time. They were boundaries common to the estates of two or more persons. The free-lords whose estates touched one another were called associate mark-men, *comarcani*. Vid. Lex Baiw. XI. 5: quotiens de commarchanis contentis nascitur, ubi evidentia signa non apparent in arboribus, aut in montibus nec in fluminibus . . . We shall give the whole passage in Note 53. Cf. the passage cited above from Lex. Rip. The tenants of the *hubae* in the passage cited from Fulda Codex would be called *comarcani*. They lived together within a common boundary: and if Warinus had left these *hubae* to his descendants, they too would have been called *comarcani*. Again, it often happened that a group of free-lords settled in isolated farms or villas, which, inasmuch as they were isolated from other settlements, had a common mark. These lords would be described as *comarcani*, land-owners within a common mark, *consortes in marca*. Accordingly we have marks in which there are several villas. See Fulda Codex 392: in villa Urdorpf et Chizicha

NOTES AND REFERENCES. 161

et Adalfrideshuson et in marca illarum villarum. So also in Ibid. 429. The land-owners in these villas would be called *consortes in marca* or *comarcani*. The same terms might be used to describe their dependants and slaves. The existence of two classes of *vicini* is referred to in the first Capitulary added to Lex Salica. See Cap. 9 (Behrend, p. 91): vicini illi . . . qui meliores sunt . . . minoflidis vero. Cf. Capitula Add. ad Leg. Alam. 22, 39. All this will be elucidated more fully, as we go on in our argument. The point to be considered here is, that the mark was in the early time simply a boundary of uncultivated land separating one settlement from another. The *comarcani* were those persons who held this boundary in common. They were neighbors, *vicini*. The *comarcani* were separated one from another by marks, and groups of *comarcani* were separated from one another by marks. We have the *villa cum marca* and the *marca villarum*.

NOTE 50. — PAGE 17.

We hear a great deal of talk about house communities in which the holding of property was communistic. The holding of property in the Teutonic house communities was certainly not communistic. The head of the household was the lord of the land, and owner of all the live-stock and slaves set out upon it. When the head of the household died, his sons stepped into his place; when the sons died, the grandsons stepped into it: so it often happened that several persons were lords of the land and owners of the stock and slaves set out upon it. But we must not assume that the holding of the property was communistic. The evidence goes to show, as we shall see as we go on in our argument, that, although there was unity of possession, there was diversity of title. The title vested in the founder of the community was distributed among his descendants from generation to generation: so that each one could, if he pleased, appropriate some of the land, and some of the stock and slaves. When the individual was thought to have taken more than his share, a systematic division of the property was called for, a division in equal shares, an *exaequatio*. Then the unity of possession was broken up, and instead of one household we have several or many. The heads of these new households stood quite independent one of another, like their progenitor, the founder of the family and first lord of the land. The new households became house communities in the same way. The heirs increased in each one. They held their lands, stock, and slaves in common for a while; but with this unity of possession there was diversity of title, which led after a while to a division of the property among the heirs. The property being divided, the heirs distributed themselves in new households. The process went on indefinitely. We do not deny that there were house communities among the early Germans; but we do not believe that their constitution was in any respect communistic. The evidence goes to show that the principle of individual property was dominant everywhere.

Sometimes one son took the household, the stock, slaves, and land, — the boldest and best son, or the eldest. Cf. Germ. 32: inter familiam et penates et jura successionum equi traduntur: excipit filius, non ut cetera, maximus natu, sed prout ferox bello et melior. This is said of the Tencteri. In such cases the disinherited sons were maintained as dependants, or went off to seek their fortunes in other places. When they remained at home, they were vassals in the house of their father, vassals of their brother. In this condition of things we have the germ of a feudal system. All this, however, will be brought out more clearly as we go on through our argument.

Note 51. — Page 18.

Caesar VI. 22: Agriculturae non student; majorque pars victus corum in lacte, caseo, carne consistit: neque quisquam agri modum certum aut fines habet proprios; sed magistratus ac principes in annos singulos gentibus cognationibusque hominum, qui una coierunt, quantum et quo loco visum est agri attribuunt, atque anno post alio transire cogunt. Ejus rei multas afferunt causas, ne assidua consuetudine capti studium belli gerendi agricultura commutent: ne latos fines parare student, potentioresque humiliores possessionibus expellant, ne accuratius ad frigora atque aestus vitandos aedificent; ne qua oriatur pecuniae cupiditas, qua ex re factiones dissensionesque nascuntur: ut animi aequitate plebem contineant, cum suas quisque opes cum potentissimis aequari videat.

Note 52. — Page 19.

Tacitus Germ. 25 (given in Note 2). Ibid. 26 (given in Note 9).

Note 53. — Page 20.

Lex Baiw. XVI. Cap. I. 1 : Si quis homo pratum vel agrum vel exartum alterius contra legem malo ordine invaserit, et dicit suum esse, propter praesumptionem, cum sex solidis componat, et exeat. 2. Si autem suum voluerit vindicare illum agrum aut pratum vel exartum, vel unde illa contentio est, taliter vindicet. Juret cum sex sacramentalibus, et dicat: Ego in tua opera priore non invasi contra legem, nec cum sex solidis componere debeo, nec exire, quia mea opera et labor prior hic est quam tuus. Tunc dicat ille qui quaerit: Ego habeo testes qui hoc sciunt, quod labores de isto campo semper ego tuli, nemine contradicente exartavi, mundavi, possedi usque hodie, et pater meus reliquit mihi in possessione sua. Ille homo qui hoc testificare voluerit, commarchanus eius debet esse, et debet habere sex solidorum pecuniam et similem agrum. Tunc ille testis iuret taliter: Quia ego hoc meis auribus audivi et oculis meis vidi, quod istius hominis prior opera fuit in isto agro quam tua, et labores fructuum ille tulit. Post sacramentum reddat agrum. Tunc ille defensor, si sperat quod institia de illo agro suo fuisset, et hoc in praesenti populo fiat, ne per invidiam aliquis pereat, dicat ad illum testem : Mendacium iurasti contra me. Sponde mihi pugnam duorum, et manifestet Deus si mendacium an veritatem iurasti contra me ; et componere debes cum duodecim solidis, et illam terram reddere quam mendacitur abstulisti. Si vicerit ille qui quaerit, componat cum duodecim solidis, et illam terram reddat. Et si illam terram non potuerit donare, donet aliam in proximo quantum iactus est de securi saiga volente : Et si in proximo non habet, nec comparare potest, iuret secundum pretium agri ut ipsum agrum cum pretio valente nec cum duplo nec cum triplo conquirere non potuisset, et donet ubi habet : et ipsum agrum qui donet iuret quod talis sit qualis suus fuerat.

Lex Baiw. XVII. Cap. II : De his qui propriam alodem vendunt vel quascunque res, et ab emptore alter abstrahere voluerit et sibi sociare in patrimonium, tunc dicat emptor ad venditorem : Terram, aut quaecunque fuerit res, abstrahere mihi vult vicinus meus, dicens quod sua fuerit. Et iste respondet: Ego quod tibi donavi, cum lege integra et verbis testificatione firmare volo. Super septem noctes fiat constitutum. Si dicit, cum utrisque utraeque partes conveniunt: Cur invadere conaris territorium quod ego iuste iure hereditatis donavi. Ille alius contra: Cur meum donare debuisti, quod antecessores mei antea tenuerunt? Iste vero dicit: Non ita, sed mei antecessores tenuerunt, et mihi in alodem relinquerunt, et vestita est illius manus cui tradidi, et firmare volo cum lege. Si statim voluerit, liberam habeat potestatem. Sin autem, postea super tres dies aut quinque aut certe septem ea ratione firmet. Per quatuor angulos campi, aut designatis terminis, per haec verba tollat de ipsa terra vel aratrum circumducat, vel de herbis, aut ramis, silva si fuerit: Ego tibi tradidi, et legitime firmabo per ternas vices. Dicat haec verba, et cum dextera manu tradat; cum sinistra vero porrigat wadium huic qui de ipsa terra cum mallat, per haec verba: Ecce wadium tibi do quod terram tuam alteri non do, legem faciendo. Tunc ille alter suscipiat wadium et donet illum vicessoribus istius ad legem faciendam. Si causa fuerit inter illos pugnae, dicat ille qui wadium suscepit: Iniuste territorium meum alteri firmasti, id est, farsvirotos. Ipsum mihi debes reddere, et cum duodecim solidis componere. Tunc spondeant pugnam duorum, et ad Dei pertineat indicium. Sin autem, cum sacramento se defendat, id est, cum duodecim, quod suam terram iniuste non firmaret alteri, nec suae ditioni restituere deberet, nec cum duodecim solidis componere.

Lex Baiw. XI. Cap. V: Quotiens de commarchanis contentio nascitur, ubi evidentia signa non apparent in arboribus, aut in montibus nec in fluminibus, et iste dicit: Hucusque antecessores mei tenuerunt, et in alodem mihi reliquerunt, et ostendit secundum proprium arbitrium locum: alter vero nihilominus in istius partem ingreditur, alium ostendit locum, secundum prioris verba suum et suorum antecessorum semper fuisse usque in praesens asserit. Et si alia probatio nusquam inveniri dinoscitur, nec utriusque invasionem compensare voluerint, tunc spondeant invicem wehadine quod dicimus, et in campiones non sortiantur, sed cui Deus fortiam dederit et victoriam, ad ipsius partem designata pars, ut quaerit, pertineat.

NOTES AND REFERENCES. 165

NOTE 54.—PAGE 21.

Lex Sax. XVI: De terra aliena invasa. 1. Qui terram suam occupatam ab altero dixerit, adhibitis idoneis testibus, probet eam suam fuisse; si occupator contradixerit, campo diiudicetur. 2. Si occupator sibi concrediderit, reddat hoc quod occupavit, non amplius.

NOTE 55.—PAGE 21.

Lex Rip. LXVII. 5: Si quis pro hereditate vel pro ingenuitate certare coeperit post malo ordine cum sex in Ecclesia coniuret, et cum duodecim ad stappulum Regis in circulo et in hasla hoc est in ramo, cum verborum contemplatione coniurare studeat. Si non adimpleverit, cum legis beneficio restituat. Aut si quis eum contra prendere voluerit, aut cum armis suis se defensare studeat ante Regem, aut omnem repetitionem cum legis beneficio restituat. The litigants did not always fight themselves, in person. It became customary to appoint representative champions. The fighting was then done by proxy. There is a case in illustration of this in Ritz Urk. 41 (p. 56): Nulla melior visa est sententia diffinitio quam per juditiarium campum super hoc fieret examinatio sic deinde statuto die et collata utrimque magna populorum affluentia nobis et ipsis presentibus advocatis duo ex utraque parte homines ad hoc preelecti ut fieri solet agressi sunt singulariter et noster homo propitiante deo et sancto Remaclo victor factus est et ecclesia nostra sua possessio ut ante a nostris premonstrata et preambulata fuerat jure adjudicata et per legem restituta est hinc ipsi homini qui est Gisleberto nomine qui posuit quasi in mortem animam suam pro nostra fidelitate delegavimus imo dedimus quartariam terre et cortilium jacens in dominicatu . . .

NOTE 56.—PAGE 21.

Lex Alam. LXXXIV: De his qui de terra sua inter se contendunt. Si qua contentio orta fuerit inter duas genealogias de termino terrae eorum, et unus dicit: Hic est noster terminus, alius revadit in alium locum, et dicit: Hic est noster terminus, ibi praesens sit Comes de plebe illa, et ponat signum ubi iste voluerit, et ubi ille alius voluerit terminum, et girent ipsam contentionem,

Postquam girata fuerit veniant in medium, et praesente Comite tollant de ipsa terra, quod Alamanni curtfodi dicunt, et ramos de ipsis arboribus infigant in ipsam terram quam tollunt, et illae genealogiae quae contendunt levent illam terram praesente Comite, et commendent in sua manu: ille involvat in fanone, et ponat sigillum, et commendet fideli manu usque ad statutum placitum. Tunc spondeant inter se pugnam duorum. Quando parati sunt ad pugnam, tunc ponant ipsam terram in medio, et tangant ipsam cum spatis suis, cum quibus pugnare debent, et testificentur Deum creatorem ut cuius sit iustitia, ipsius sit et victoria; et pugnent. Qualis de ipsis vicerit, ipse possideat illam contentionem; et illi alii praesumptiosi, quia proprietatem contradixerunt, duodecim solidos componant.

Rothar CCXXXI: Si quis alium de re mobile aut immobile pulsaverit dicendo, quod malo ordine possideat, et possessor negaverit, ita prospeximus: quod si per annos quinque fuerit possessor, tunc ipse qui possedit, aut per sacramentum debeat negare, aut per pugnam se defendere, si potuerit.

Grimoald IV: Si quis per xxx annos possederit casam, familiam vel terras, et cognitum fuerit, quod eius possessio fuit per xxx annorum curricula. ad pugnam non perveniat: nisi ipse, qui possedit secundum qualitatem pecuniae cum sacramento suo defendat: nam per pugnam, ut supra diximus, non fatigetur.

Whether the custom of fighting for land obtained in England before the Conquest is doubtful. After the Conquest it obtained generally, except in regard to lands in Kent held according to the custom of Gavelkind. Cf. Kent Custum. XXI: Of the tenements which are holden in Gauelkinde, there shall no battail be joined. nor graund assise taken by xii Knights, as it is used in other places of the realme. Then read the account of a judicial combat in Melsa Chron. II. pp. 97–102. The date of the combat is between A. D. 1249 and 1269. The last case of battle for land before English judges was, we believe, that which took place in Tothill-fields, Westminster, in the reign of Elizabeth, A. D. 1571. Spelman, who was present on the occasion, describes the procedures in his Glossary, sub. voc. *campus*. Fighting for land was lawful, however. until the year 1819, when an Act was passed (59 Geo. III., c. 46) abolishing "Wager of Battel, or joining Issue and Trial by Battel in Writs of Right." See Kent Custum. p. 278.

Note 57. — Page 22.

Lex Alam. LXXXIV : Si qua contentio orta fuerit inter duas genealogias . . . See Note 56, where the passage is given in full. The procedure was the same whether the dispute was between individuals or between clans. The title of the passage is: De his qui de terra sua inter se contendunt.

Note 58. — Page 22.

Caesar VI. 22. The passage is given in Note 51.

Note 59. — Page 22.

See Du Cange sub voc. *guerra*. It is perhaps going too far to say that "*gewere* is without doubt the same word as *guerra*." In my own mind there is little or no doubt upon this point. The passages of Fulda Cod. (447, 448) which are cited to prove that the *gewerida* was the *restitio* do not prove this. Cf. 447: testes qui vestitionem viderunt; and 448: testes qui hoc audierunt, et viderunt giweridam. The *restitio* has reference to the giving over of the land, the transfer of it to the grantee; the *gewerida* has reference to the taking possession of the land by the grantee, and, perhaps, to a demonstration by him of his newly acquired dominion over it. The alienation on the one hand, and the taking possession on the other, were, in this early period, two distinct procedures. Cf. Lex Sal. XLVI: De affatomie. The reader will find the passage cited in Note 153. The fundamental idea of the word *gewere* seems to have been a demonstration or exertion of force to secure possession. We may be wrong, however, in this matter. The student should read Andreas Heusler's book entitled, Die Gewere (Weimar, 1872, 8°). It contains a valuable bibliography. See also Grimm Rechtsalt. pp. 555, 556.

Note 60. — Page 22.

Henneb. Urkb. XL: discordia sive gwerra. Mon. Weihensteph. p. 467: prediolum hereditario jure dicens sibi debere succedere, werram fratribus intulit, que ita decisa est. Cf. Wirtemb. Urkb.

CLIII : hereditatem injuste invasam, quasi hereditario jure sibi vindicavit. Note the words *non invasi contra legem* in Lex Baiw. XVI. 2. The passage is given in Note 53. Cf. Hist. Frising. Num. DCCII : Odalschalc Triente Episcopus per malorum suasionem ad Pauzanam vinearum Sancte Marie invasionem fecit injuste.

Note 61. — Page 22.

Cod. S. Galli 164 : conquesitum nostrum, quam conquesivimus adque coulaboravimus. Ibid. 181 : conquesitio in villa. Ibid. 186 : conquesitum meum cum omni marca sua (cf. Tacitus Germ. 16 : colunt discreti ac diversi ut fons ut campus ut nemus placuit.) Ibid. 190 : quicquid ibidem pater meus conquesivit et mihi in hereditatem dimisit . . . conquesitionem patris. Ibid. 198 : conquestum meum. Beyer Urkb. 119 : proprisum.
Fulda Codex 472 : capturam in terminis villae comprehensam. Ibid. 479 : comprehensio. See also Nos. 513, 515, 520, 532 : decem capturas ; 631 : captam capturam. Lauresham Codex CCXLIX : unum proprisum cum aedificio, et mansis, campis, pratis, etc. (cf. again Germ. 16). Ibid. CCLII : proprisum qui jacet in illo angulo ubi Suarzaha intrat in fluvium Wisscoz. Fulda Cod. 311 : capturam in silvis. Ibid. 313 : quartam partem unius capturae. See also 377, 391, 412, 462, 465 : capturam in silva Bochonia comprehensam. Cod. S. Galli 547 : quicquid in illo saltu conprehensum habuit. Hist. Frising. Num. DXVIII : hereditatem meam cum omni conquestu meo (cf. Note 35). Ibid. DXXXIV : conquesto atque conlaborato. Cf. DCI : quicquid ad colendum comprehensum habuissent. Lauresham Cod. MMCCLXXXV : capturas. Ibid. CCCXIII : meum proprisum. So in DCXXVIII : proprisum quem pater meus proprisit. Cod. S. Galli 325 : conquestum meum. Ibid. 360 : meam conquisitionem. See also 373 : conquestu meo. References to *Capturae* abound in Fulda Trad. See for examples Cap. 42, Nos. 16, 18, 102, 104, 105, 120, 139, 143, 158, 195, 196, 204, 219, 221, 222, 286, 310, and so on. The student will easily find as many examples as he wishes, by simply glancing over the pages.

Note 62. — Page 23.

Formula CCCXIII (Rozière I. p. 373). Cf. Mon. Weihensteph. p. 364: predium quale tunc in potestate habuit. Wirtemb. Urkb. XC: res in potestate. Ibid. CXIX: potestativa dominatione integriter habere. Ibid. CXLVIII: proprias res potestative possidere. Trad. Wiz. CLXXVIII: habere et dominare. So in CI and CXIII. Chart. Sithiense, p. 22: possedere vel dominare. Cod. S. Galli 219: sicut in hac die potestativa manu videar habere. Ibid. 619: potestativa manu possidere. Hist. Frising. CCCLXV: jure dominationis habere. Allodial property is constantly described as a *possessio vel dominatio*. See Formula CXVIII: quantumcumque in ipso loco mea videtur esse possessio vel dominatio. So also in CXXX, CLXXII, CXCIV, and in any number of others. Also in the documents Chart. Sithiense, p. 49, and p. 70; Wirtemb. Urkb. LXII; Cod. Trad. Lunaelac. XIX, XLIX, LXIV, LXX, XCVIII; Hist. Frising. Num. CCCIX. It is a common formula. Innumerable examples might be adduced. It is worth while to observe that the phrase *possessio vel dominatio* is applied to all kinds of land, — meadows, pastures, and forests, as well as house lots and arable lots. The landlordship, the dominion, of the allodial proprietor, was not limited to house lots and arable lots, as some writers have told us. It extended over meadows, pastures, and forests as well: campis, pratis, pascuis, silvis; and even over the *communiis*: that is to say, over lands held in common, or in undivided shares. See, for example, Formula CXVIII; and Mohr Cod. Dipl. 35 (Cod. S. Galli 680): talem usum habuimus, qualem unus quisque liber homo *de sua proprietate* juste et legaliter decet habere, in campis, pascuis, silvis, lignorumque succisionibus, atque porcorum pastu, pratis, viis, agnis, aquarumque decursibus, piscationibus, exitibus et reditibus. The existence of private rights in common land will, however, be considered at length in another connection.

Note 63. — Page 23.

As time went on, the chiefs and the kings assumed the right to distribute the land as they pleased. Certain tracts of land were assigned to certain persons by formal grants, usually in writing, and authenticated by the signatures or names of witnesses. The written grant is described in the Lex Rip. as a *testamentum Regis*. See Tit. LX. It is described as a *boc* by the English. Hence *boc-land*, i. e. land held by a document from the chief or king. See Alfred 42; and the Laws of Henry I. LXX. 21 (Thorpe, p. 575). See also Cnut 13 and 78. The *folc-land* appears to have been the land occupied by the mass of the people, in which titles were based upon priority of possession. The title to *boc-land* was based upon the possession of a *boc*, or written grant. Many men had property both in *folc-land* and *boc-land*. See Edward, § 2. The kings held property in *folc-land*. We meet with *cyniges folc-land* in Kemble's Codex CCLXXXI. There is a famous passage upon the *folc-land* in Baed's letter to Archbishop Ecgbirht. See Smith's edition of Baed, p. 309.

Among the Ostrogoths the word *pictatium* was used to describe the written grant. Cassiodorus Varia I. 18: si Romani praedium sine delegatoris cujusquam pictatio presumptor barbarus occupavit, cum priori domino submota dilatione restituat. The reading *petitione* for *pictatio* is senseless. The word *pictatium* occurs again in Varia III. 35: presenti jussione censemus, ut quicquid ex nostra ordinatione patritium Liberium tibi matrique tuae per pictatium constiterit deputasse, in suo robore debeat permanere. The word occurs also in Theoderic's Edict.

The possession of written documents gave to the land-owners a great sense of security. They were everywhere sought for, and generally obtained. A whole chapter in the history of land-holding is contained in the following few lines of one of the Fulda records. Fulda Cod. 261: proprisit sibi Amalungus partem quendam de silva quae vocatur Bocchonia, quam moriens dereliquit filio suo Bennit, qui ad nostram accedens clementiam postulavit celsitudini nostrae auctoritatis praeceptum circa eum confirmare deberemus, quatenus ipse quoad veniret absque ullius prejudicio tenere et possidere quieto ordine deberet ... Precipientes ergo jubemus ut nullus fidelium nostrorum presentium scilicet et futurorum prefatum Bennit vel heredes illius de hoc propriso quod in lingua eorum dicitur binane expoliare aut inquietare ullo modo presumatis sed liceat sicut diximus ei per hoc nostrum preceptum ipsam terram quantumcunque pater illius proprisit et ei in hereditate demisit tenere atque possedere ut prescriptum est: et ut hec auctoritas firmior habeatur vel per tempora melius construetur de anulo nostro subter sigillare jussimus. The date of this document is A. D. 811, Dec. 1st.

By means of these documents, *testamenta* or *praecepta* (cf. Lex Sal. XIV. 4), a direct relationship was created between the chief or king and the provincial land-owners. Cf. the formula CCCCXII: Relatione Pagensium ad Rege Directa. When a man held his lands by a document or documents from the king, he was thereby brought into a direct personal relationship with him. It would not, perhaps, be too much to say, that the consolidation of the Merovingian and Carolingian Empire was chiefly due to the introduction of title deeds held from the head of the Empire. The consolidation of England was in the same way chiefly due to the conversion of *folk-land* into *boc-land*.

Note 64. — Page 24.

Before the introduction of written documents and title deeds, the people spread over the country and settled wherever they pleased, more or less under the direction of their chiefs and kings. Cf. Caesar VI. 22: magistratus ac principes in annos singulos gentibus cognationibusque hominum, qui una coierunt, quantum et quo loco visum est, agri attribuunt . . . The chiefs appear to have had nothing to do, at this time, with the settlement of the individual members of the *gens* or *cognatio*. We infer from the *colunt discreti ac diversi ut fons ut nemus ut campus placuit* of Germania 16, that the individual settled wherever he pleased, wherever he found a pleasant place, and room enough for his slaves and his cattle. This inference is more than confirmed by the testimony of the later records. See references to *comprehensiones, proprisa, conquesta*, and *capturae* in Note 61. To these references we may add those which follow. Lex Baiw. XVI. 2: Ego in tua opera priore non invasi contra legem, quia mea opera et labor prior hic est quam tuus. (See Note 53 for the rest.) Cod. S. Galli 25: quod ego adquesivi vel laboravi. Ibid. 202: novale ad Segalpah; 239: roncale meo nuncupatum nomine; 334: novale Adalrammiswilare, quantum ibidem genitor Adalram excolere videbatur; 337: unam runcalem; 352: novales III; 439: locum, qualiter tunc per denotata signa segregatus est securiter nos haberemus, nec ullus incidendi vel extirpandi infra denotata signa habeat potestatem ; 447 : runcalem, 1 hobam et amplius continentem ; 514 : potestatem quam habuerunt in Goldahun marcha ; 643 : silvulam ab aliorum potestate segregatam cum legitimis marchis. Hist. Frising. Num. CCLXII : exaratum ; DCI : quicquid in ipso die habere viderentur culti vel inculti, vel ad colendum comprehensum habuissent ; DCXXXIII : cinctadam unam. Trad. Wiz. LXXVI : quicquid ibidem laboratum habeo aut inceps laborare potuero ; CLXXXVI : duas stirpis ad stirpand. Beyer Urkb. 108 : bifangum unum ubi possunt edificari mansa centum [*agri pro c cultoribus*] necnon insaginari porci mille ; 512 : terram novalium ad viginti mansos vel amplius. Lauresham Codex CLXXXXIX : bifangos III ; CCXVII : bifangum qui dicitur Geroldeshufa . . . bifango Engilhelmi ; CCXI : quicquid in silva adjacenti conlaborare, aut stirpare, vel aedificare seu attrahere potuero ; CCXLIV : rem nostram in Basinheimer marcha, illum bifangum, stirpatum, et proprisum ad stirpandum ; CCXLV : bifangum vel mastunga ; CCLXII : terram factam et adhuc in silva faciendam ad x jurnales ; CCCLXIV : collaboratum meum quem modo habeo, et quidquid videtur esse mea possessio. For *possessiones* and *dominationes* see Note 62. Lauresham Cod. CCCLXXVII : stirpo, habente in longitudine perticas xxx in latitudine xx ; CCCX : occupationem ad decem hubas [*agri pro x cultoribus*] ; DCCCCXCVI : laboratum ; MMCCCLXXXIII : stirpum in marca ; MMDCCCXXXV : bivangum. Fulda Cod. 88 : hereditatem a parentibus et a nobis elaboratum aut exquisitum ; 99 : septum id est bifang ; 223 : unum ambitum quem nos bifang appellamus ; 300 : in illo septo duas hobas unam in silva alteram in terra ; 323 : bifangis et novalibus quae capta et possessa sunt ex his duabus forestis . . . de territoriis, de novalibus, vel de villis ; 395 : bifang in marcu villarum ; 413 : unam bizunnam cujus longitudo xxx virgarum est, latitudo vero xv ; 460 : bifang ; 465 : ambitus capturae ; 501 : elaboratum meum in pago ; 542 : unum ambitum in marcu ; 757 : biuanc. Lisch. Urkb. II. No. VII : incultam silvam a novalibus extirpaverint. Cod. Morav. CXXXVI : circuitum meum in Prahensi provincia, has villas cum hominibus et terris, silvis et pratis continentem. Cf. also CXXXVII, CXLVI, CXLXIX, CCXXIII ; CXCI : villam et circuitionem silve ; CCLXXV (CCXCII?) : cum omnibus circuitionibus silvarum, sive rivulorum aut agrorum. Cf. Zahn Urkb. 8 : res proprietatis nostre, id est terra exartata, parata scilicet ad arandum, mansos integros VIII [*agri pro* VIII *cultoribus*], id est ad unamquamque coloniam [i. e. *mansum*] jugera xc, et de silva undique, in gyrum scilicet ac per omnes partes, miliarium unum cum terris, pratis, pascuis, etc. Here we have almost the type of the primitive settlement: only in the earliest time the breadth of the mark, or border land, was not defined. As Cæsar says: neque quisquam agri modum certum aut fines habet proprios. The free-lord did not know how far his domain extended. Cf. Cod. Morav. XXXV: in hanc partem silve sine termini conclusione; and Ibid. XLVI: hereditas et proprietas in omnibus marchis. The mark was defined, at first roughly, as in the case above cited, then more and more exactly. See Notes 32, 33, 34. Even after estates came to be defined by exact boundaries, the free-lords extended their possessions by appropriating unoccupied or uncultivated lands. See Notes 35–41.

Note 65.—Page 24.

See Orig. Nassoic. LXXIII. Cod. S. Galli 117. Mon. Nideralt. Dipl. XIV (p. 121): Avus noster Carolus licentiam tribuit suis fidelibus in augmentatione rerum Ecclesiarum Dei in Pannonia carpere et possidere hereditatem. The document is printed also in Cod. Dip. Morav. I. pp. 30, 31.

Note 66.—Page 24.

This etymology has been questioned, but no good reasons have, so far as we know, been raised against it. See the Wörterbücher of Grimm, Fick, and then that of Kluge. The root from which both *erbe* and *arbeit* appear to be derived is *rabh*, or *rab*, meaning to seize, to lay hold of, to take eagerly or vehemently. See, in Skeat's Etymological Dictionary of the English Language, the list of Aryan Roots. The *erbe* would be, accordingly, first a seizure or appropriation, a "take" of land; then, when it was transmitted from father to sons, from sons to grandsons, it would be regarded as an inheritance. The original meaning of the word would become obsolete. This is our theory, and it is supported by testimony of peculiar interest. In the first place, we have the passage in the Lex Baiw. (XVI. 2) to show that he who first cultivated a piece of land was regarded as the owner of it. In vindicating his right to it he says: mea opera et labor prior hic est quam tuus. We should expect, therefore, to find some word used to describe landed property, in which the idea of prior occupation and labor would be expressed. Searching in our records we find the very word. We find property in land described as a *vorwerc*. Du Cange cites a passage from the Life of St. Mainwerc: ut unum vorwerc cum xx lidis et xii aratris ei concederetur. See the Glossarium sub voc. *vorwerc*. Then we find, in Cod. Dipl. Lubec. II. viii, the following gloss: *allodium* melius dixisset, nam *vorwerc* latinum non est, sed vulgare. So the word *vorwerc* was used by the common people instead of the word *allodium*. How beautifully our theory about the history of the word *erbe* is illustrated in this fact! And the history of the word *alod* is elucidated. The word appears to have signified, originally, a farmstead and land held from most ancient times; therefore an inheritance or patrimony. See Skeat's Dictionary sub voc. *allodial*. Cf. Lex Baiw. XVI. 2: habeo testes qui hoc sciunt, quod labores de isto campo semper ego tuli, nemine contradicente exartavi, mundavi, possedi usque hodie, et pater meus reliquit mihi in possessione sua. The *alod* was primarily a "take" of land; then, as it was held from generation to generation and no longer "taken," it came to be simply an inheritance. It was an inheritance secured by appropriation or conquest, and then maintained, when necessary, by force. At a later time we have *allodia* held, not in virtue of prior occupation, but in virtue of grants from prior occupants. They are then property in a modern sense of the term.

NOTE 67. — PAGE 24.

What is said in the preceding note about the *arbeit* and *erbe*, the *vorwerc* and *allodium*, is further illustrated in the following passages from early records. Chart. Werth. 23 (Lacomblet Urkb. 19): pro haereditate comprehendi a rivulo qui dicitur Burgbeki usque ad illum rivulum qui in occidentali parte Widubergi decursit, cum omni integritate usque ad ripam Rurae, excepta illa particula, quam Folebertus in proximo angulo inter Ruram et Widubergam olim stirpare inchoavit. Fulda Cod. 88: hereditates a parentibus et a nobis elaboratum aut exquisitum. Ibid. 117, 118, 119. It appears in these documents that a certain man named Swidmot made an appropriation or "take" of land: *captura circa fluvium Elmaha*. When he died this "take" was an inheritance for his sons. Each one received a share: *quicquid in eadem captura ad meam proprietatem ex paterna hereditate pertinere dinoscitur*. These shares were afterwards alienated by their respective owners to St. Boniface at Fulda. A whole chapter in the history of property in land might be written upon the text of these three documents. Many others of a similar nature might be cited. See Notes 61 and 64, and consider how all the *occupationes, capturae, conquesta*, would, had they not been given to the Church by the occupiers, captors, and conquerors, have passed to sons and grandsons, as inheritances.

NOTE 68. — PAGE 25.

Chart. Werth. 5, or Lacomblet Urkb. No. 6. Cf. again Ibid. 19: *tradidi comprehensionem illam quam ego in propria hereditate comprehendi*. Also 27: *quicquid ibi habuimus aut per jus hereditatis aut per comprehensionem*. We find in our note-books a great quantity of such references; but these will be sufficient. The student can easily find others for himself.

NOTE 69. — PAGE 27.

The word *Einzelhof* means an isolated farmstead. The word *Gehöferschaft* means a number of farmsteads clustered together. The *Gehöferschaft* was an outgrowth or extension of the *Einzelhof*. The heirs in the *Einzelhof* became too numerous to live in one house. New houses had to be builit. Then we have several houses where there was originally one, a *Gehöferschaft*. The number of houses in the *Gehöferschaft* increased with the number of heirs. The *Gehöferschaft* is described as an *Erbschaft*. The inhabitants are described as an *Erbgenossenschaft*.

It is sometimes argued, that the *Gehöferschaft* or *Erbgenossenschaft* is, as an institution, antecedent to the *Einzelhof*. The argument is inconclusive. It assumes that the association of heirs, the *Erbgenossenschaft*, existed before any inheritance, *Erbe*, existed for them. This seems to us an illegitimate assumption. We meet with *gentes* and *cognationes hominum* in Caesar VI. 22 : but have we any right to assume that these associations were not previously formed by the multiplication of heirs upon isolated domains? Caesar says that the people were constantly migrating. But have we any right to assume that they had been always migrating? It is quite possible, if not probable, that a period of permanent settlement preceded the migrations of Caesar's time.

At the time of the Folk-Laws we find that associations of kinsmen were formed by the multiplication of heirs upon isolated domains. Why assume that they were formed in a different way in earlier times?

We hear a good deal of talk about a tribal system which existed among the Germans up to the time of Caesar and Tacitus. It may be that a tribal system did exist up to that time: but what do we know about it? Nothing, of course. Why talk about it then?

We are told that the tribal system of the Germans closely resembled that of the ancient Irish: but why should it? Differences are as common in history as coincidences. Different people have different ideas, different ways of doing things, different modes of life, different institutions.

How many different departures are made from the family, the elementary group, according to variable conditions and circumstances! Give the family bows, arrows, and fish-hooks, and no other means of support, it will at once seek some good ground for hunting and fishing. If the game and fish are plentiful, the family may remain united for many generations; but if game and fish are scarce, the members of the family have to separate in order to live. Given large flocks and herds, and plenty of pasture ground, the family may continue united for a while; but when the pasture ground is limited, the stock has to be divided, and then the family is scattered. Given large numbers of slaves, the family may remain united, and the slaves may be established in village communities round about the residence of the family. We have, then, a village of lords surrounded by villages of serfs. Or if the slaves are divided, the lords establish themselves in isolated farmsteads, with communities of serfs under their over-lordship. In other words, the course of history is not predetermined. It is divergent according to variable conditions. Starting with the family, we see that many different departures may be made from it. Different departures mean different results. In some places we may have a tribal organization; in other places, a system of village communities; in other places we may have a system of isolated farms, or a manorial system.

Taking any one of these various modes of life, and varying conditions and circumstances, many new departures will be made, which will have very different issues.

Coincidences are, nevertheless, very common. The reason of this is that the family, the elementary group from which the others are directly or indirectly derived, is always preserved. It is a physiological, if not a sociological fact, in all forms of society. The family can be isolated at any time, and then the processes of differentiation begin again. The simpler forms of sociological development are naturally reproduced,—the life in isolated farmsteads, the manorial system, the house community, and the village community.

Note 70.—Page 28.

The fact that the common land was subject to appropriation by individuals (see Notes 61, 64, 65, 66, 67, 68) is evidence to show that the common land was simply undivided land. But it will be urged, Suppose the amount of the common land was limited, and objections were made to appropriations; what was done then? We find an answer to this question in the Appendix to the Burgundian Law. Lex Burg. Add. I. Tit. I. 5: agri quoque communis nullis terminis limitati exaequationem inter consortes nullo tempore denegandam. If objection was made to *ad libitum* appropriations, the land was divided among the heads of the different households.

It was not always easy to make these divisions. Disputes arose. Among the Visigoths it was decided that the best men, or a majority, should decide matters of dispute. See Lex Wisig. X. Tit. I. 1, 3, 8, cited in Note 33. Among the Franks, however, these disputes were referred to the king or his *missus*. See Formula CXXVII: De divisione ubi rege accederit missus. The passage will be cited in Note 74. The division of a common mark into a number of private estates (*inter fiscum regis et populares possessiones*) is described in Formula CCCCII (No. XI, in Salomo Form.).

When disputes arose in regard to rights of enjoyment in common land, the land was usually divided. It was regarded, therefore, as undivided land, in which every man had a share that he could have assigned to him, if he pleased. That it was so regarded appears clearly in a multitude of documents. In one of the Lauresham records (Cod. MCCXXXVI), for example, a man alienates his inheritance in the common forest: *quantum jure hereditario ad me pertinere videtur de illa silva communi*. Other references will be given in other connections. See, especially, Notes 92–95, 99, and 100.

NOTE 71. — PAGE 28.

Lacomblet Urkb. 21: Dum omnibus vicinis suis non habetur incognitum qualiter Hembaldus filius Heribaldi tradidit suam comprehensionem illam quam ipse Hembaldus in propria hereditate et in communione proximorum proprio labore et adjutorio amicorum suorum legibus comprehendit et stirpavit. The *communio proximorum* is described in Font. Rer. Austr. XXXI. p. 20 (A. D. 861) as the *confinium coheredum*. Cf. Hist. Frising. DXVIII: hereditatem meam cum omni conquestu meo. Lacomblet Urkb. 27: quicquid habuimus aut per jus hereditatis aut per conprehensionem. Cod. S. Galli 373: quicquid ibidem de paternica portione sive de conquestu meo, seu de conquestu Irminhardi fratris mei sit. Beyer Urkb. 108: in commarca ipsius ville bifangum unum ubi possunt edificari mansa centum. Ibid. 465 (b): novalia ad xx mansos vel amplius. In this way inheritances were indefinitely enlarged. If a man had no room for his people in the *Gehöferschaft*, he sent them out into the forest or waste. There they settled down; houses were built; arable lots (*hubae*) were assigned; and the animals were turned out to pasture. Around the *Gehöferschaft*, several, and sometimes a great many, subject communities were thus established, — *Hubengemeinden*. The lord of the *Hubengemeinde* was an heir in the *Gehöferschaft*. But the *Hubengemeinde* was an inheritance for the heirs of the founder. The *Hubengemeinde* became in most cases an *Erbschaft*, the heirs in the *Hubengemeinde* forming an *Erbgenossenschaft*. In many cases the distinction between the *Hubengemeinden* and the *Gehöferschaften* was obliterated. This happened when the lands of the *Gehöfer-*

schaft were distributed in *hubae*, i. e. in tenant allotments. In the course of the early and middle ages the *Hubengemeinden* and *Gehöferschaften* became quite confounded.

Note 72. — Page 29.

Lex Burg. Add. I. Tit. I. 6 : Sylvarum, montium, et pascuorum unicuique pro rata suppetit esse communionem. Ibid. 5 : Agri quoque communis nullis terminis limitati exaequationem inter consortes nullo tempore denegandam. Ibid. LXVII : De sylvis hoc observandum. Quicunque agrum aut colonicas tenent, secundum terrarum modum vel possessionis suae ratam, sic sylvam inter se noverint dividendam: Romano tamen de sylvis medietate ex exartis servata. Cf. Add. II. 11 : De Romanis vero hoc ordinavimus, ut non amplius a Burgundionibus, qui infra venerunt, requiratur, quam ad praesens necessitas fuerit, medietas terrae. Alia vero medietas cum integritate mancipiorum a Romanis teneatur : nec exinde ullam violentiam patiantur. Then read Lex Burg. XXXI. 1 : Inter Burgundiones et Romanos id censuimus observandum, ut quicunque in communi campo nullo contradicente vineam fortasse plantaverit, similem campum illi restituat, in cuius campo vineam posuit. 2 : Si vero post interdictum quicunque in campo alterius vineam plantare praesumpserit, laborem suum perdat, et vineam cuius est campus accipiat. Also Ibid. XIII : Si quis tam Burgundio quam Romanus in sylva communi exartum fecerit, aliud tantum spatii de sylva hospiti suo consignit, et exartum, quem fecit, remota hospitis communione, possideat.

Note 73. — Page 30.

See Alsat. Dipl. IX, XII, XXXII, XXXIII. Trad. Wiz. IX, X, XIII. Neugart Cod. Dipl. V. Cod. S. Galli 186, 334, 352, 438, 676. Wirtemb. Urkb. XLVII, CCLXVII. Mon. Scheftl. p. 377 (XXVI). Cod. Patav. I. XIII and LXII. Hist. Frising. I. p. 35 (53?). Ibid. Nos. CLXXIX, CCXLVII, CCXC, CCXCIII, CCCLXV, CD. Two cases may be given as examples.

Hist. Frising. CXVII : tres germani fuerunt, et uno defuncto duo superstites fuerunt fratres, et dividere debuerunt aequaliter inter se ipsam hereditatem defuncti fratris Scatto, et Poapo, sed antequam divisio haec facta est, et mortuus est Poapo relinquens portionem suam filio suo Kejoni, et ipse Kejo bene valens portionem, quod ei accedere debuit contra patruum suum tradidit Deo, et Sancto Tertuliano ad Slechdorf. Sed nolente Kejone renuit omnia haec Scatto, et reliquid filio suo Reginberto. Tunc ipsi missi cum Orendilo judice, et ceteris veracibus hominibus tractaverunt, pro qua causa Reginperht possidere debuisset portionem nepotis sui Kejoni hereditas, quod ipse pro anima sua Deo tradidit, et Sanctis ejus. Tunc convictus cum lege et justitia Reginpertus de presente reddidit Advocato ipsius Ecclesiae et Archipresbytero ipsius Episcopi Ellannodo loca nuncupata Allingas, Kupingas, et in Germareskavve, ut amplius eas possiderent praesules loci ipsius absque ulla contradictione evindicatas jure perpetuo, et ita finita est contentio coram resedentibus, et adstantibus multis. Et testes usu Bajowariorum per aures ex utrisque partibus tracti, ut amplius exinde finita esset contentio.

Ibid. CCCLXXIX: De traditione, quam fecit Isanhart Clericus filius Saxoni ad Steinhard. Ipse quidem Isanhard eo modo hanc traditionem cum matre sua Tunna nomine fecerunt, post obitum Saxoni patris sui coeperunt fratres illius ei contradicere propriam hereditatem a patre suo legitime derelictam, ipseque Isanhart junior erat fratribus suis, et propter infantiam non potuit contendere contra fratres suos jam annorum aetate viginti. Veniens ad venerabilem Hittonem Pontificem et enarrabit ei omnem necessitatem, atque angustiam, quam eis fratres ejus in propria hereditate actam habuerunt, at ille blande consolavit eum, ipseque accepta consolatione ab Episcopo accessit ad altare Sanctae Mariae, et tradidit seipsum in servitium Sanctae Mariae semper Virginis cum omnibus, quae habuit, vel quodcumque pater ejus Saxo ei in propriam hereditatem dereliquid, nihil enim praetermisit cum omni integritate, quae habuit, et hanc, quod juste, et legitime ad fratres suos conquiri debuit, cum seipso Domui Sanctae Mariae in servitium tradidit, et firmiter confirmavit.

Note 74. — Page 30.

Formula CXXV: In Dei nomen. Placuit adque convenit inter illus et illus germanus ut inter se de res eorum dividere debuerunt, quod ita et fecerunt . . . et hec paccio divisionis omni tempore firma permaneat.

Formula CXXVI: Pactum divisiones inter fratres, id sunt illi et illi, heredes illui et illei quondam, qualiter se de alote corum dividere vel exequare deberent, quod ita et fecerunt.

Formula CXXVII: De divissione, ubi rege accederit missus. Dum et divisio vel exsequatio inter illum et illum seu consortes corum de alode lui aut de agro illo caelebrare debetur, et quatenus petitio illorum adfuit ut missus de palatio nostro ad hoc inter eos dividendum vel exequandum accedere deberet ideo cognoscite nos misso nostro, inlustris viro illo, ad hoc inter eos exequando visi fuimus di[re]xisse. Propterea per praesentem praeceptum [decrevimus ac iubemus] ut ipsum in hoc vos recipere faciatis, et unicuique ex ipsis iusti debita portionem terminetur, et decimo illo suntellitis quod exinde in fisci ditionibus, tam de terra, vincis, mancipia vel undecumque redebetur, ipsi vir ille habeat ex nostra indulgentia concessum, vel quicquid exinde facere voluerit, liberam habeat potestatem.

Formula CXXIV: Pactum inter parentes de corum hereditate. Quicquid enim inter propinquos de alode parentum, non ad iudiciaria potestate coacti, sed sponti, manente caritate, iusti debitum uniquique portio terminatur, non de rebus detrimentum, sed augmentum potius potest esse consendum. Et ideo necesse est inter se corum facta scribturarum series alligari, ne ab aliquibus in posterum valeat refragari. Ideo dum inter illo et germano suo illo de alode genitoribus corum illis et illis bone pacis placuit atque convinit ut eam inter se, manentem caritatem, dividere vel exaequare deberent, quod ita et fecerunt. Accepit itaque ille villas nuncupantes illas, sitas ibi, cum mancipia tanta illa. Similiter et ille accepit econtra in compensatione alias villas, nuncupantes illas, sitas ibi, cum mancipia tanta illa. De presidio vero, drappos, fabricaturas vel omni supellectile domus, quicquid dici aut nominare potes, aequalentia inter se visi sunt dividisse vel exaequasse, et hoc invicem pars parte tradidisse, et per fistuca omnia partitum esse dixisse.

Note 75.—Page 30.

Lex Alam. LXXXVIII: Si quis fratres post mortem patris corum aliquanti fuerint, dividant portionem patris corum. Dum hoc non fuerit factum, nullus rem suam dissipare faciat usque dum aequaliter partiant. For descriptions of inheritances see Cod. S. Galli 28, 72, 142, 159, 174, 185, 373, 459, etc. We have selected these cases as good examples.

Note 76. — Page 30.

Lex Baiw. XIV. Cap. VIII: De divisione inter fratres. Ut fratres hereditatem patris aequaliter dividant. Inheritances are described in Hist. Frising. I. p. 52; Ibid. p. 85; and in Nos. LXIII, LXXX, CLXXV, CDXVI, DCI, DCXCIX. See also Mon. Schlehdorf. Dipl. VIII; and Cod. Patav. I. xxxviii, xlvi.

Note 77. — Page 30.

See Notes 73-76. Then Lex Sal. LIX: De alodis. Cf. Herold Text of the same (Merkel, p. 72). See also the Capitulary of A. D. 560, § 2; and the edict of Chilperic, circ. A. D. 575, § 3. Lex Rip. LVI: De alodis. Lex Fris. XIX. Lex Angl. Werin. VI. Lex Sax. VII. Lex Wisig. Lib. IV. Tit. II. 2: quod in hereditatis successione filii primi sunt. Cf. Ibid. § 1: ut sorores cum fratribus aequaliter succedant. This comes without doubt from the Roman Law. See also Lex Burg. Tit. I. 1. In Lex Wisig., and also in Lex Burg., the primitive custom of inheritance is somewhat modified by subsequent legislation. This is so also in the Lombard Law. See Rothar CLIV, CLV. Here natural sons take shares with legitimate sons, only their shares are smaller. Then read Grimoald V. If a son dies, his sons are allowed to step into his place and take shares with their uncles. The principle of representation is admitted. It appears to have been introduced in some places by means of adoption. The grandsons were adopted as heirs in the place of their father. See Formulae CXXXI, CXXXII, CXXXIV.

There is very little regarding the law of inheritance in the early English records; still we find a few passages. See Kemble's Codex CXLVII: rus etiam hoc modo donatum est, ut suum masculum possideat et non femininum. Cf. Alfred LI: if a man have boc-land, he must not give it out of his *mæg-burg*, if to do so was forbidden by those who first acquired it and gave it to him. King Alfred says in his will that the persons, his kinsmen, who have received freehold land from him, must not let it go out of the family. If left to descendants, it must go to males. Lib. de Hyd. p. 332. That the principle of inheritance was fully recognized at this time appears evident. Cf. Kemble's Codex CXCI : et jure hereditario firmiter fixa permaneat. That the heirs divided their inheritances appears in Cnut 79 : let the heirs succeed to the land and the property, and divide it very justly. It must not be inferred from the above that women were always, or even regularly, excluded from the right of inheritance. Cf. Kemble's Codex CCXXXII : possessoribus quorum propria haereditas, id sunt tres sorores. Probably, except in special cases like those cited above, daughters took the inheritance when there were no sons. This is the rule of Kent Custum. X. The early law of inheritance appears to be here preserved. In other parts of England, primogeniture was introduced.

Although the law of inheritance differs somewhat in different countries, it is quite safe to say that sons were generally preferred to other persons ; that they came into their inheritance with equal claims ; that the inheritance was consequently divided among them in equal shares.

Note 78. — Page 31.

Liutprand LXIX : Si inter fratres per XL annos possessio fuerit de rebus, seu de casis, vel de terris, quae indivisae sunt, vel inter parentes, qui per XL annos possedit, qualiter praesumit dicere, per sacramentum ad sancta Dei Evangelia affirmet, quod de avo, aut de patre, aut de fratre, aut de aliquo parente ipsas res suas habeat factas, aut per donationem, aut commutationem, aut per aestimationem, aut per comparationem, aut quomodo praesumpserit dicere aut affirmare : et liceat ei postea ipsas res illibatas habere, et possidere. Aliae vero res, quae divisae fuerint inter fratres seu nepotes, vel ubi mensura tracta est, sorte stante adaequentur. Nam ubi per XL annos mensura minime ambulaverit, et caussa probat, fuerit, quod iure quieto possedisset, sicut supra legitur, per sacramentum finiatur, excepto si communiter aliquid possedisset.

Cf. Hist. Frising. DLV : Kerolt et Kernod qui communem hereditatem habuerunt, non inter se divisum sed communiter sine divisione usitaverunt, sicut amabiles fratres Dei amore usitare debuerunt. See also Num. CDLXVI.

Note 79. — Page 31.

Lacomblet Urkb. 16 : notum fieri desideramus omnibus tam presentibus quam futuris qualiter nos coheredes et conparticipes et consanguinei his nominibus . . . tradidimus agrum hereditarii juris nostri. Ibid. 17 : idcirco placuit nobis coheredibus et conparticipibus in uno patrimonio, his nominibus . . . tradere aliquam particulam hereditatis nostre. Cf. Cod. S. Galli 386 : quidquid proprietatis visus sum habere sive ex paterna hereditate seu ex adquisita, sive divisum habeam cum meis coheredibus, seu indivisum. Ibid. 480 : hereditatem in Ludolteswilare in meam portionem a coheredibus accepi. Ibid. 594 : silvulae medietatem, quam ibi habemus ego et coheredes mei. See also Ibid. Anhang 9 : quidam fratres K, C, R, K, E, M, B, et coheredes illorum interpellati pro decimatione hereditatis sue. Beyer Urkb. 119 : Terra Wolfgrammi et Ruodiconis et consanguincorum ipsorum . . . et silvam communem S. Goaris que ad ipsum monasterium pertinet et aliorum coheredum . . . ad terram Hildinuodi et Waltarii et corum heredum. Ibid. 640 : Henricus de Tris cum filiis, cum ceteris ejusdem ville coheredibus allodium suum quod commune habuerunt contulerunt. Then read Fulda Cod. 366 : isti habent hereditatem in Dienenheim. Hruodpraht (Comes) and twenty-two other persons are mentioned as holders of the inheritance, and coheirs therein.

Note 80. — Page 32.

Cod. S. Galli 439 : inter nos et Rihwinum et coheredes ejus fuit contentio in loco, qui dicitur Seppenwane; quapropter illuc illuc venit Huodalrihus comes et prepositus noster Hartmuotus et advocatus Ruodpertus necnon et Rihwinus et coheredes ejus. Et jactatis inter se causis conplacuit Rihwino et Otgero atque Geroloo fratribus necnon ceteris coheredibus, ut aliquid nobis de sua proprietate donarent, quod et fecerunt, ita ut a nobis pagalium firmitatis acciperent ; ea videlicet ratione, ut nos supra nominatum locum, qualiter tunc per denotata signa segregatus est, securiter nos haberemus, nec ullus incidenti vel extirpandi infra denotata signa habeat potestatem. Et similiter Rihwinus et coheredes ejus suas portiones contra ipsum locum per se habeant excepto ut pascua communia in agris habeamus.

Note 81.—Page 32.

Hist. Frising. I. p. 49: dum erga eodem loco conexae arvae ducali pascua non sufficerant; appetivi locum ad proprios heredes, quo vocatur Erichinga, et ibidem pro necessitate domos construxi, quia antea jam temporibus plurimis inculta atque deserta remansit, omnis autem possessores hujus loci prumptis viribus donantes atque tradentes . . . Tassilo Dux Bajoarorum quicquid ad Feringas pertinebat pariter ipsis consentientibus Alfrid cum fratribus suis et participibus eorum atque consortiis, reliquas autem partes quicquid ad genealogiam quae vocatur Fagana pertinebat, tradiderunt ipsi, id sunt Ragino, Anulo, Wetti, Vurmhart, et cuncti participes eorum, donantes atque transfundentes seu firmitatem secundum jus Bajoarorum facientes, ut ipsaque hujus loci, id est Erichinga, fines utrorumque genealogiarum sine fraude ditionibus beatae praedictae Dei Genetricis Mariae consistere in perpetuum firma permaneat. The land alienated appears to have been the undivided inheritance of two groups of heirs, — the members of the ducal family, the Agilolfingi, and the members of the Fagana family. These families are mentioned in Lex Baiw. Tit. II. Cap. XX.

Note 82. — Page 32.

See Reg. Hist. Westf. XX. and Beyer Urkb. Nachlese I. No. 3: quod contra allodiones meos recepi totum ad integrum dono atque trado, terris silvis, etc., quantum cumque mihi obvenit. The heirs in an undivided inheritance are usually called *coheredes* (see Notes 79. 80. 81); or else they are called *consortes* (see Note 81). Alsat. Dipl. IX: quicquid nos de Animgo seu consortes ipsius, vel de quibuscumque hominibus comparavimus. Cod. S. Galli 155: quicquid in pago Durgauense genitor meus a consortibus suis in partem visus fuit accepisse et ille postea suis dividenda dimisit heredibus. Ibid. 199: pratum quod cum consortibus meis adhuc in commune visa sum possidere, reliqua omnia que in predicta villa mihi in hereditate succedunt volo esse concessum.

Lauresham Cod. X: rubo per Agilolfum et suos consortes pro signo incisus.

The word *socii* occurs instead of the word *consortes* in Fulda Cod. 165: traditio Waltoni et sociorum. Fifteen persons are mentioned as donors of a certain undivided appropriation: capturam que de villa B. capta est et haec sunt nomina locorum quibus illa per gyrum determinatur. In Ibid. 471, fourteen persons unite in selling a *captura*. They receive payment severally. A claim is afterwards put in by two other persons, that a portion (*portiuncula*) of the property belonged to them. They gave up their claim upon the receipt of the following articles: duos boves et duo pallia, lanea et linea, duos gladios. They then declared: quod ulterius in illa captura nullam communionem habeant. The word *communio* is used here, as elsewhere, to describe a right in undivided land, a right to a portion of it, or, the land remaining undivided, a right of enjoyment in it. Cf. Note 72. The word *potestas* is often used instead of the word *communio*. See, for example, Cod. S. Galli 514: et jam dicti fratres omnem potestatem, quam habuerunt in Goldahun marcha et in eadem silva ad monasterium Sancti Galli vendiderunt, et xxx solidos pro pretio acceperunt.

When, in the early time, a group of kinsmen took possession of a tract of land, every individual member of the group had a *potestas* or *communio* in the land, — a right to appropriate as much as he wanted of it, or to use and enjoy it without stint. But as time went on it became necessary to define the amount of land which the individual might appropriate, or, if the land remained undivided, to define rights of enjoyment. A right of appropriation being defined, it was held as property. It was transmitted from father to sons, and it was alienated. Rights of enjoyment in undivided lands were held in the same way. They were hereditary and alienable rights. But we shall speak of this matter at length presently.

NOTE 83. — PAGE 32.

The passage is given in Note 72. In Notes 73–78, and in Note 82, we learned how inheritances were divided among the heirs. The heirs are called parceners (*participes*) in the passage cited from Hist. Frising. in Note 82. Divisions of land among kinsmen are described in Lex Wisig. X. Tit. I. See passages cited in Note 33.

Note 84. — Page 32.

Liutprand LXXIII: Si infans dum intra aetatem est, res suas cum fratribus, aut cum parentibus suis dividere voluerit, aut si ipsi cum ipso infante dividere voluerint, faciant Iudici notitiam; et ipse Iudex faciat venire parentes ipsius propinquos, ut una cum ipsis, aut per se, aut per missum suum bonam personam Deum timentem res ipsas dividat, sic tamen, ut omni tempore sortes stare debeant, et adaequatio percurrat.

Formula. Petre te appellat Martinus, quod tu tenes sibi malo ordine terram in tali loco. Illa terra dico esse mea, quia quando tu eras infra aetatem, voluisti dividere mecum, et Comes divisit ipsam terram, aut per se, aut per Missum suum, et tui parentes fuerunt: Aut probet, quod sic fuisset facta divisio; aut perdat.

Note 85. — Page 32.

Formula CXXVII. See Note 74.

Note 86. — Page 33.

Beyer Urkb. Nachlese I. No. 3. Cited in Note 82.

Note 87. — Page 33.

Cod. S. Galli 480. Cited in Note 79.

Note 88. — Page 33.

This text of Lex Salica, De alodis, is first found in the "Originum ac Germanorum Antiquitatum Libri" of B. J. Herold (Basileae, 1555, folio). It is probably the text of a MS. once preserved at Fulda, but now lost. It is a simple, logical amplification of the ordinary texts. It is safe, therefore, for us to use it. If it were inconsistent with the ordinary texts, if it were in any sense contradictory of them, we could not use it. It will be remembered that we possess no MS. for the Lex Frisionum ; that the citations which we use are from the Editio Princeps of Herold. The text of the De alodis which we have cited has, therefore, precisely the same authority that a passage of Lex Fris. has: no more, no less.

The phrase *nepotes aut pronepotes* should be noted. The division was supposed to be made between grandsons *or* great-grandsons. Can we infer, therefore, that this text of the De alodis antedates the introduction of the principle of representation? Cf. Formula CXXXIV (in Note 155). It is hardly safe to put so much stress upon the word *aut*, it is so constantly used for *et* in our early records.

NOTE 89. — PAGE 35.

See Joshua xviii. There remained among the children of Israel seven tribes, which had not yet received their inheritance. The land was accordingly divided into seven parts, one for each tribe. Joshua then cast lots, and divided the land unto the children of Israel according to their divisions; according to their tribes and according to the families within the tribes. Ibid. xix: The second lot came forth for the tribe of the children of Simeon according to their families: and their inheritance was within that of the children of Judah. See also Numbers xxxvi: The Lord commanded that the land should be given for an inheritance by lot to the children of Israel, and the inheritance of Zelophehad went to his daughters. See also Chronicles vi. 63, where the land is given " by lot throughout their families."

We do not suppose that the land was distributed in this manner among the German clans, but within the limits of the clan and family, distributions were made upon this principle, without doubt. Reference is made to *per stirpes* divisions in the Herold text of Lex Salica, De alodis. See Note 88. Divisions among brothers were made by lot. See, for example, Cod. Patav. I. LXII: quod mihi pater meus moriens dereliquid et quod mihi sortie accedit erga fratres meos; id est in domibus, mancipiis, campis, pratis, silvis, etc. Divisions among brothers were made by lot: why should divisions among grandsons and great-grandsons be made upon any different principle? We see, in Liutprand LXIX, that divisions among grandsons were made by lot. See the passage in Note 79. In

Liutprand LXXIII (in Note 84) we see that divisions between kinsmen (*parentes*) were made by lot.

We read in Rothar CLIII: Omnis parentela usque in septimum genuculum numeretur, ut parens parenti per gradum et parentelam heres succedat, sic tamen ut ille qui succedere vult, nominatim unuscujusque nomina parentum suorum antecessorum dicat. It is a fact beyond question that the knowledge of genealogical relationships was as carefully preserved among the Germans as among other people in early times. How is this to be explained, unless the knowledge was useful in some way? The hypothesis suggests itself: that the knowledge of genealogical relationships was preserved as a means of determining rights of property by inheritance; that the knowledge of relationships was preserved for the same reason that title deeds are preserved among us. If this is so, it is possible that ancestor worship was introduced as an aid to the memory; ancestors being so soon forgotten if not repeatedly remembered. We can imagine the house-father saying to his children: Let us institute a festival in honor of our progenitor in order that we may not forget him: for we may some day lose our inheritance by forgetting him. But all this is mere hypothesis.

Note 90. — Page 35.

Lex Burg. Tit. LXXVIII: De hereditatum successione adtentius pertractantes, statuimus ut si pater cum filiis sortem suam diviserit . . . Cf. Liutprand LXXIII, in Note 84, and Ibid. LXIX, in Note 79: aliae vero res, quae divisae fuerint inter fratres seu nepotes, vel ubi mensura tracta est, sorte stante adaequentur. Inheritances, being distributed by lot, were very properly called *sortes*. So in Cassiodorus, Varia VIII. 26: quae necessitas ad injusta compellat, cum vos et sortes alant propriae, et munera nostra, domino adjuvante ditificent?

Note 91. — Page 35.

See Formula CXXVII in Note 74. It is from the collection of Marculf (I. 20), who lived in the time of Landeric, Archbishop of Paris, in the second half of the seventh century. The shareholders in the *alod* were *consortes*; the *alod* was their *sors*. Then see passages cited in Notes 79, 82, and 90. The phrase *terra sortis titulo acquisita* occurs in Lex Burg. Tit. I. 1.

Note 92. — Page 36.

We have already cited Cod. S. Galli 199: pratum carrorum quinque, quod cum consortibus meis adhuc in commune visa sum possidere. Cf. Hist. Frising. DCCCLXXVI: de pratis carradas xxx, excepto quod commune est cum aliis. So in Ibid. CCCXLVIII: territorium jurnales xxx. de pratis carradas L, et in alio loco pratas communes, sicut alii coheredes habent.

Note 93. — Page 36.

Formula CCXXXIX: dedi eidem sponsae meae futuraeque uxori dotis nomine curtem sepe cinctam et in eadem marcha de arvea terra juchos c, de pratis juchos totidem, de silva proprii mei juris juchos CL, communem pascuam communesque silvarum usus, etc. Part of the pasture land had been divided, or appropriated. The rest remained common. It was held in undivided shares, which were, it appears, alienable. The shares of the common land were probably proportioned to the shares of land held in severalty. See Chart. Sithiense, p. 103: mansam cum castitiis; de prato bunaria XVI. de terra arabili bunaria CLVIII, de silva grossa bunaria XVIII ad saginandos porcos XX, de silva minuta bunaria LI, de pastura communi sufficienter. Cf. the passages cited from Lex Burg. in Note 72; also Lacomblet Urkb. 3: unum modicum curtile cum agris III. cum waterscapis, perviis, communiis pascuis; et dedi ei potestatem habere in silvam que dicitur Sitroth. Cod. Trad. Lunaelac CV: trado atque transfirmo partes duos hereditatis meae ... in omnibus firmabo, cum domibus, edificiis, curtiferis, cum terris arabilis, cum campis, pratis, pascuis communiis, etc. Here we have *pascua communia*, i. e. undivided shares of a common pasture, included within an inheritance. Two thirds of these undivided shares of common pasture are alienated to the Church of St. Michael at Lunaelac, or Mondsee.

The word *conpascua* is often used instead of the phrase *pascua communia*. See Beyer Urkb. 280. Hist. Frising. MCCXXXI. Wirtemb. Urkb. CCCVII. Günther Cod. Dipl. 34. In Ibid. 59

we have *communibus pascuis* alienated with a *mansus:* quendam mansum ex proprietatibus cum omnibus appenditiis; videlicet vineis, areis, agris, communibus pascuis. The *communia pascua* belonged to the owner of the *mansus.* We have *conpascua* again in Orig. Nassoic. LXVIII. These common pastures are not, strictly speaking, common pastures. They are not the property of the community. They are the undivided property of neighboring land-owners. It is property held in common, not common property. With unity of possession we have diversity of title. The undivided shares are hereditary, divisible, and even alienable, — alienable as wholes or in fractions. We must not infer communism from the word *communis.* Many writers have done this. They have fallen, consequently, into very serious errors.

Note 94. — Page 36.

Lex Burg. Add. I. Tit. I. 6: sylvarum, montium, et pascuorum, unicuique pro rata suppetit esse communionem. Note the force of the words *pro rata.* The arable land of an inheritance being divided, the rest of the land was often held in undivided shares proportioned to the shares of land held in severalty: secundum terrarum modum vel possessionis ratam. See passage of Lex Burg. (Tit. LXVII) cited in Note 72. When a man alienated his severalty lands he alienated with them proportionate but undivided shares in all the common lands. See, for example, Westf. Urkb. 3: mansos duos cum terris cultis et incultis et silvis communibus ad eos mansos pertinentibus. In Cod. Trad. Lunaelac LXIV, an estate is alienated including *silvis communiis.* In Ibid. CXXX a *silva communia* is included under *res suas proprias.* Cod. S. Galli 466: pars silve quae in ipsa marcha ad meam pertinet proprietatem. So in No. 531: de communi silva quantum ad portionem nostram pertinet . . . de silva juxta estimationem nostre portionem in communi silve. Lauresham Cod. MMMDCXCVI: portionem suam de silva inter ambas marcas. Ibid. MCCXXXVI: de illa silva communi, quantum jure hereditario ad me pertinere videtur. MMMDCCXVI: de silva portionem suam, item sextam partem. MMMDCCXLVI: de silva quod ad se pertinuit. Trad. Wiz. LXIX: tres partes de illa marca silvatica portione sua. Ibid. CC: sortes IIII, et silva in communiis que possunt porci saginari numero cc si fructus evenerit. In Hist. Frising. DCCCLXI a man alienates a *silvam communem cum ceteris viris*. Cf. DCCCCIX : maximam partem de silva optimā communem cum ceteris nobilibus viris. Brev. Not. Salzb. XV. 2 : silvam cum participibus suis. Then read Formula CCCCII : silviculam propriam vel cum suis coheredibus communem.

It is evident from these examples, and many more which might be cited, that the *silva communis* was simply undivided property, or property held in undivided shares. The shares of it were held as private property. They were hereditary, divisible, and even alienable. The *silva communis* did not belong to the community. It belonged to the members of it. Among them there was unity of possession, but diversity of title.

Note 95. — Page 36.

Lex Rip. Tit. LX. 2.

Note 96. — Page 36.

Communia are described as private property, as hereditary and alienable, in Formulae CXVIII, CLXXII (observe how the *communia* are included under the head of *possessiones vel dominationes*), CC (here they are alienated *per festucam*, included within a *possessio vel dominatio*, under a *jus vel dominatio*), CCII (here they have been acquired *de alode, de comparato, seu de adtracto*, and are included under a *jus et dominatio*), CCCI, CCCXLVI, CCCLXVII : usus saltuum communium (described as private property, in the same category with *mancipiis, jumentis, pecoribus, curtilibus et hobis possessis*). See, lastly, Formula CCCCII. Then Kemble's Codex LXVI, XCVI, CVIII, CXC, CCLXXVI : communionem marisci quae ad illam villam antiquitus cum recto pertinebat. See also CCLXXXVIII, CCCCXXXII. Then Chart. Sithiense, p. 61 : where a man alienates two thirds of his estate including *communiis*. Cf. p. 62, where a whole estate is alienated including *communiis*. Then read Lex Burg. Add. I. 6 again (given in Note 72). See also Chart. Sithiense, p. 117 : curtilem, id est cum casticiis ; et, inter ipsum curtilem et pratum ac terram arabilem, bunaria XL ; et de silva bunaria X, una cum ipsorum locorum communiis.

The *communia* were rights in common lands supplementary to property held in severalty. Rights in severalty lands being alienated, *communia* went with them, — the *communia ipsorum locorum*.

In Lacomblet Urkb. 6, a *comprehensio in silva* is alienated and with it a *communio in eandem silvam*. In Ibid. 3, the phrase *potestas in silva* is used instead of *communio in silva*. In No. 5 we have the phrase *dominatio in silvam*. Cf. No. 8: portionem hereditatis mee . . . in terra aratoria, seu in pratis, et in pascuis, et in omnem communionem mecum in silvam. Hist. Frising. DCCLXXXIII: dedit episcopus . . . in silva communem usum cum aliis. Ibid. MXXX: communionem in silvis, etiam in marchis. Ibid. MCXCVII: praedium cum privatis et communibus usibus legaliter ad eundem locum pertinentibus. Brev. Not. Salzb. VII: portionem venationis communem cum cohaeredibus suis. Beyer Urkb. 400: coheres est in communione que pertinet ad Tris. Wirtemb. Urkb. XXXVII: utilitatibus, quam in ipsam supradictam marcam et ad ipsam supradictam rem legitime pertinet. Ibid. LXXVIII: commoditatibus. Osnabrk. Gesch. XXVI: utilitatibus ad eadem loca pertinentibus. Cod. S. Galli 514: potestatem quam habuerunt in marcha; 680: usum habuimus qualem unusquisque liber homo de sua proprietate [*note this*] juste et legaliter debet habere in campis, pascuis, silvis lignorumque succissionibus, atque porcorum pastu, pratis, viis, aquis, aquarumque decursibus, piscationibus, exitibus et reditibus. See also Ibid. 738, 740, 742: in silva usus ad focos et ad sepes et ad edificia quantum sufficerent ad curtile. Ibid. No. 806: quicquid hereditario jure possidemus . . . agris, pratis, silvis, omnibusque usibus ad ea cedentibus. See also No. 808.

It is evident, from the above examples, that rights of enjoyment in common land were based upon rights of property therein. The common land was simply undivided land, in which two or more persons owned shares. It was in virtue of this shareholding that they had rights of enjoyment. It appears that these rights of enjoyment were of the nature of real property. They were held as real property, inherited, divided, and alienated.

Note 97. — Page 37.

Wirtemberg. Urkb. LXIII, or Cod. S. Galli 199.   See Note 92.

Note 98. — Page 37.

Trad. Wiz. CCLXXII. Kemble's Codex CCXCII. Cf. Ibid. LXVI: communa pasturae pro omni genere animalium omnibus scionis sibi et hominibus suis sive tenentibus. Ibid. CVIII: unius gregis porcorum pascuam in saltu Andoredo. See Chartularium Abbathiae de Novo Monasterii (published by the Surtees Society, Durham, 1878, 8°), p. 72: communem pasturam ad IIII equos domitos, et ad x boves et xxx vaccas cum vitulis earum donec superenentur, et ad quadringentas oves cum agnis earum. There are other similar passages in this Cartulary; which, by the way, has been accidentally omitted from our list of sources.

In addition to the passages cited above, two passages may be given from the Visigothic Law. Lex Wisig. VIII. Tit. 5, 2: Si inter consortes de glandibus fuerit orta contentio, pro eo quod unus ab alio plures porcos habeat: tunc qui minus habuerit, liceat ei secundum quod terram dividit, porcos ad glandem in portione sua suscipere, dummodo aequalis numerus ab utraque parte ponatur. Et postmodum decimas dividant. Sicut et terras diviserunt.

See also Ibid. 5: Si in pascua grex alienus intraverit, sive ovium, sive vaccarum, hoc quod de porcis constitutum est praecipimus custodiri. Consortes vero vel hospites nulli calumniae subiaceant: quia illis usum herbarum, quae conclusae non fuerant, constat esse communem. Qui vero sortem suam totam forte concluserit, et aliena pascua absente domino invadit, sine pascuario non praesumat, nisi forte dominus pascuae voluerit.

It is evident that the common pasture was simply the undivided pasture; that rights of enjoyment were unregulated, or else proportioned to undivided shares.

Note 99. — Page 38.

Lauresham Cod. MCCXXXVI. Cod. S. Galli, No. 531. Westf. Urkb. No. 3. The passages were cited in Note 94.

A share of the common forest was attached to every *mansus* or *huba;* so that if a man owned two *mansi* or *hubae,* he owned two shares of the common forest. The tenants of the *mansi* or *hubae* had rights of common in the common forest. The owners or lords of the *hubae* had shares of the common forest: their tenants had rights of common in it, by grant or by prescription. We may again refer the reader to Mr. Joshua Williams's "Rights of Common," and to Mr. Charles Elton's "Law of Commons and Waste Lands."

Through the early period the common forests were owned by a great many persons. Some owned a few shares, some owned many; but in the course of time there was an enormous concentration of ownership, and a substitution of tenancy in its place. The common forest came to be the property of one or more great lords, and the mass of the people had merely rights of common therein. During the following centuries, however, the tenants succeeded, in many places, in getting rid of their landlords. In the mean time they had grouped themselves in corporations; so the landlordship which they took away from their landlords was assumed, not by individuals but by corporations of individuals. — by communes, or communities. This theory differs very much from that which is commonly held; but we recommend it to the reader for his consideration.

Note 100. — Page 39.

Hist. Frising. DCCCLXXVI. Ibid. DCCCXV. Ibid. DCCCCIX.

Note 101. — Page 40.

The possession of undivided land was almost the first bond of union between the allodial land-owners. There was no other in the early time, except the bond of kinship; and even the bond of kinship was very loose except where there were undivided inheritances to keep the kinsmen together. As long as there was plenty of land, and every man could take as much of it as he wanted, rights in the land were seldom disputed, and seldom brought for discussion before the assembly of land-owners. In the course of time, however, the good land became scarce. Quarrels arose in regard to the rights of property in it. Systematic divisions of the undivided lands were called for. These divisions were usually made by the assembly of land-owners. But in regard to pasture and forest lands, it was often thought best not to divide them, but to have rights of enjoyment in them defined. The definitions were seldom permanent, however. Disputes continued to arise, and these disputes were settled by the assembly of land-owners; and when the right of the individual was opposed to that of the majority it was apt to be annihilated. Strangers were sometimes admitted to rights in the common land, by the assembly. In this way the sovereign control over the common land came to be vested in the community or corporation, rather than in the members. It is generally true, that wherever the control of undivided property is vested in a majority of the shareholders, rather than in the majority of shares as represnted by their owners, the property becomes, sooner or later, the property of the community or corporation. The majority vote may be described as the root of communism. Most of the communism which the world has seen has been an outgrowth from it.

Note 102. — Page 40.

Take, for example, the *almend* of Switzerland. Was it, in the early time, land held in common, — i. e. undivided land, held in undivided shares, — or was it land which belonged to an association or corporation of persons, in which the individual had merely a usufruct? No careful student of the records will hesitate in concluding, the question being put to him in this way, that the *almend* was undivided land, land held in undivided shares. He will remember perhaps the passage of Cod. S. Galli 680 (A. D. 890): talem usum habuimus qualem unusquisque liber homo de sua proprietate [*note these words*] juste et legaliter debet habere in campis, pascuis, silvis, lignorumque succisionibus atque porcorum pastu, pratis, viis, aquis, aquarumque decursibus, piscationibus, exitibus et reditibus. See Notes 92–94, 96–99. The student will remember also the innumerable documents in which shares of the undivided and common land are described as hereditary, divisible, and alienable. That the nature of the *almend* has changed in the course of the Middle Ages, that at the present time the ownership of it is vested rather in the villages and communes than in individuals, is to be

NOTES AND REFERENCES. 197

granted, of course. The change in the constitution of the *almend* may be explained as the result of giving the control of the *almend* to the majority of the shareholders, rather than to the majority of shares as represented by their holders.

But this is not the only explanation of the present constitution of the *almend*, nor perhaps the best. The *almend* was, in many cases the property of one or two great lords; but it was occupied by the tenants of these lords. They had rights of common in it, by grant or by prescription. The tenants then formed themselves into corporations or communes, and succeeded in overthrowing the lord or lords, and in getting possession of the landlordship. They then emerge with rights of common under their own landlordship. Of these two explanations the reader may take whichever he prefers, or both. It is probable that the history of the *almend* has been different in different cases. See remarks and citations in Note 17.

What has been said here of the *almend* refers equally well to communal lands in Belgium, in England, and elsewhere.

Note 103. — Page 41.

Lauresham Cod. CCCLXXVII. Cf. Cod. Morav. CCCXXXVII: portio Reinoldi in via quam vendebat. We have the *via alicujus* in Lex Baiw. IX. 13. In Wirtemb. Urkb. XLIII *viis* are included under the head of *omnes res meas*. Cf. Ibid. LXI. See Formulae CCXXXI, CCXXXIX. Many other instances might be cited. It was some time before roads and ways ceased to be regarded and described as undivided property. They were held in undivided shares, — *communiter divisam*, as the phrase was. See Lex Burg. Add. I. Tit. I. 1 : Observandum viam publicam, vel inter agros communiter divisam, nec possideri, nec intercludi, nec exartari posse.

Note 104. — Page 41.

Lex Burg. Add. I. 4 : Viam in actum, hoc est, ubi carpenta vel carra ducuntur, similiter biennio amitti, et adquiri posse.

Note 105.—Page 42.

Lex Baiw. IX. 13: Si quis viam publicam, ubi Rex vel Dux egreditur, vel viam aequalem alicuius [*note the force of this word*] clauserit contra legem, cum duodecim componat, et illam sepem tollat. Et si negare voluerit, cum duodecim sacramentalibus iuret. If a man could get twelve witnesses to swear that the road was his, he might appropriate it: if he could not do this, he paid twelve solidi to the owner, the king or duke, or any one else (*aliquis*) who happened to be the owner.

Lex Baiw. IX. 14: De via convicinali vel pastorali, qui eam alicui contra legem clauserit, cum sex solidis componat et aperiat, vel cum sex sacramentalibus iuret. Ibid. 15: De semita convicinali, si quis eam clausevit, cum tribus solidis componat, aut cum uno sacramentali juret.

Note 106.—Page 43.

The formula *aquis aquarumve decursibus* occurs in almost all the descriptions of property which we have, of the early period. One example will be sufficient,—Formula CCXXXVI: curtem clausam cum ceteris edificiis, cum terra salice, id est jurnales tantos, prata ad carradas tantes, et hobas tantas, cum agris, pratis, silvis, pascuis, aquis aquarumve decursibus, ut a die presente habeas, teneas, atque possideas. Cf. Cod. S. Galli 619: potestative manu possidere usque in medium Hrenum. See also Hist. Frising. DCCLXXXVII: terminum fluminis pertinentem. Cod. Trad. Lunaelae V: donavimus unam aquam. Fulda Trad. Cap. 5. 69: capturam unam et duas partes fluminis supra et infra. Ibid. Cap. 42. 1: agrum in quo fons ebullit. Ibid. No. 215: pratum unum et fontem in eo manentem. Fulda Cod. 410: talem partem in illo fonte ubi nascetur sal qualis mihi contingit in eodem fonte. Lauresham Cod. MMCXVII: fontem I in Sigulfingheim. Cf. Alsat. Dipl. LXIX. Formula CC. Kemble's Codex XXVII: fontanis vel mariscum. Beyer Urkb. 22: de illa fontana, quantum ad nos pertinet. Ibid. 465 (b): xx mansos cum fontibus inde manentibus. Cf. Lib. Eli. II. 21: unum gurgitem quem Eanflead moriens partim dimisit Wine, et partim emit ipse a cognatis suis.

Note 107. — Page 43.

Lex Burg. Add. I. Tit. I. 3: Aquae cursum et adquiri et amitti biennio constat.

Note 108. — Page 43.

Lex Baiw. IX. 16: De fonte. 1. Si fontem quacumque immunditia coinquinaverit vel maculaverit, emundet, cum prius, ut nulla sit suspicio coinquinationis, et cum sex solidis componat, aut cum sex sacramentalibus iuret. 2. Si autem plurimorum in vicinia putens fuerit, compositione inter se multentur. 3. Ille vero puteum in pristinum restituat gradum. Another stage in the history of wells is described in Rothar CCCXI: Si animal in puteo alterius ceciderit, et mortuum aut debilitatum fuerit, non requiratur, cujus putens est; quia putei aqua communis omnium utilitatibus invenitur esse. Here the well is supposed to belong to somebody, but the water is free to all. The individual was no longer allowed to hold an exclusive right to the water of his well. He must allow others to partake of it.

Note 109. — Page 44.

Lauresham Cod. DCCCCXLVII. See also Cod. S. Galli 731: dimidium curtem cum arboribus positum et dimidium domum. Hist. Frising. CCCLXXVII: quicquid ipso die propriae hereditatis se habere videbatur totum tradidit . . . hoc est curtem medium et domum mediam cum alia edificia, tota media. Brev. Not. Salzb. XVII. 3: Gotschalh dedit medietatem domus suae et omnia ad eam pertinentia. So in Mon. Weihensteph. p. 471: dimidiam domum suam delegavit. Lastly, see Münst. Beitr. III. 6: curtim in unum congregare commutatione. When several persons held a house in shares, the shares could be united again by means of purchases and exchanges. One of the shareholders bought out the others. Then he had the house to himself. Unless this was done, the house would come to be the undivided property of a great many persons, representing the original proprietor. We have already cited the passage of the Lombard Law, Rothar CLXVII: si fratres post mortem patris in casa communi remanserint . . . Doubtless grandsons and even great-grandsons sometimes remained together under the same roof, forming a house community. The house community arises from the multiplication of heirs within the house of an ancestor.

House communities of this kind may be seen in the Slavonic countries, especially in Slavonia, Croatia, Dalmatia, Servia, and Montenegro. They may be seen also in India and in other countries. They are, in all cases we believe, assemblages of heirs holding an undivided inheritance. The inheritance (the ancestral homestead) being in its nature indivisible, the heirs are bound together by it into a unit. They separate only when their inheritance will no longer contain them.

Note 110. — Page 44.

Salem Reg. p. 327. See also Wirtemb. Urkb. XXXVIII: mediam partem de uno molendino. Ibid. XLVII. Lauresham Cod. DXVI: tertiam partem de uno molino. Ibid. MMCXXIV: dimidium molendinum. Cod. S. Galli 127: mediam partem de uno molendino. Münst. Beitr. I. No. VI: ego Goscalcus, cum pleno consensu uxoris me, et germani mei, ejusque uxoris et corum natorum; item et sororis mee, aliorumque tam heredum quam coheredum meorum libero arbitrio vendidisse molendinum cum omnibus suis emolumentis.

In this connection the following passage of the Chart. Sithiense is interesting: p. 67: quod mirabile nostris hactenus monstratur temporibus [A. D. 800?] molendinum fecit [Orlandus, abbas] volvere aquis contra montem currentibus; constituitque ut nullus hominum molendinum extra locum jam dictum [villa Arecas, Arques?] construere presumeret: quod ad utilitatem monasterii Sithiu ad tempus fuit conservatum. This is a very early case of copyright!

Note 111. — Page 44.

Fulda Cod. 68. Hist. Frising. CXXIX. Capit. Wormat. A. D. 829. See also Capit., Additio Tertia LI (Corp. Jur. Germ. II. p. 805): perlatum ad nos est quod inter heredes ecclesiae in rebus propriis constitutae dividantur, et tanta per eandem divisionem simultas oriatur, ut unius altaris quatuor partes fiant, et singulae partes singulos habeant presbyteros: quod sine discordia et simultate nullo modo geri potest. Unde nobis visum est quod hujuscemodi ecclesiae inter heredes dividi non debeant. Et si in contentionem venerint . . . References to shares of churches owned by individuals are very common.

Alsat. Dipl. CCXLVIII: quarta pars ecclesiae. Formula CCCXIV: partem in basilica. Lacomblet Urkb. 289: octavam partem ecclesiae. Ritz Urk. 5: portio mea de illa basilica. Fulda Cod. 161: partem illius ecclesiae quam pater noster nobis in hereditatem dereliquit. Lauresham Cod. LXXXIII: duas partes basilicae. Ibid. MDCCCCLXV: portionem meam de basilica. So also in MDCCCCLXVI, MDCCCCLXVII, MDCCCCLXIX–MDCCCCLXXII, and MDCCCCLXXIV. In these documents different persons are mentioned as shareholders in the same church; that of St. Lanpert in Mainz. See also Trad. Wiz. CLXXVIII. Cod. S. Galli 13: de illa ecclesia, de v partibus duas partes. Ibid. 108: de illa ecclesia portionem, quicquid mihi legitime obtingit. Ibid. 155: partem ecclesie, vel quicquid in predicto pago genitor meus a consortibus suis in partem visus fuit accepisse et ille postea suis dividenda dimisit heredibus. Ibid. 185: partem basilice. See also Hist. Frising. CDXIV: tunc interrogavit Episcopus Fridupertum et coheredes sui, si illorum portionem, quod eis contigisset in ipsa Ecclesia donare voluissent. Num. CDLXXII is also interesting, and DCCXXXI. Wirtemb. Urkb. CXXXVI, CLIV, CCLVII. Lastly, see Reg. Hist. Westf. XX, where we have *successores alodii* in a church.

Note 112. — Page 45.

Hist. Frising. CCCLXVII: mancipias II et III um dimidium. Ibid. CDIII: unum mancipium et alium dimidium, quem communem habuit cum fratre suo nomine Erlolf. Fulda Cod. 445: unius pueri communis duae partes, nomine Ruadhelm. Ibid. 573: mancipia quorum quaedam mea, quaedam vero meorum propinquorum et mea communia, quorum haec sunt nomina. Cf. Trad. Corb. 383: tradidit mansum cum medietate familie.

Note 113.—Page 45.

Brev. Not. Salzb. VII. 3: Madelhelmus quidem vir nobilis cum caeteris rebus suis portionem venationis suae ad istam dei ecclesiam juxta ripam, quae vocatur Albina, hanc esse communem cum cohaeredibus suis. Cf. Ibid. VIII. 1: illa genealogia supradictorum hominum de Albina. We have here a clan holding a hunting ground in undivided shares, the shares being hereditary, divisible, and alienable. *Venationes* are frequently referred to in the documents, where they are alienated with other property. See Cod. Quedlinb. XXVII, XXVIII, XXIX, XXX, and Juvavia II. Num. VI. p. 22.

Note 114.—Page 45.

Lauresham Cod. CCCCLXVIII. See also Indic. Arnon. VII. 4: prata et silva et medietatem de lacu piscatione. Lib. Eli. II. 20: dedit unius gurgitis piscationem. Lisch. Urk. II. No. I: piscatura dimidiam juxta mare. Juvavia II. p. 22. Lacomblet Urkb. 5. Cod. Quedlinb. XXVII–XXX.

Note 115.—Page 46.

Pez Thesaurus VI. Part I. p. 72: de curte, qui dicitur Atarholf, inde licet piscari in Maninsco hebdomadas duas circa natale Domini. This is one of the Mondsee records. Sometimes a man was obliged to fish with a small net. See Stenzel XLVIII: piscaturam cum parvo rete. On the sea-coast the number of boats which a man might send out was sometimes limited. See Lisch. Urk. LVIII: libertatem capiendi rumbos [*flounders*] cum una navi et retibus in mari salso terre nostre dominio adjacenti. In early times, of course, hunting and fishing were enjoyed *ad libitum*. It was a long while before rights were defined or limited. The passage last cited dates from the year 1265. Just as soon as there was a scarcity of game or fish, disputes arose regarding hunting and fishing grounds, and rights of property in them, and rights of enjoyment in them were defined. Rights to hunt and fish were, in most cases, assumed by the landlords, who distributed them in the form of rights of common among their tenants. The right to fish in the lord's waters is called, in the English law, the "common of piscary." A "common of fowling" is not unheard of. All such rights fall under the general head of "profits à prendre."

NOTE 116. — PAGE 46.

The German family, or clan growing out of it, is best described by the German word *Erbgenossenschaft*. It was a group of heirs bound together by the possession of an inheritance in the land. The inheritance was the main bond of union or association among them. There was no other, in the early time, except the bond of kinship, which, in itself, was a rather loose one.

The *Erbgenossenschaft* must be very carefully distinguished from the association of *huba*-holders, the *Hubengemeinde*. The *Hubengemeinde* was an association of tenants holding allotments of land (*hubae*) from a landlord or landlords. The *Erbgenossenschaft* was, at the time of which we are speaking, the association of landlords. The *Erbgenossenschaft* very often embraced one or more *Hubengemeinden*. That is to say, the inheritances of the *Erbgenossen* consisted of *Huben*. An inheritance in the *Erbgenossenschaft* consisted of one, two, or more *Huben* of the *Hubengemeinden*.

In later times the distinction here drawn is of no importance. We have *Erbgenossenschaften* of tenants, and *Hubengemeinden* of landlords. The two institutions are so confounded that they cannot be distinguished. We shall consider this matter at greater length presently.

It is worth while here to speak of the resemblance between the Teutonic *Erbgenossenschaft* and the Hindu village community. The resemblance is very striking. The landholders in the Hindu village almost always trace their descent from a common progenitor, the founder of the village and first holder of the village lands. The landholders in the village are the heirs and representatives of this person. Sometimes the inheritance is undivided for several generations. During this time the heirs are apt to live in the ancestral house, forming a house community; and the land is held in undivided shares, in common. After a while, however, the heirs in the inheritance become too numerous to live together in one house. They have to separate. New houses are built in which they distribute themselves. At the same time, the land, or as much of it as is required, is divided among the different households. Every house has then an inheritance in severalty. The distribution of the land is usually made according to the law of inheritance applied to a table of descents from the common progenitor, i. e. *per stirpes et jure hereditario.* As the heirs increase in the different households of the village, the inheritances of the households have to be divided and subdivided among the members, and the number of households increases constantly. The heir in an undivided inheritance is allowed, at any time he pleases, to have his portion of the inheritance divided off and assigned to him as a severalty. From time to time, as the land becomes exhausted, the fields of the village are shifted to a new locality. In such cases the households of the village receive equivalent inheritances, and the individual receives a share of the land assigned to the household of which he is a member. The divisions are regularly made according to descents and the law of inheritance. The undivided, common land of the village is regarded as the undivided inheritance of the different households, and of the individuals within these households. The Hindu family or clan, like the German family or clan, is not, properly speaking, a land-owning corporation. It is simply a group of heirs, with a partly divided, partly undivided, inheritance in the land and the things on the land. The corporate character which the observers of the Hindu village community have described, and so much insisted upon, is due to the fact that the heirs in the village are held collectively responsible for the payment of state taxes. The villagers are taxed, not as individuals, but as a group. They are taxed as a corporation. Apart from their relations with the state, however, they must be regarded as a group of parceners rather than as a body corporate. A man dies holding certain taxable property. The property passes to his heirs, who hold it in undivided shares. They are collectively responsible for the taxes, but they are not properly speaking a body corporate. According to our system of law, when the property is divided the shareholders pay their taxes severally and individually. There is no collective responsibility among them. But in India the collective responsibility remains, whether the property is divided or not. A certain tax being laid upon the property, it is paid by the holders of the property, whether they hold it in undivided shares or in severalties. They distribute the burden among themselves as they please.

The mode in which state taxes are levied, and distributed among the landholders, has nothing to do with the internal constitution of the village, except in so far as it may be the means of altering that constitution. We have no reason to believe that the revenue system of the Hindu kings, or of their conquerors, has to any appreciable degree changed the constitution of the Indian village community. The taxes have always been paid according to the extent of the different inheritances; and the principle of private property has been persistently adhered to.

Note 117. — Page 46.

Formula CCCXVIII: in vico et genealogia quae dicuntur, ubi rivolis ille intrat in illum flumen, curtiles duos et aforis a terra arabili jurnales tantos et de pratis ad carradas tantum et molendinum unum; et e contra in conpensatione harum rerum dedit memoratus vir ex suo proprio prefato episcopo ad partem episcopum, in pago illo, in villa vocabulo illo, prope fluvium illum, curtilem unum et aforis de terra jurnales tantos, lucos duos, molendina duo. We see here that the principle of private property was fully recognized within the *vicus vel genealogia*. Cf. also Brev. Not. Salzb. VII. 3: portio venationis communis cum cohaeredibus. It was alienated to the church at Salzburg by a member of the *genealogia* de Albina. See Ibid. VIII. 1. And read again Lex Alam. LXXXIV: contentio inter genealogias de termino terrae eorum. The passage is given in full in Note 56. It must be remembered that within the limits of the clan land the law of inheritance was in operation. By it the right of property in the land was being distributed among the individual clansmen from generation to generation. In connection with Lex Alam. LXXXIV, Lex Alam. LXXXVIII must not be forgotten: ut fratres post mortem patris eorum hereditatem non dissipent antequam dividant eam. Nor must we forget the documents of Cod. S. Galli in which individual inheritances of clan land are described: *cum campis, pratis, pascuis, silvis*, etc.

Note 118. — Page 47.

See Kemble's Saxons in England, Vol. I., Appendix A (I, p. 449 of the new edition, London, 1876, 8°).

Note 119. — Page 47.

Ethelbert 3, 5, 13, 17.

Note 120. — Page 48.

See Dr. Ernst Förstemann: Die deutschen Ortsnamen (Nordhausen, 1863, 8°); his Altdeutsches Namenbuch, Zweiter Band: Ostsnamen (Nordhausen, 1872, 4°); Prof. Wilhelm Arnold's Ansiedelungen und Wanderungen Deutscher Stämme (Marburg, 1875, 8°); the Rev. Isaac Taylor's Words and Places (London, 1865, 8°); and Mr. F. Seebohm's English Village Community (published this year by Longman & Co., in London, 8°).

Besides examining the lists of local names in the above-mentioned works, the student will find it worth his while to look over the geographical indices of the Cod. S. Galli and Hist. Frising., and over some good map of Germany that gives the names of small villages.

Note 121. — Page 48.

See the genealogies in Angl. Sax. Chron. at the years 547, 552, 560, 597, 611, 617. Take for example the last-named year, where Edwin the son of Aella is described as Eadwine Aelling. There would be as many Aellings in England as there were sons of men named Aella; but they would not necessarily be related one to another.

Note 122. — Page 49.

Edictus domni Hilperici regis (in Merkel's Lex Salica, p. 37), § 3: Simili modo placuit atque convenit, ut si cumque vicinos habens aut filios aut filias post obitum suum superstitutus fuerit, quamdiu filii advixerint terra habeant, sicut et lex salica habet. Et si subito filios defuncti fuerint, filia simili modo accipiant terras ipsas, sicut et filii si vivi fuissent aut habuissent. Et si moritur, frater alter superstitutus fuerit, frater terras accipiant non vicini. Et subito frater moriens, frater non derelinquerit superstitem, tunc soror ad terra ipsa accedat possidenda. Det illi vero et conveniat singula de terras istas qui si adveniunt, ut leodis qui patri nostro fuerunt consuaetudinem qua habuerunt de hac re intra se debeant.

Note 123. — Page 49.

Lex Burg. Add. I. Tit. I. 5. Formula CXXVII. See Notes 72, 74, 82.

Note 124. — Page 50.

Lex Wisig. X. Tit. I. 1, 2, 3, 8. See Notes 74-91.

Note 125. — Page 50.

Lex Sal. XLV: De Migrantibus. 1. Si quis super alterum in villa migrare voluerit, si unus vel aliqui de ipsis qui in villa consistunt cum suscipere voluerit, si vel unus exteterit qui contradicat, migranti ibidem licentiam non habebit. 2. Si vero contra interdicto unius vel duorum in villa ipsa adsedere praesumpserit, tunc ei testare debet et si noluerit inde exire ille qui testat cum testibus sic ei debet testare: Hic tibi testo in hac nocte proxima in hoc quod lex Saliga habet sedeas et testo tibi ut in x noctes de villa ipsa egredere debeas. Postea adhuc post decem noctes iterum veniat ad ipsum et ei testet ut iterum in decem noctes exeat. Si adhuc noluerit exire, item tertio decem noctis ad placitum suum addatur ut sic xxx noctes impleatur. Si nec tunc voluerit exire, tunc maniat eum ad mallum et testes super singula placita qui fuerunt ibi praestos habeat. Si ipse cui testatum est noluerit inde exire et eum aliqua sunnis non tenuerit et ista omnia quae superius diximus secundum legem est testatus, tunc ipse qui testavit super furtuna sua ponat et roget grafionem ut accedat ad locum et eum inde expellat. Et quia legem noluit audire, quod ibi laboravit demittat et insuper MCC dinarios qui faciunt solidos xxx cuipabilis judicetur. 3. Si vero quis migraverit et infra xii menses nullus testatus fuerit, securus sicut et alii vicini maneat.

Note 126. — Page 53.

See Notes 92-100.

Note 127. — Page 54.

Lex Angl. Werin. VI: De Alodibus. 1. Hereditatem defuncti filius, non filia suscipiat. Si filium non habuit qui defunctus est, ad filiam pecunia et mancipia, terra vero ad proximum paternae generationis consanguineum pertineat. 2. Si autem nec filiam habuit, soror eius pecuniam et mancipia: terram proximus paternae generationis accipiat. 3. Si autem nec filium, nec filiam, neque sororem habuit, sed matrem tantum superstitem reliquit, quod filia vel soror debuerat, mater suscipiat, id est, pecuniam et mancipia. 4. Quod si nec filium, nec filiam, nec sororem, aut matrem dimisit superstites, proximus qui fuerit paternae generationis, heres ex toto succedat, tam in pecunia atque, mancipiis, quam in terra. 5. Ad quemcunque hereditas terrae pervenerit, ad illum vestis bellica, id est lorica, et ultio proximi, et solutio lendis, debet pertinere. 6. Mater moriens filio terram, mancipia, pecuniam dimittat, filiae vero spolia colli, id est murenas, nuscas, monilia, inaures, vestes, armillas, vel quidquid ornamenti proprii videbatur habuisse. 7. Si nec filium, nec filiam habuerit, sorori pecuniam et mancipia, proximo vero paterni generis terram relinquat. 8. Usque ad quintam generationem paterna generatio succedat. Post quintam autem filia ex toto, sive de patris sive matris parte, in hereditatem succedat, et tunc demum hereditas ad fisum a lancea transeat.

Note 128.— Page 54.

Rothar CLIII: Omnis parentela usque in septimum genuculum numeretur, ut parens parenti per gradum et parentelam heres succedat. Sic tamen ut ille qui succedere vult, nominatim uniuscuiusque nomina parentum suorum antecessorum dicat. Et si intentio fuerit contra Curtem Regis, tunc ille uni quaerit, praebeat sacramentum cum legitimis sacramentalibus suis duodecim, et dicat per ordinem, quod parentela nostra sic fuit; et illi sic fuere nobis parentes quomodo nos dicimus.

An explanation of the *septimum genuculum* is to be found in the Sachsenspiegel I. 3, § 3.

The classification of collateral heirs appears to have been determined, among the Germans, with reference to the natural divisions of the family and clan. It was not an artificial classification like that of the ancient Irish, described in the Book of Aicill. See Ancient Laws and Institutes of Ireland, Vol. III.

Although the classification of collateral heirs was based upon the natural divisions of the family, and clan growing out of it, the question has been raised whether the grandson of a father was preferred to the son of a grandfather; whether the grandson of a grandfather would be preferred to the son of a great-grandfather. That is to say, were near descendants of a remote ancestor preferred to distant descendants of a near ancestor? We do not propose to enter into a discussion of this question. If the reader cares to go into it, he should read the following books and essays. See first Johann Christian Majer's Deutsche Erbfolge (Stuttgart, 1804, 8°), and his Gemeinrechtliche Erbfolge-Ordnung (Stuttgart, 1805, 8°). Then Heinrich Siegel's Germanische Verwandschafts-berechnung (Giessen, 1853, 8°), and his Deutsche Erbrecht (Heidelberg, 1853, 8°). Then Dr. H. Wasserschleben's Prinzip der Successionsordnung (Gotha, 1860, 8°), and a Replik by the same author (Giessen, 1861, 8°). Next in order, the controversy still raging, comes a summing up of arguments by Lewis in the Kritische Vierteljahrschrift für Gesetzgebung und Rechtswissenschaft (IX. p. 23). Then we have Dr. Heinrich Brunner's Anglonormannische Erbfolgsystem (Leipzig, 1869, 8°) ; and, lastly, Karl von Amira's Erbfolge und Verwandschafts-Gliederung (München, 1871, 8°). Unless the student has a taste for controversies he will hardly be tempted into this one. There is very little to be ascertained from it.

NOTE 129. — PAGE 55.

Hist. Frising. CDXCII, DLXXIV. Mon. Scheftl. I (p. 363) See also Hist. Frising. XIII : congregavi multitudinem parentum meorum nobilium virorum, per quandam dubitationem filiorum meorum, consiliavi cum illis sicut ipsi consilium eorum mihi per fidem dederunt ut hereditatem tradidissem; and Ibid. LXXX : haec sunt nomina proximorum suorum, qui hanc convenientiam cum ipso Waldkero fecerunt [Tradedit hereditatem]. Ibid. CII : tradedi hereditatem et propinqui mei consenserunt et firmaverunt cum verbis eorum. Ibid. CXLII : factum est in presentia matris eorum nomine Iudit, et aliorum plurimorum qui ibidem de familia adfuerunt. Ibid. CCCVIII : traditionem feci ; contigit autem mihi, ut ego valida infirmitate depressus vocari ad me proximos et vicinos meos et in manus illorum totam dictam rem meam per wadium posui, ut ipsi perfecissent traditionem. Cf. also Ibid. I. p. 49, — the passage cited in Note 81. Then read Fulda Cod. 189 : talem portionem que mihi a parentibus meis in proprietatem hereditario jure contigit, consentientibus atque simul conlaudantibus fratribus ac sororibus meis uterinis, nulloque parentum meorum et affinium contradicente coram testibus idoneis et cognatis meis trado. This is as good a case as we could find. Cf. Chron. Benedictob. p. 74 : tradidit absque ullius contradictione quidquid proprietatis habebat in villa Taerzins, edificia, curtes, animalia, sive in agris, in pratis, silvis, calminis, montibus aquis, etc. Mon. Schlehdorf. p. 1 : hereditatem propriam transfundavi, per consensum illustrissimi Ducis Tassilonis et Satrabum ejus, atque confinitimorum nostrorum consentientium. Some more references will be given under Note 164.

Note 130. — Page 56.

Formula CCXXXIX. In a majority of the documents the heirs, collateral as well as descendant, are warned that no claim on their part will be deemed valid. The following formula is that which is commonly used : si quis, quod futurum esse non credimus, aliquis de heredibus nostris, vel quicumque, contra hanc cessionem nostram agere aut ipsa rem tibi auferre conaverit, inferat tibi cum cogente fisco auri tantum, et hanc epistola firma permaneat cum stipulatione subnexa.

Note 131. — Page 57.

See the last paragraph on p. 12; then pp. 17–19. It may be argued from the words of Caesar, *privati ac separati agri apud eos [Suevos] nihil est*, that private estates were unknown; but the argument is inconclusive. The *agri* may have been, probably were, occupied and cultivated by serfs, and the lords and owners of the serfs were lords and owners of the land which they cultivated. It is probable that in the time of Caesar, as in the time of Tacitus, *agri* were occupied according to the number of cultivators; that the cultivators were serfs; that *agri* having been thus occupied (*pro numero cultorum*) were redistributed in sections, *spatia camporum*, and so intermixed. That being the case, it might very well be said : *privati ac separati agri apud eos nihil est*. The phrase may refer, however, simply to the absence of boundaries between the possessions of one free-lord and another. It may not mean any more than the passage in VI. 22 : neque quisquam agri modum certum aut fines habet proprios. The conclusion to which these considerations lead is, that there is nothing in the statements of Cæsar which can legitimately lead us to suppose that the holding of land was communistic. It is quite possible that the principle of individual property was fully recognized. We must not assume that the life of the people had always been migratory. There were, doubtless, periods of permanent settlement before the beginning of recorded history. Private property in land may have existed among the Germans hundreds of years before we meet with them in the Commentary of Cæsar. The reasons which the Germans gave Cæsar as accounting for their migratory life would indicate that they had had some experience of the *régime* of private property. They were afraid, if they settled anywhere permanently, that the rich would drive the poor from their possessions, and so make great estates for themselves. See Note 31.

Note 132. — Page 57.

The testimony of Tacitus has been pretty thoroughly discussed in the previous pages and in previous notes. Enough has been said about it perhaps. Besides the passages already considered, however, — Germ. 5, 16, 20, 25, 26, 32, — it may be well to cite the following passage from the Annals. An. IV. 72 : ac primo boves ipsos, mox agros, postremo corpora conjugum aut liberorum servitio tradebant [Frisii, transrhenanus populus]. This would indicate that the Frisians held *agri* as property, that their property consisted chiefly of cattle and lands. We know from the concurrent testimony of the later records that this was the case. Without doubt, the testimony of Tacitus goes to prove the existence of private property in land. Communistic holding of land was probably quite unknown. There is no reference of any kind to it.

Note 133. — Page 57.

This will appear like a very bold statement: but we have spent the best part of six years in reading through the early records with the question in mind: Is there any evidence of the existence of communism in respect to land? We have found none. We make our statement, therefore, not rashly, but calmly, with the assurance of approximately complete knowledge.

Note 134. — Page 58.

See pp. 27–46 inclusive, and the Notes referred to.

Note 135. — Page 58.

See pp. 21–23, and Notes referred to.

Note 136. — Page 58.

Formula CCCCXII: Relatione pagensium ad rege directa. Formula CXXVII: De divisione ubi rege accederit missus. See Notes 63, 74. Cf. Liutprand LXXIII: et ipse judex faciat venire parentes ipsius propinquos, ut una cum ipsis, aut per se, aut per missum suum res ipsas dividat, sic tamen ut omni tempore sortes stare debeant et adaequatio percurrat. The only exception to the statement that when fighting was given up disputes were referred to the chief or king, or an agent, *missus*, is found in Lex Wisig. X. Tit. I. 3: si plures fuerint in divisione consortes, quod a multis vel melioribus juste constitutum est a paucis vel deterioribus non convenit aliquatenus immutari.

Among the Visigoths the voice of the best men, or of a majority, was referred to in disputes regarding the division of land. But this fact is no evidence of communism, because it is assumed that the shareholders have rights. The best men, or the majority, are referred to as judges to decide disputed claims. Observe the force of the words *juste constitutum est*.

Then it must be remembered that the division of land once made was permanent. The decision of the best men, or of the majority, was not to be revoked: sed quod a parentibus vel vicinis divisum est, posteritas immutare non tentet. See Lex Wisig. X. Tit. I. 8.

Note 137. — Page 59.

See Notes 73–77. Whenever a tract of territory was occupied, there was at once a distribution or appropriation of inheritances;

and these inheritances passed from the original holders to their descendants to be divided and subdivided among them. This appears very clearly in the first three paragraphs of the Edict of Chilperic (A. D. 573–575). They are as follows: 1. Pertractantes in Dei nomen cum viris magnificentissimis obtimatibus, vel antrustionibus, et omni populo nostro, convenit qui fluvium Caronna [*Garonne*] hereditas non transiebat, ubi et ubi in regione nostra hereditas detur [*leodibus nostris*], sicut et reliqua loca ut et Turrovaninsis hereditatem dare debent et accipere [*for as in other places so now in the country of Tours inheritances must be distributed and received*]. 2. Similiter convenit ut reibus [*rebus, res, i. e. hereditates*] concederemus omnibus leodibus nostris, ut per modicam rem scandalos [*ill-feeling, discontent, disturbance*] non generetur in regione nostra [*it was decided that everybody should have an inheritance*]. 3. Simili modo placuit atque convenit, ut quicumque vicinos [*proximi, parentes vel vicini*] aut filios aut filias post obitum suum superstitutus fuerit, quamdiu filii advixerint terra habeant, sicut et lex Salica habet . . . The rest of the passage may be read in Note 122.

These paragraphs have been much misunderstood. The assumption that the word *reibus*, in § 2, has reference to the sum of money which he who married a widow was obliged to pay to the relatives (see the first of the Capitularies appended to Lex Salica, § 7, on p. 90 of Behrend's edition) is absurd. The word *reibus* stands for *rebus*, and *rebus* stands for *res*, without doubt. Merkel gives us the reading *rebus* (p. 37), and makes no reference to any other. The use of the ablative instead of the accusative is not uncommon in these early writings. The accusative *loca* is used for *locis* in § 1.

The localities referred to in § 1 are fixed for us in Greg. Turon. IV. 48.

Note 138. — Page 59.

Given a law of inheritance in land, the inference is that all undivided lands are undivided inheritances, until we have the means of proving them to be something else.

Given an undivided inheritance, the inference is that with unity of possession there is diversity of title. We must assume that the inheritance is divisible among the heirs, until evidence is adduced to show that it is indivisible.

Unless the student keeps these rules in mind, he will fall into serious errors. Undivided property must not be called common property. Holding in common must not be described as communistic holding.

Note 139. — Page 59.

All these points have been so fully considered in the preceding pages, and so fully illustrated in the notes, that it will not be necessary to dwell upon them much longer. Undivided lands were, without doubt, regarded as undivided inheritances. See once more the words in the Edict of Chilperic (Note 137): convenit, quia fluvium Caronna hereditas non transiebat, ubi et ubi in regione nostra hereditas detur. Newly occupied lands were speedily divided into inheritances, and if any land remained undivided it belonged to these inheritances in *pro rata* shares. See once more the passages of the Burgundian law, cited in Note 72; and Formula CCCCII, in which the division of mark-land *inter fiscum regis et populares possessiones* is described. The Formula was referred to in Note 70.

Note 140. — Page 60.

Lex Sal. LX: De eum qui se de parentilla tollere vult. 1. In mallo ante thunginum ambulare debet et ibi tres fustis alninus super caput suum frangere debet. Et illos per quattuor partes in mallo jactare debet et ibi dicere debet, quod juramento et de hereditatem et totam rationem illorum se tollat. 2. Et sic postea aliquis de suis parentibus aut occidatur aut moriatur, nulla ad eum nec hereditas nec compositio perteneat sed hereditatem ipsius fiscus adquirat.

If any doubt remains in the reader's mind, whether the inheritances which passed to kinsmen and neighbors were divisible among them or not, the passage above cited is likely to remove it. It is evident that the kinsmen and neighbors received their inheritances distributively, as a body of heirs, and not collectively, as a body corporate. Note the force of the words *nulla ad eum nec hereditas nec conpositio perteneat*. When a man died without sons, and his inheritance passed to his kinsmen and neighbors, every one of them came in for a share. The only question which remains unsettled is the question, How was the inheritance distributed among the neighbors and kinsmen? We know that it was subject to distribution, but we do not know upon what principle the distribution was made. Perhaps it was made *per capita;* perhaps it was made *per stirpes.* Perhaps it was made upon some other principle. We know nothing about it.

NOTE 141. — PAGE 60.

See pp. 48–56, and the Notes referred to. See also the preceding Note, No. 140.

NOTE 142. — PAGE 63.

The passage is cited from a document of A. D. 1173, first printed, "aus der schönen Urschrift," in Bodmann's Rheingauische Alterthümer. p. 453.

NOTE 143. — PAGE 64.

It is said, that we have in the agricultural community of the Middle Ages the remains of an ancient community antedating all forms of landlordship. It is said that landlordship was introduced afterwards; that the primitive community was, in one way or another, drawn under this landlordship; that we have in the manor of the Middle Ages a union of the two institutions, — landlordship and the ancient village community. In other words, according to a generally received theory, the manorial group has been evolved out of the village community, by the imposition upon the village community of an over-lord, with a right of property in the village lands and authority over its inhabitants. The process has been described as the transformation of the mark into the manor.

There is a very serious objection to be raised against this theory. The agricultural community of the Middle Ages is a community of tenants under landlordship; and it is nothing else in the very earliest period of its recorded history. According to the records landlordship is at least as old as the agricultural community included under it. What right have we, therefore, to assume that the agricultural community antedates the institution of landlordship? Why not assume that landlordship existed first, that the village community arose under it, — a community of serfs or dependants? It must not be forgotten that, according to the earliest records we have, the freemen had dependants and slaves attached to their households. Why not, therefore, derive the manor out of this group? Why not derive the manor out of the patriarchal household with its company of dependants and servants?

It is said that the manor has grown out of the village community. Why not say that the village community has grown out of the manor? We can show, first, how at the dawning of our history landlordship existed everywhere; how there were groups of tenants arising under it. Then we can describe how, as time went on, these groups of tenants assumed a communal character; how they became village communities. Lastly, we can describe how these communities waxed stronger and stronger, until they were able to overthrow the incubus of landlordship which oppressed them, and how they then emerged as independent free communes.

Take, for example, the little commonwealths of Uri, Schwyz, and Unterwalden, in Switzerland. We are told that they are the remains primitive of agricultural communities and democratic villages. We are told how, during the Middle Ages, they became subject to feudal lords; how, afterwards, they recovered their independence again. But what right have we to suppose that they were independent communities before the feudal period? Why not suppose that they were associations of tenants under allodial lords, — that they became organized into communities during the periods of allodial and feudal landlordship, — that they became strong enough at last to fight for, and to secure, their independence? Is there anything in the records inconsistent with this theory? After a careful examination of them, we can say with confidence that there is not. On the contrary, there is a great deal to support and establish it. We cannot go into this matter in detail. We are glad, however, to be able to refer the reader to M. J. J. Hisely's admirable essay entitled, L'Origine et le Développement des Libertés des Waldstetten, published in three parts (Lausanne, 1838-43, 8°), by the Société d'Histoire de la Suisse Romande.

We have a theory, that in most cases the village community has originated within the manor and grown out of it, that the manor has disappeared leaving the village community as a legacy to the future. Had we space, we should be able to illustrate this theory by many examples. Only consider the multitude of village communes in France and in Germany, which were manorial villages during the early and middle ages; which have succeeded in throwing off the overlordship which oppressed them so long; which appear now as independent, free communes!

The theory that these communes existed before there was any landlordship, that they were not in their origin manorial villages, is probably erroneous, except, perhaps, in regard to a few cases.

NOTE 144.—PAGE 65.

The advocates of the communism theory assume, in the first place, that private property has arisen from the disentanglement of individual from collective rights,—the rights of the family from those of the tribe or clan, the rights of the individual from those of the family. Then, wherever they find any communism, no matter where it is, or what its date is, they seize upon it and describe it as a vestige of the primitive condition of things. And wherever they find private property, they say at once, the communistic stage of development has been passed. Then, even where they find no evidence that communism ever existed, they assume that it existed, "because it existed everywhere in early times." Again and again they fall back upon their original assumption, that progress has been from communism towards individualism; and they convince the uninitiated simply by incessant reiteration of this idea. They assume what they have to prove, and prove it by reiteration.

The evidence adduced to prove the universality of communism in early society, has very little value from a scientific point of view. It consists of fragments of communism gathered from all parts of the world and from all periods of time, classified in a most imperfect manner.

It may be thought that we are too severe in this judgment. We are, therefore, glad to cite the following passage from an essay of M. Fustel de Coulanges, read before the French Academy in November, 1879. The subject of the essay is "La Propriété à Sparte." The essay was printed in the "Séances," in the "Journal des Savants," and afterwards separately (Alph. Picard, Paris, 1880, 8°).

"Il s'est produit, dans ces dernières années, une opinion historique qui nous paraît mériter une sérieuse attention, mais dont l'exactitude a besoin d'être vérifiée. On a soutenu que le droit de propriété sur le sol avait été inconnu aux antiques sociétés, qu'elles avaient longtemps cultivé la terre en commun, et qu'elles n'étaient passées au régime de l'appropriation que tardivement et par degrés. . . . L'expression la plus claire de l'opinion nouvelle se trouve dans le livre qu'un esprit fort distingué, M. Em. de Laveleye, a publié en 1874, sous ce titre: *De la propriété et de ses formes primitives*. L'auteur passe en revue presque tous les peuples du monde, la Russie, l'île de Java et l'Inde, la *marke* germanique et les communautés agraires des Arabes, Rome et l'Égypte, l'ancienne Grèce et la Suisse moderne. . . . Je ne conteste pas que la méthode comparative ne soit fort utile en histoire; elle peut devenir une source féconde de découvertes; mais l'abus en est dangereux. Vous apercevez certaines communautés de village dans l'Inde; vous rencontrez quelque chose d'analogue dans le *mir* russe et dans les petits villages de Croatie; vous entrevoyez les mêmes traits dans les *allmenden* de la Suisse; vous rapprochez de tout cela deux lignes de César sur les anciens Germains, une phrase de Diodore sur un petit peuple des îles Lipari, et quelques fantaisies des poètes latins sur l'âge d'or; vous accumulez ainsi quelques indices, mais hâtivement recueillis, imparfaitement étudiés, pris çà et là en mêlant les époques et en confondant les peuples. Est-ce assez de cela pour déduire une loi générale de l'humanité? Une telle méthode manque de rigueur. La comparison entre les peuples ne devrait venir qu'après une étude scrupuleuse et complète de chaque peuple. L'analyse doit précéder la synthèse. Je voudrais que l'histoire du *mir* russe, celle du village indou ou javanais, celle de la communauté agricole de Croatie, et même celle de la *marke* germanique, fussent plus nettement connues qu'elles ne le sont, avant qu'on tirât du rapprochement de ces connaissances une conclusion générale. Je souhaiterais qu'une génération de travailleurs s'appliquât séparément à chacun de ces objets et qu'on laissât à la génération suivante le soin de chercher la loi qui se dégagera, peut-être, de ces études particulières."

No criticism could be more just, no advice better or more timely.

Note 145. — Page 67.

The reference is to Numbers xxxvi. Cf. Tacitus Germ. 17: prope soli barbarorum singulis uxoribus contenti sunt, exceptis admodum paucis, qui non libidine sed ob nobilitatem pluribus nuptiis ambiuntur. The only rule which was imposed regarding marriages was that the husband and wife should be of equal rank. See Rudolfi Transl. S. Alex. in M. G. H. Script. II, p. 675: Quatuor igitur differentiis gens illa consistit, nobilium scilicet et liberorum, libertorum atque servorum. Et id legibus firmatum ut nulla pars in copulandis conjugiis propriae sortis terminos transferat, sed nobilis nobilem ducat uxorem et liber liberam, libertus conjugatur libertae et servus ancillae. Si vero quispiam horum sibi non congruentem et genere praestantiorem duxerit uxorem, cum vitae suae damno componat. See the passage of Lib. Eli. cited in Thorpe I. p. 192, note *a* (Gale, II. c. 40).

Intermarriages between clans were very common. This proposition could be proved, if it were worth while, by reference to particular cases, but we may venture to take it for granted.

Note 146. — Page 67.

Lex Angl. Werin. VI: De alodibus, 8: Usque ad quintam generationem paterna generatio succedat [proximus paternae generationis consanguineus]. Post quintam generationem filia ex toto, sive de patris, sive de matris parte, in hereditatem succedat, et tunc demum hereditas ad fusum a lancea transeat. We assume that the limit of collateral inheritance was also the limit of the clan. The limit of the clan was probably determined by the limit of collateral inheritance. Among the Lombards the clan appears to have included the male descendants of seven successive generations. This was the limit for collateral inheritance. See Rothar CLIII: Omnis parentela usque in septimum genuculum numeretur, ut parens parenti per gradum et parentelam heres succedat.

Cf. Lex Baiw. XIV. Cap. IX. 4: Quod si maritus et mulier sine heredes mortui fuerint, et nullus usque ad septimum gradum de propinquis et quibuscumque parentibus invenitur, tunc illas res fiscus adquirat. As among the Lombards, so among the Bavarians, seven generations was the limit of collateral inheritance. It was without doubt the limit of the clan as well.

The subject of clan relationships and collateral inheritance is, however, very difficult. We are by no means sure that we understand it. The records bearing upon the subject are few. They are vague in their terms, and to a certain extent contradictory. It is doubtful whether any definite general conclusions can be drawn from them.

Note 147. — Page 68.

We have already seen how, at the time of Lex Salica, when a man died without sons, the neighbors, *vicini*, took the inheritance. We have seen how at the same time neighbors were regularly kinsmen, *parentes*, *proximi*. See pp. 46–56, and the Notes referred to. The classification of collateral heirs was inaugurated, apparently, by the Edict of Chilperic, A. D. 573–575. See passage cited in Note 122.

We are speaking here, and in the text also, of the right of inheritance in land. We are not speaking of the right of inheritance in movable property.

We know, from Lex Sal. LIX. De alodis 1–4, that inheritances of movable property passed from the family of the deceased to distant relatives in the order of their proximity: quicumque proximior fuerit ille in hereditatem succedat. While collateral heirs in land remained unclassified, collateral heirs in movable property were, it appears, very carefully distinguished one from another, according to relative degrees of proximity. This is very curious and inexplicable. What is still more curious and inexplicable, however, is the fact that, when collateral heirs in land came to be classified, they were classified without reference to the classification of collateral heirs in movable property, so far as we can make this clear from the De alodis.

In Lex Sal. LVIII De creneeruda, still another classification of relatives is hinted at. Reference is made to tres de generatione matris et tres de generatione patris qui proximiores sunt.

After much puzzling over these inconsistencies, we conclude that it is impossible to explain them in any satisfactory manner under one theory; that it is best, on the whole, to take De alodis 5 (qui fratres fuerint tota terra perteneat), and the passage (§ 3) of the Edict of Chilperic (referred to above), and to consider these passages by themselves, without reference to De alodis 1–4, and without reference to the De chrenecruda, as these passages appear to have no direct bearing upon the question of inheritance in land.

Accordingly, when we say that the kinsmen were not classified among the Franks, as among the Angli and Werini, we are speaking of them as heirs in the land simply. Without this qualification the statement is of course open to criticism. We may say, once more, what we have said before, that it is probably impossible to reach any very definite conclusions in regard to clan relationships and collateral inheritance among the early Germans. What we have said upon the subject has accordingly been said with no little diffidence.

Note 148. — Page 68.

Lex Sal. LIX: De alodis. Lex Rip. LVI: De alodibus. It may be stated, as a general rule, that a practice is not forbidden until it actually obtains, or has its advocates. So, when we read that women had no right of succession in the ancestral inheritance, we may assume that women had in certain instances received ancestral inheritances, or else, that there were persons who desired that they might receive them.

Note 149. — Page 68.

Formula CXXXVI. Cf. Formula CXXXV: Dulcissima atque in omnibus amantissima filia mea illa, ego enim vir magnificus ille. Omnibus non habetur incognitum que, sicut lex Salica contenit, de res meas, quod mihi de alode parentum meorum obvenit, apud germanos tuos filios meos minime in hereditate succidere potebas.

Note 150. — Page 69.

According to the Edict of Chilperic, A. D. 573–575, cited in Note 122.

Note 151. — Page 69.

Lex Alam. LXXXVIII, and LVII: Si autem duae sorores absque fratre relictae post mortem patris fuerint, et ad ipsas hereditas paterna pertingat, et una nupserit sibi coaequali libero, alia autem nupserit aut colono Regis aut colono Ecclesiae, illa quae illi libero nupsit sibi coaequali, teneat terram patris earum. Res autem alias aequaliter dividant. Illa enim quae illo colono nupsit, non intret in portionem terrae, quia coaequali non nupsit.

Lex Baiw. XIV. 8: Ut fratres hereditatem patris aequaliter dividant. Ibid. 9: De eo qui sine filiis et filiabus mortuus est, mulier accipiat portionem suam, dum viduitatem custodierit, id est, medietatem pecuniae. Medietas autem ad propinquos mariti pertineat. The word *pecunia* is used to describe land as well as other property; as in Cod. Trad. Lunaelac XXXIII, and Fulda Cod. 355: agris seu alia pecunia.

Lex Sax. VII. 1: Pater aut mater defuncti filio non filiae haereditatem relinquit. Ibid. 5: Qui defunctus non filios, sed filias reliquerit, ad eas omnis haereditas pertineat, tutela vero earum fratri vel proximo paterni generis deputetur.

In regard to England, see what was said in Note 77.

NOTE 152. — PAGE 69.

Cassiodorus Varia IV. 2: Per arma fieri posse filium . . . Damus quidem tibi equos, enses, clypeos, et reliqua instrumenta bellorum. Ibid. VIII. 1: Vos genitorem meum in Italia palmatae claritate decorastis. Desiderio quoque concordiae factus est per arma filius, quiau nis nobis [vobis?] pene videbatur equaevus . . . In parentelae locum [*note this*] noster jam transire debet affectus. Nam ex filio vestro genitus, naturae legibus vobis non habetur extraneus. See also Ibid. VIII. 9: solum armis filius factus . . .

Cf. Tacitus Germ. 13: Sed arma sumere non ante cuiquam moris quam civitas suffecturum probaverit. Tum in concilio vel principum aliquis vel pater vel propinqui scuto frameaque juvenem ornant: haec apud illos toga, hic primus juventae honos; ante hoc domus pars videntur, mox rei publicae.

In Formula CXXXIV we have grandsons adopted into a right of inheritance in lands, houses, and other things, — terris, domibus, et cetera. Quidquid in jam dicto loco genitor vester et filios meos illos et illas dividere et exsequare deberet, vos quoque, nepotes mei, per hanc affatimum post [diem] obitus mei dividere [et] exsequare faciatis.

See also Formula CXVII: Si quis extraneo homine in loco filiorum adoptaverit; and CXVIII: Si quis in loco filii aliquem adoptare voluerit; and Formulae CLXVIII, CLXXII. Then read Capitulare IV, A. D. 803, vii: Qui filios non habuerit, et alium quemlibet heredem facere sibi voluerit, coram Rege vel Comite et Scabiniis vel Missis dominicis, qui tunc ad justitias faciendas in provincia fuerint ordinati, traditionem faciat.

A similar practice appears to have obtained in England. See Lib. de Hyd. p. 7: egressus de fonte loco filii susceptus est [Athelwoldus]. In cujus signum adoptionis Ulfere, rex Merciorum, duas illi provincias donavit. . . . Reference is made to an adopted relative, *adoptivo parenti*, in Abingdon Chron. I, p. 205.

NOTE 153. — PAGE 70.

Lex Sal. XLVI: De affatomie. 1. Hoc convenit observare ut thunginus aut centenarius mallo indicant et scutum in illo mallo habere debent et tres homines tres causas demandare debent. Postea requirent hominem qui ei non perteneat et sic fistucam in laisum jactet. Et ipse in cui laisum fistucam jactavit, de furtuna sua dicat verbum quantum voluerit aut totam furtunam suam cui voluerit dare. Ipse in cujus laisum fistucam jactavit, in casa ipsius manere debet. Et hospites tres vel amplius collegere debet et de facultatem quantum ei creditum est in potestatem suam habere debet. Et postea ipse cui isto creditum est, ista omnia cum testibus collectis agere debet. Postea aut ante rege aut in mallo illi cui furtuna sua depotavit reddere debet et accipiat fistucam in mallo ipso. Ante xii menses quos heredes appellavit in laisum jactet; nec minus nec majus nisi quantum ei creditum est. 2. Et si contra hoc aliquis aliquid dicere voluerit, debent tres testes jurati dicere quod ibi fuissent in mallo quem thunginus aut centenarius indixerit et quomodo vidissent hominem illum qui furtuna sua dare voluerit in laisum illius quem jam elegit fistucam jactare: debent denominare illo qui fortuna sua in laiso jactat et illo quem heredem appellit similiter nominent. Et alteri tres testes jurati dicere debent quod in casa illius qui furtuna sua donavit ille in cujus laisu fistuca jactata est ibidem mansisset et hospites tres vel amplius ibidem collegisset et in beodum pultis manducassent et testes collegissent et illi hospites ei de susceptione gratias egissent.

Ista omnia illi alii testis jurato dicere debent et hoc, quod in mallo ante regem vel legitimo mallo publico ille, qui accepit in laisum furtuna ipsa aut ante regem aut in mallo publico legitimo hoc est in mallobergo ante teoda aut thunginum furtunam illam, quos heredes appellavit publice coram populo listueam in laiso jactasset; hoc est novem testes ista omnia debent adfirmare.

Some of this passage is almost unintelligible. The gist of it, however, may be gathered out. It is an adoption (*adoptio*) effected by means of an alienation of property (*traditio*). Cf. the passage cited, in Note 152, from the Capitulare IV of A. D. 803.

Note 154. — Page 70.

Lex Rip. XLVIII: Si quis procreationem filiorum vel filiarum non habuerit, omnem facultatem suam in praesentia Regis, sive vir mulieri, vel mulier viro, seu cuicunque libet de proximis vel extraneis adoptare in hereditatem vel adfatimi per scripturarum seriem seu per traditionem, et testibus adhibitis secundum legem Ripuariam licentiam habeat.

Ibid. XLIX: Quod si adfatimus fuerit inter virum et mulierum, post discessum amborum ad legitimos heredes revertatur, nisi tantum, qui parem suum supervixerit, in eleemosyna vel in sua necessitate expenderit.

Note 155. — Page 71.

Formula CXXXIV: Affatimum. Dulcissimis nepotis meis illis, ego avus aut ego ille. Dum et cognitum est qualiter genitor vester et filius meus, nomine illo, complenta fine naturae, de hac luce discessit, et vos in alode minime accedere poteratis, ideo pensantes causa consanguinitatis dabo vobis per hanc affatimum omni proportione in loco nuncupante illo, in pago illo, in centena illa, hoc est in iam dicto loco tam terris, domibus, et cetera. Quicquid in iam dicto loco genitor vester et filios meos illos et illas dividere et exsequare deberet, vos quoque, nepotes mei, per hanc affatimum post [diem] obitus mei dividere [et] exsequare faciatis. Illud etiam in hanc affatimum conscribere rogavimus, ut si fuerit aliquis de heredibus meis propinquos, avunculos vestros, aut de aliis heredibus, vel quislibet in eorum causas, nulla calumnia nec repetitione generare non praesumat, sed iure firmissimo in omnibus habeatis potestatem faciendi, tenendi, dandi, commutandi, vel quicquid exinde facere elegeritis, liberam in omnibus perfruatur potestas faciendi. Sed si fuerit aliquis de heredibus meis, qui contra hanc affatimum venire aut refragare praesumpserit, socio fisco solidos tantos contra quem litem intulerit suis partibus multa componat, et ille qui repetit nihil vindicet sed praesens affatimus diuturnum tempore firmus et inviolatus valeat permanere, quam manu propria subterfirmavimus et bonis operibus viris magnificis roborare decrevimus.

Note 156. — Page 71.

Formula CCLVI. Hist. Frising. DCVII. Cf. also Formulae CCLV and CCLVIII: per hanc titulum traditionis, vel per servo meo, et per hostium de ipsas domus, et cispitae de illa terra, seu vitis de ipsas vineas, et ramos de illas arbores; et quantumcumque in ipsa donatione continet; id sunt tam terris, vineis, pratis, silvis, exenis, aiacentiis, omnia ex omnibus, sicut in illa donatione loquitur vel in ista traditione insertum est. See also No. VI. of the Capitularia in lege salica mittenda (Merkel p. 47): De his qui ad casam Dei res suas tradere voluerint . . . domi traditionem faciat coram testibus legitimis.

According to Lex Sal. LVIII, De chrenecruda, the debtor for homicide, having no movable property, *supra terra nec subtus terra*, with which to pay his debt, has to mortgage his land. This he does by a procedure in his house, and upon the threshold of it, looking into it: et postea debet in casa sua intrare et de quatuor angulos terra in pugno collegere, et sic postea in duropalo hoc est in limitare stare debet et intus in casa respiciens et sic de sinistra manu de illa terra trans scapulas jactare super illum quem proximiorem parentem habet. The nearest relative, or relatives, took the mortgage and paid the debt, if they could, rather than allow a stranger to come into possession of any of the clan land. Of course it was very undesirable to allow the heirs of him who had been murdered or killed to come into the possession of any of it. In connection with the *De chrenecruda*, it is worth while to read the Capitulary of Childebert, A. D. 595, § 15: De chrenechruda lex, quam paganorum tempore observabant, deinceps nunquam valeat, quia per ipsam cecidit multorum potestas.

It appears, from the passages cited, that the *casa* was the regular place for alienations of land. It cannot, therefore, be maintained that the *De affatomie* procedure was employed for the alienation of movable property only, on the ground that property in land would not be alienated *in casa*.

Before leaving this point we may refer the reader to the interesting passage of the Lex Alam., from which it appears that a man received an inheritance from his wife who had died in childbirth, only in case the child had opened its eyes to see the roof and four walls of the house, — Lex Alam. XCII.

Note 157. — Page 72.

Diplomata Merowing. 12. For other examples of the use of the word *facultas* to describe landed property, see Fulda Trad. Cap. 4. 74 and 127; Cap. 39. 73; Beyer Urkb. 6; Trad. Wiz. CCII; Cod. S. Galli 19 and 199: facultates meas excepto una silva et pratum. The ancestral inheritance is described by the word *facultas* in Lex Burg. LXXV, Lex Wisig. IV. Tit. II. 1, and elsewhere.

Note 158. — Page 72.

Fulda Cod. 355: agris seu alia pecunia. Kemble's Codex DCXXI: x mansas . . . numinis mei particulam. See also Cod. Trad. Lunaelac XXXIII, where the word *pecunia* is used to describe a *curtem cum domos, terram, pratas, rures, campos, silvas, aquas, cultum et incultum*, etc.

Note 159. — Page 73.

See Formulae CXXXIV, CLXVIII, CXXXI, CXXXII, and CXXXIII. Until the principle of representation was admitted, fatherless grandsons were constantly adopted into the inheritances of their respective fathers. For a long time a man was expected, if he gave away his property, to give it either to the Church, or to increase the possessions of his kinsmen. See Formula CLXXI. The passage referred to will be cited in Note 161.

Note 160. — Page 73.

See Notes 152–154.

Note 161. — Page 73.

Formula CLXXI : Licet unicuique de rebus suis quas in presente seculo viditur [habere], tam ad sanctorum loca seu parentum meliorare, et lex manet et consuetudo longinquam percurrit facere quod voluerit.

Note 162. — Page 73.

Hist. Trev. XXXII (A. D. 709), XXXIV (A. D. 711), XXXV (A. D. 712). The alienation of Folker *secundum Legem Ripuariam et Salicam* is given in Münst. Beitr. II. Num. III. See also Formula CCXXXI : dono tibi donatumque secundum legem Salicam in tua dote a die praesenti jure legitimo in perpetuum esse volo, et de meo in tuum jus et dominationem trado atque transcribo, hoc est mansum juris mei indominicatum, cum aliis mansis servilibus, silvis, pratis, campis, etc. The conclusion at which we arrived, that land was alienable according to Lex Salica, is by these records completely verified.

In Diplomata Merowing. 15, of the date A. D. 635, a man named Dado alienates certain lands to the Church *per festuca*, and it is recorded that his brother and his father had done likewise, before him. This takes the practice of alienating land back quite to the time of Lex Salica. The fact that the land was alienated *per festuca* takes us to the passage *De affatomie*. The procedure of the *De affatomie* was certainly used for alienating land.

That the right to alienate land was exercised freely everywhere, from the time of Lex Salica on, is proved by the concurrent testimony of Folk-Laws, Formulae, and Documents. No fact is more clearly recorded, more indisputable, than this.

Note 163. — Page 74.

Lex Sax. XV : De traditionibus. 1. Traditiones et venditiones omnes legitimae, stabiles permaneant. 2. Nulli liceat traditionem haereditatis suae facere, praeter ad Ecclesiam, vel Regi, ut haeredem suum exhaeredem faciat. 3. Nisi forte famis necessitate coactus, ut ab illo, qui hoc acceperit, sustentetur, mancipia liceat illi dare ac vendere. Rothar CLXVIII.

Note 164. — Page 74.

The consent of heirs is very often referred to in grants of land. See Beyer Urkb. 341: filiorumque meorum consensu, ceterorumque mei amicorum suggestione. Osnabrk. Gesch. XLIV: consensu et collaudatione legitimorum heredum suorum. Ibid. XLVII: laudantibus et consentientibus duobus eorum filiis. Wirtemb. Urkb. CCLXIII: liberis meis consentientibus. Lisch. Urkb. XXVIII: cunctis heredibus sibi consentibus. Ibid. LXVI: de pleno consensu heredum nostrorum, filiorum nostrorum videlicet ac filiorum fratris nostri.

Hist. Frising. I. p. 35 (53?): propriam portionem quam de fratribus meis recepi dono atque transfundo, per consensum fratrum meorum, colonias VIIII. See also the references given under Note 129.

Note 165. — Page 74.

The evidence for this statement may be found on p. 55 and in Note 129.

Note 166. — Page 74.

Lex Burg. LXXXIV: 1. Quia cognovimus Burgundiones sortes suas nimia facilitate distrahere, hoc praesenti lege credidimus statuendum, ut nulli vendere terram suam liceat, nisi illi qui alio loco sortem aut possessiones habet. 2. Hoc etiam interdictum, ut quisque habens alibi terram, vendendi necessitatem habet, in comparando, quam Burgundio venalem habet, nullus extraneus Romano hospiti praeponatur nec extraneo per quodlibet argumentum terram liceat comparare.

Note 167. — Page 74.

Lex Burg. I: 1. Quia nihil de praestita patribus donandi licentia vel munificentia dominantium legibus fuerat constitutum, praesenti constitutione omnium uno voto et voluntate decrevimus, ut patri etiam antequam dividat, de communi facultate et de labore suo cuilibet donare liceat, absque terra sortis titulo acquisita, de qua prioris legis ordo servabitur. 2. Aut si cum filiis diviserit, et portionem suam tulerit, et postea de alia uxore filios habuerit aut unum aut plures, illi filii, qui de secunda uxore sunt, in illam, quam pater accepit, portionem succedant: et illi, qui cum patre dividentes portiones suas fuerant consecuti, ab eis penitus nihil requirant.

Ibid. LXXVIII: De hereditatum successione adtentius pertractantes statuimus, ut si pater cum filiis sortem suam diviserit, et postea mori filium vivo patre contigerit sine filiis, pater facultatum filii integram usufructuario iure vindicet portionem: quam inter filios et nepotes ita moriens dimittat, ut quanti nepotes ex uno filio fuerint qui patrem non habent, portionem patris sui vindicent, qualem pater eorum habiturus erat. Illam vero partem, quam pater cum filiis dividendam habuisset, superstitibus filiis derelinquat, et nepotes in eam partem non succedant. Praesens tamen lex ad masculos tantummodo pertinebit.

Lex Baiw. I. 1: Ut si quis liber Baiuarius vel quiscumque alodem suam ad Ecclesiam vel quamcunque rem donare voluerit, liberam habeat potestatem. Ut si quis liber persona voluerit et dederit res suas ad Ecclesiam pro redemptione animae suae, licentiam habeat de portione sua, postquam cum filiis suis pertivit. Nullus eum prohibeat, non Rex, non Dux, nec ulla persona habeat potestatem prohibendi ei. Et quicquid donaverit, villas, terram, mancipia, vel aliquam pecuniam, omnia quaecunque donaverit pro redemptione animae suae, hoc per epistolam confirmet propria manu sua ipse, et testes adhibeat sex vel amplius si voluerit, et imponat manus suas in epistola, et nomina eorum notent ibi quos ipse rogaverit.

Cf. Trad. Wiz. CLII: jurnales terre xxxx quas contra heredes meos mihi parciendo sors contulit. Cod. S. Galli 360: quicquid contra filios meos in portionem et in meam swascaram accepi. Hist. Frising. CLXXXVIII: tradidit quidquid in suam partem ei evenit hereditatis, quando cum filiis partivit. Ibid. DLVIII (b): quicquid de patre vel fratre suo in proprietatem divisum ab illis accepisset. See also Ibid. CXII, CXV, DCVII, and Mon. Schefft. p. 364: tradidi ego Atto et filius meus Ammo que nobis in partem contigerunt, quando divisimus cum Albrico filio meo omnia. A **great many more cases might be adduced, but these will suffice.**

Note 168. — Page 75.

See Grimm Rechtsalt., 2d ed., p. 530. See also Prof. Hanssen's "Abhandlungen." p. 48, note; where he refers to Jüt. Low I. 34, and Erich-seel. Ges. III. 2. M. Paul Viollet cites an interesting passage from the Guta-Lagh in his article in the Bibliothèque de l'École des Chartes, Vol. XXXIII., 1872. We have not ourselves had access to these records. The prior right of purchase which neighbors obtained must have been based upon the opinion, that of two prospective purchasers the neighbor should be preferred to the stranger, — an opinion which naturally recommends itself where the population is increasing and inheritances are small. The right had its *raison d'être* in economic conditions which are known to have existed in many places during the Middle Ages.

Note 169. — Page 76.

See Lex Sal.: De migrantibus, in Note 125. Cf. Coutum. d'Orleans CCCCLXXXVI: On acquiert possession d'heritage, droict corporel ou incorporel, en jouissant par an et jour. See Coutum. Gen. III. p. 807. See also Ibid. p. 37; Coutum. de Paris XCVI. So in the Coutumes de Beauvoisis (Beaumanoir, Cap. XXIV. 4): Uzages de an et jor pesiblement soufist à aquerre saizine.

Note 170. — Page 76.

Twelve Tables VI. 3 (in Ortolan, Instituts de Justinien, 9th ed., Vol. I. p. 110) : Usus auctoritas fundi biennium. Cf. Gaius II. 42; Ulpian XIX. 8.

Note 171. — Page 76.

Lex Burg. Add. I. Tit. I. 1, 3: Observandum viam publicam, vel inter agros communiter divisam nec possideri, nec intercludi, nec exartari posse . . . viam in actum, hoc est ubi carpenta vel carra ducuntur, biennio amitti et adquiri posse.

Note 172. — Page 76.

The passage cited in the text is from Lex Wisig. X. Tit. II. 5. See also Lex Burg. LXXIX: De praescriptione temporum.

Note 173.—Page 77.

Rothar CCXXXI, and Grimoald IV, given in Note 56.

Note 174.—Page 77.

See Notes 53-60.

Note 175.—Page 78.

The proprietors in the village were called shareholders, *participes villae*. See Greg. Turon. VII. 47: Cum autem haec Chramnisindus audisset, commonitis parentibus et amicis, ad domum ejus [Sicharii] properat. Quibus spoliatis, interemtis nonnullis servorum, domus omnes, tam Sicharii quam reliquorum, qui participes hujus villae erant, incendio concremavit, abducens secum pecora et quaecumque movere potuit. We get a glimpse of the Teutonic village in this passage.

Note 176.—Page 79.

If it were not for the statement of Tacitus, in Germ. 16, *colunt discreti ac diversi ut fons ut campus ut nemus placuit*, we might infer that the freemen who had only a few slaves settled down in village groups; that they built houses for themselves and houses for their slaves; that arable lots, *agri*, were marked off, one for every freeman and one for every slave; that the freeman in the village had one lot for himself and one for each of his slaves; that the slaves cultivated their own lots, and those of their respective lords as well. In view of the statement, *colunt discreti ac diversi*, however, we are not at liberty to suppose that the freemen settled down in village groups. Such villages as there were must have been villages of dependants or slaves connected with the isolated farmsteads, the *Einzelhöfe*, of different free-lords. There were, accordingly, no independent free village communities in Tacitus's time. As soon, however, as the migrations were over and settlements were permanent, heirs began to multiply upon the isolated domains, and we have consequently house communities, and then clan villages. In this way village life was introduced among the freemen. Then new villages were founded, in the manner described. Several freemen went out together, built houses for themselves and houses for their dependents and slaves, and took shares in the land according to the number of houses (*mansi*) each one owned. Each of the free proprietors in the village then owned one, two, or more *mansi, cum campis, pratis, pascuis, silvis, aquis*, etc. The *portio in villa* is regularly described by this formula, or some equivalent.

Note 177. — Page 80.

See the maps in Prof. Meitzen's introduction to Cod. Dipl. Siles. IV. pp. 72, 82. The same maps are given in his statistical work, Der Boden des Preussischen Staates, I. pp. 358, 360, and in an article in the Jahrb. für Nationalökonomie und Statistik, Jahrg. XVII. Bd. I. See also the map in Schröder's Niederländischen Kolonien (Berlin, 1880, 8°), — Flurkarte der Dörfer Borstel und Wester-Jork.

Note 178. — Page 81.

In regard to the division and distribution of arable lots, see pp. 5-8 and the Notes referred to. In addition to the passages cited in Note 13, the student should read the following passage from Lex Wisig. X. Tit. I. 14 : Si inter eum qui accipit terras vel silvas, et qui praestitit, de spatio unde praestiterit, fuerit orta contentio : tunc si superest ipse qui praestitit, aut si certe mortuus fuerit, eius heredes praebeant sacramenta, quod non amplius auctor eorum dederit, quam ipsi designanter ostendunt ; et sic posteaquam iuraverint, praesentibus testibus quae observentur signa constituant : ut pro ea re nulla deinceps accedat caussatio. Si vero consortes eius non dignentur iurare aut forte noluerint : vel aliquam dubietatem habuerint, quantum vel ipsi dederint, vel antecessores eorum : ipsi ut animas suas non condempnent, nec sacramentum praestent : sed ad tota aratra, quantum ipsi vel parentes eorum in sua sorte susceperant, per singula aratra quinquagenos aripennes dare debent. Ea tamen conditione, ut quantum occupatum habuerint, vel cultum *mixti quinquaginta aripennes* concludant; nec plus quam in eisdem mensuratum fuerat aut ostensum, nisi terrarum dominus forte praestiterit, audeant usurpare. Quod vero amplius usurpaverint, in duplum reddant invasa.

Note 179.—Page 81.

See Commons Inclosure Report of 1844, No. 296 (p. 27), and Nos. 372-383 (pp. 35, 36).

Note 180.—Page 82.

See pp. 21, 22, and Notes 53-60.

Note 181.—Page 83.

There is little or no evidence that redistributions of the same land among the same persons, or representatives, took place in the early period. The custom was introduced here and there, we cannot say when, and in certain places it has survived down to our own time. It is doubtful whether we have any right to argue from the modern instances that the custom is an ancient one; and perhaps the custom was introduced in the tenant communities only, and not at all among free proprietors.

Note 182.—Page 83.

The rotation system is one of the many institutions which have been, in their origin, remedies against violence, devices to prevent quarrelling and fighting, or compromises to reconcile conflicting claims. It was an improvement on redistributions by lot; and redistributions by lot were an improvement on the grab-system which obtained generally in the early period. It is probable that redistributions by lot and the rotation system originated in the tenant colonies. In that case they were introduced by adoption into the colonies of freemen.

It is possible, however, that the rotation system was introduced into the tenant communities only, and not at all among the free proprietors. There is no evidence of the existence of the system in any early records. It appears to have been introduced during the Middle Ages. We cannot say when. The custom has survived in certain places to our own time. That is all we know about it.

Note 183. — Page 83.

See Mr. Elton's Observations on the Commons Bill, 1876, p. 38.

Note 184. — Page 84.

See Notes 20, 21, 92, 96, 97, and the pages of the text referred to.

Note 185. — Page 84.

See note 22. In regard to the "marks" used in casting lots, see, besides the writings referred to in Note 22, Mr. Benjamin Williams's articles in the Archaeologia, vol. 35. p. 471, and vol. 37, p. 382; also A. L. J. Michelsen's Hausmarke, Jena, 1853.

It must be remembered that the free colony we are describing was cast in the mould of the tenant colony of earlier time, and what is true of the one is probably true of the other. During the Middle Ages the free colonies became, in most cases, subject to over-lords; either by being conquered, or in consequence of a voluntary surrender of independence for the sake of the protection which the over-lords offered in return. We have then only the tenant colonies; and we cannot say which of them were in their origin colonies of proprietors.

Note 186. — Page 84.

See Ine 42: If ceorls [i. e. husbandmen] have a common meadow or other partible land (*gedal-land*) to enclose, and some have enclosed their portion and some have neglected to do this, and [cattle come in] and eat the grass; let those go who own the gap and compensate the others for the damage done. Then they may demand such justice on the cattle as may be right. The landholders took equal portions of the fence or enclosure only when they held equal shares of the land enclosed. If the land was distributed in unequal shares, the burden of fencing and enclosing was distributed accordingly.

Note 187. — Page 84.

The best source of information upon this point is the Commons Inclosure Report of 1844. See especially Nos. 293-300, the testimony of W. Blamire, Esq.

Note 188. — Page 85.

See Notes 25, 93, 96, 98.

Note 189. — Page 85.

See Notes 94, 96, 99, 100.

Note 190. — Page 85.

See Note 20.

Note 191. — Page 86.

Lex Sal. XXVII. 9.

Note 192. — Page 86.

See Lacomblet Urkb. 61 : hoc est quod tradidi in pago Sutrachi, in villa que dicitur Aldgrepeshem, terram xx animalium et dimidium unius, et in alia villa terram xv animalium. In such cases, it is probable that the pasture was divided into severalties; that it was a common pasture, however, in spite of this fact. That is to say, it was unenclosed.

The severalties were unenclosed and the animals ranged at large. At the same time no man turned out more animals than could be supported upon his own land. By this system the labor and expense of enclosures were avoided. See references under Note 25.

Note 193. — Page 86.

See Lex Burg. XXVIII. 1: Si quis Burgundio aut Romanus sylvam non habeat, incidendi ligna ad usus suos de jacentivis et sine fructu arboribus in cujuslibet sylva habeat liberam potestatem, neque ab illo cujus sylva est repellatur.

Note 194.—Page 86.

Lex Sal. XXVII. 18 : Si quis ligna aliena in silva aliena furaverit solidos III culpabilis judicetur. Capitularia A. D. 615, XXI : sylvas Ecclesiarum aut privatorum. See also Lex Baiw. XXI ; Lex Burg. XXVIII ; Lex Wisig. Lib. VIII. Tit. II. 2, Tit. III. 8, Tit. IV. 27, Tit. V : Rothar CCXLIV, CCXLV, CCCXXIV et seq. ; Alfred 12 : if a man burn or hew another's wood ; and Ibid. 13 : he who owns the wood. Capitularia A. D. 813, III. 40 : hereditas de sylva. Alsat. Dipl. XI : possessio in silvis. See also Ibid. XXXV, LXVII, LXXXVII : de silva quasi jugera septem . . . holzmarcha. Formulae CCXXXIX, CCLXXXII, CCCXIV : unam silvam suae singularis ac propriae potestatis ; CCCLXV : de terra vero silvativa duas hobas ; CCCLXVII : nemoribus propriis ; CCCXCVIII, CCCCII. Kemble's Codex CCXIII (cf. CCLXV), CCXCVII. Lacomblet Urkb. 7 : scara in silva juxta formam houe plene ; 65 : in illa silva scaras LX ; 93 : duos speciales forastas. Fulda Trad. Cap. 6. 67 : Reginbraht Trad. unam holzmarcham ; 91 ; 98 ; 104 : ambitum de silva ; 130 : unum nemus. See also Ibid. Cap. 5. 4, and Cap. 38. 201 : trad. holzmarcham ad x hubas ; Cap. 39. 77 : tria novalia proprie silve ; 82 : huba in silvis. Fulda Codex 298 : x jugera saltus ; 506, where property in woodland is exchanged for arable land, in the same villa.

Lauresham Cod. XXXIII, MMCCCXXI, MMDCCCXCIII, MMMDLXXII, MMMDCCCVIII : silvam in qua saginari possunt c porci. Trad. Wiz. XXI, LIII : silva quod ego mea uxore condonavi. Ibid. CLXXVIII, CCVI, CCVIII : in marca forastum meum et portione de illa harde. Ibid. CCIX, CCXI, CCXIX, CCXXVII, CCXXXV, CCXLIV : de ipsa silva sua portione, perticas nonaginta et una. Then Ibid. CCLXIII. Cod. S. Galli 85, 102, 110 : in villa silva quod pater meus reliquid mihi ; 123, 331 : tres silvas conservatas ; 373, 381 : silvam habentem hobas v ; 410, 444, 586, 619, 643 : silvulam ab aliorum potestate segregatam ; 701, 775 : silvulam unam bonam. Hist. Frising. I. p. 199. Then Ibid. XXX, XLIX, CXCVIII, CCIII : partem propriae silvae ; CCCXXVII : suam silvam ; CDXLII, DIV, DXVIII : partem de propria silva ; DXL, DXLVI, DLXXIV, DCI, DCVIII, DCXVIII, DCXXXVII, DCXCIII, DCCIX : unum lucum : DCCXXXVII, DCCXXXIX, DCCXLVII, DCCLXVII, DCCLXXIV : de silva hobas II. Ried

Cod. Dipl. XXXIII, XL, LXXXII, LXXXIII, XC: communi utilitate silvae, sive in speciali comprehensione; XCVII: forestum cum forestario. Wirtemb. Urkb. XXVIII: silva mea. So elsewhere, in numberless places. The references to undivided and common forests are comparatively rare. In many cases the *silva* is not described either as undivided or as divided property; as, for example, in the formula, *cum campis, pratis, pascuis, silvis*, etc. In such cases the question whether it was held in severalty or in common remains open.

Note 195. — Page 87.

Given the formula, *cum campis, pratis, pascuis, silvis*, etc., it remains an open question whether the lands referred to were held in common or in severalty; because we find lands held in common, and also lands held in severalty, in records of the same date. In order to prove that the *silvis* of the formula were common lands, it would be necessary to show that private forests did not exist at the time. This cannot be done in any case. We know that severalties of forest land existed everywhere from the time of Lex Salica on. See Note 194.

Note 196. — Page 87.

See Notes 96, 97, 98.

Note 197. — Page 88.

See Notes 101, 102.

Note 198. — Page 89.

According to the laws of inheritance. See pp. 29, 30, and Notes 73-77.

Note 199. — Page 89.

Although in some cases the original divisions were obliterated, they usually remained. A village which originally consisted of ten allotments, *mansi* or *hubae*, continued to consist of ten allotments;

in spite of the fact that the allotments were divided and distributed among several or many persons. The preservation of the original allotments facilitated very much the division and distribution of undivided lands. The owners of the different allotments had different marks, which were used in casting lots. See Notes 22, 185. The holders of the same mark received their lands together, and then divided them among themselves according to individual shares. The villagers as a body took no part in the subdivision of the allotments. They were assigned to the owners, and divided by them, among themselves. See references in Note 200.

NOTE 200. — PAGE 89.

See Prof. Hanssen's essay upon the "Gehöferschaften in Regierungsbezirk Trier," in the Proceedings of the Berlin Academy of Sciences, 1883. The essay is reprinted in his " Agrarhistorische Abhandlungen." See also Dr. Achenbach's " Haubergs-Genossenschaften des Siegerlandes " (Bonn, 1863).

NOTE 201. — PAGE 90.

Dionysius Halicarnassensis IV. 14.

NOTE 202. — PAGE 91.

This was the condition of things until the feudal system was introduced. We have first the system of isolated farms, — *Einzelhöfe;* then a system of clan villages and free colonies, — a system of *Gehöferschaften.* Then the property in the *Gehöferschaften* came to be concentrated in a few hands. At the same time the mass of the people became dependants under over-lordship. As dependants they were distributed in tenant colonies. We have then *Gehöferschaften* of tenants, as distinguished from *Gehöferschaften* of free proprietors. These later *Gehöferschaften* must be very carefully distinguished from those of early times. They differ from them in many respects. The principle of individual property is less clearly recognized, less rigidly adhered to. Elements of democracy and communism appear in the later *Gehöferschaften* for the first time. The undivided land was often the property of the lord, and the members of the *Gehöferschaft* had only commoners' rights in it. In other cases the land was given by the lord to the *Gehöferschaft*, rather than to the members thereof. The *Gehöferschaft* appears then as a land-holding corporation. In no case, so far as we know, did the earlier *Gehöferschaften* have this character.

Note 203. — Page 92.

Mon. Schlehdorf. p. 13: mancipia in domo, tam in villis [*vici locati* in Tacitus Germ. 16?] manentibus. Cf. Hist. Frising. I. p. 126: curtem cum domo et horrea tria; infra domum mancipia vIIII . . . et ibidem ad ipsam curtem aspiciunt mansos duos vestitos; inter illos continentur mancipia decem.

Note 204. — Page 93.

Tacitus says of the Germans, that they settled apart from one another in isolated farmsteads. Then he says that they established villages, — *vicos locant*. It is evident that these must have been villages of dependants or slaves. We know, from Germ. 25, that the Germans had dependants and slaves, and that they were set out upon the land like Roman *coloni*. They must have been distributed in village communities. We have seen how this inference is supported by the testimony of the later records. It is probable that in many cases several free-lords combined in founding a village, and took shares in it according to the number of dependants or slaves each one contributed, as described in the text. There is nothing in the statements of Tacitus, nor is there anything in the later records, inconsistent with this supposition. We may, if we please, interpret Germ. 26 in accordance with it. See Note 9. The freemen occupied as a body as many arable lots as they had cultivators, and then divided the lots *secundum dignationem;* which would be according to the number of cultivators each man had in his following. He who contributed ten cultivators would receive ten lots; he who contributed five cultivators would receive five lots; and so on. Having disposed of the cultivators in this way, the free-lords might retire to their isolated farmsteads and their life of ease. They would be supported by the produce of their respective lots and the labor of the cultivators. There is a good deal to be said in favor of this view.

Note 205. — Page 93.

We have, in the first place, certain noble or patrician families as a governing body. Then we have a class of artisans, mechanics, and tradespeople, and a class of agricultural laborers, distributed in houses and upon lands belonging to members of the governing body. The history of the group thus constituted resembles in very many points the history of a Greek or Latin town. The lower classes increase in power and influence, and finally obtain a share in the government of the city and its district, in very much the same way as they did in Greece and in Italy.

Note 206. — Page 94.

In regard to the *Gehöferschaften* along the Saar and the Mosel there are two theories. According to some writers these *Gehöferschaften* were originally communities of dependants or slaves, that is to say communities of tenants under landlordship: while according to other writers they were originally free communities, without any over-lords. For our own part, we do not see how the question can be decided except in cases, if there be any, in which an origin is described in the records. We are inclined to think that these particular *Gehöferschaften* were originally communities of serfs. We believe that in most cases they are described as such in the earliest records; and we think it is best to abide by the testimony of the records. At the same time, inasmuch as the existence of free *Gehöferschaften* in early times is a pretty well established fact, we grant that it is possible, if not probable, that the aforesaid *Gehöferschaften* were originally free. If, however, we assume that they were originally free, we must not assume that they became subject to over-lords and endured over-lordship without being changed in many respects thereby. We may be sure that their original constitution was changed, though we may not know in what particular respects. We must be careful, therefore, how we use them to illustrate a primitive condition of things. It is often said that we have in the *Gehöferschaften* of the Saar and Mosel examples of a primitive village community. This, however, is an assumption. We do not know whether they were originally free communities, or communities of serfs; and even if we could be sure that they were originally free communities, we do not know to what extent their original constitution has been changed under the *régime* of the over-lords and the feudal system.

Note 207. — Page 94.

Formula CLXI: Quia si aliquis servo suo gasindo suo, aliquid concedere voluerit. Iustissimus nostris sublevatur muneribus qui nobis fideliter et instantia famulantur officio. Ego, in Dei nomen, ille, fideli nostro illi. Pro respectu fidei inservitii tui, quia circa nos inpendere non desistis, promtissima voluntate cedimus te a die praesente locello nuncupante illo, aut manso illo, infra termino villa nostra illa, cum omni adiacentia ad ipso locello aut mancello aspicientem, terris, domibus, mancipiis, vincis, pratella, silvola, vel reliquis beneficiis ibidem aspicientibus: ita ut ab hoc die ipso iure proprietario, si ita convenit, aut sub reditus terre, in tua revoces potestate, et nulla functione aut reditus terrae vel pascuario aut agrario aut quodcumque dici potest exinde solvere, nec tu, nec tua posteritas, nobis nec heredibus nostris, nec quicumque potest nos ipsa villa possidere, non debeatis, nisi tantum, si ita vult, riga, sed ipsum omnibus diebus vite tuae aut haeredis tui emuniter debeatis posedere, vel quicquid exinde facere volueritis liberam habeatis potestatem. Si quis vero, quod futurum esse non credimus, aliquis de heredibus nostris, vel quicumque, contra hanc cessionem nostram agere aut ipsa rem tibi auferre conaverit, inferat tibi cum cogente fisco auri tantum, et hanc epistola firma permaneat cum stipulatione subnexa. Cf. Rothar CCXXVIII: si aliquid in gasindio Ducis, aut privatorum hominum obsequio donum vel munus conquisierit.

Note 208. — Page 94.

Wm. Conq. XXIX: De colonis terre. Coloni et terrarum exercitores non vexentur ultra debitum et statutum: nec licet dominis removere colonos a terris, dummodo debita servicia persolvant. Cf. Ibid. XXXI: De terra colenda. Si domini terrarum non procurent idoneos cultores ad terras suas colendas, justiciarii hoc faciant. This is a rather interesting bit of legislation.

Note 209. — Page 95.

The nature of such communities may be gathered from the Coutum. de Nivernais, Chap. XXII : Des communautez et associations. See Coutum. Gen. III, pp. 1145, 1146. It will be seen how the house communities arose from the multiplication of heirs upon undivided inheritances.

Note 210. — Page 95.

The *vavassoriae* were estates held by vassals of low degree. They must be distinguished from the fiefs of the great nobles, on the one hand, and from the allotments assigned to serfs, on the other. They were held to be divisible according to the customary law of inheritance, and were as a rule very much subdivided. A *vavassoria*, belonging to the abbey at Caen in the year 1430, consisted of sixty-six acres of land. It was divided into no less than a hundred and ten parcels, which were owned by thirty-nine different persons.

Although the *vavassoria* was thus divisible among the *vavassores*, the lord had no dealings except with one person, usually the eldest male of the eldest family in the community. This person represented the *vavassores* in all relations with the lord. He paid the dues and services, and then distributed the burden thereof between himself and his associates. He was the head man of the community, and the only member thereof who came, necessarily, into connection with the outside world. See Le Grand Coustumier de Normendie, Chap. XXVI, in Coutum. Gen. IV, p. 13. See also Léopold Delisle's Études sur la Condition de la Classe Agricole en Normandie (Évreux, 1851, 8°), pp. 32–34. This work is of great value, especially as it contains many extracts from unpublished records; but, unfortunately, it has become excessively rare, and is very costly.

It is interesting to observe that the lands held according to the custom of Gavelkind in Kent, England, correspond very closely with the *vavassoriae* of Normandy. As in the case of the *vavassoriae*, so in the case of Gavelkind lands, we have partition among the heirs and "one suite for all the parceners." See Kent Custum X and XI (p. 7).

Note 211. — Page 96.

It is maintained, for example, that the Russian *mir* is an ancient form of proprietorship antedating all forms of private property and landlordship; and this view is maintained in spite of the fact that the *mir* has been an association of tenants, under over-lordship, from the earliest period of its recorded history. What right have we to assume that the *mir* is more ancient than the over-lordship under which it has always, so far as we know, existed?

The communistic *mir* is constantly cited as an example of "primitive property"; when the fact is, that it cannot be cited even as a case of primitive tenancy. The communism of the Russian *mir*, its peculiar characteristic, appears to be an innovation of comparatively recent times. The testimony of the records goes to show, we are told by good authority, that the custom of making redistributions of the land is relatively modern, having been introduced some time during the seventeenth century. The custom appears to be a result of the heavy poll-taxes which the people were obliged to pay. The village was charged with a certain rent, which was distributed among the villagers in equal shares. A natural result of this was an equalization of holdings. The result of equal taxation was an equalization of property taxed.

In regard to the custom of redistributing the land in the Russian village communities, see the very interesting article by Mr. D. Makenzie Wallace, in Macmillan's Magazine for June, 1876. See also the article, by M. Tchitcherine, upon serfdom in Russia (*Leibeigenschaft in Russland*), in Bluntschli's Staatswörterbuch.

Note 212. — Page 96.

The distinction which we should draw between tribute and rent was seldom if ever marked in early times. The receiver of tribute was regarded as the landlord, and he who paid tribute was regarded as a tenant, paying rent. So when a country was conquered and made tributary, the inhabitants were regarded as tenants paying rent. The proprietorship of the land, the landlordship, passed into the hands of the conqueror or conquerors. The inhabitants of the land, the former proprietors, became tenants.

Note 213.—Page 96.

Grants of land were constantly made upon the following condition, — in ea ratione ut, quamdiu mihi vita comis fuerit superius denominatas res habere mihi liceat et cum censu singulis annis prosolvere, infantesque mei post obitum meum similiter faciant, omnisque posteritas, quae de ipsis fuerit procreata, usque in sempiternum. Quod si evenerit ut ipse res sine herede remaneant, sine meae posteritatis legitima procreatione, quod plerumque contingit, nullus de heredibus vel proheredibus ceteris se ibidem possit adjungere, sed ubi cum censu prosolvebatur, illuc jam redeat in perpetuum. See Formula CCCLIV : Quod omnis posteritas habere debet. Examples abound. Cod. S. Galli 94 : ut annis singulis censum solvam ego et agnatio mea post me. Ibid. 113 : post obitum nostrum heres noster ipsum censum et opus reddat; similiter et tota eorum procreatio faciat legitime genita. Ibid. 193 : ipsam rem liceat mihi et filiis meis post me et filii filiorum meorum et generacionibus meis ad usum fructuario habere, et exinde censum dare debeamus solidum unum in quicquid potuerimus ad festivitate sancti Gallonis aut sancti Martini. Ibid. 211 : post obitum meum filii mei et tota agnitio eorum. Ibid. 232 : filii mei similiter faciant et illorum tota deinceps cognatio. Ibid. 279 : similiter et tota posteritas mea in eundem percipiat censum. Ibid. 318 : similiter et legitima procreatio faciat. So also in Nos. 346, 469, 742, 766, and in others besides. Cf. Alsat. Dipl. LXXVI : ut quamdiu vixero, easdem res habeam, similiter infantes et eorum posteritas, quamdiu legittima fuerit et eundem censum persolvant. Cf. also Ritz Urk. 40 : ut singulis annis ipse vel omnes posteri ejus xii ibidem persolvant denarios ; and Ibid. III. 7 : eadem bona jure hereditario recepi, pro annua pensione sc. octo maldris siliginis et quatuor titrici : que pensio tam a me quam ab omnibus dictorum bonorum successoribus in festo S. Remigii vel ante in perpetuum persolvetur.

These examples could be multiplied indefinitely.

Note 214. — Page 97.

See Du Cange, sub voc. *alodialiter.*

Note 215.—Page 97.

See the address of the Synod of Clermont to Theodebert I., in Ruinart's edition of Greg. Turon. pp. 1334–1335.

Note 216.—Page 97.

Tacitus Germ. 15.

Note 217.—Page 98.

Chlotarii Constitutio Generalis A. D. 560, Cap. XI: Agraria, pascuaria, vel decimas porcorum, Ecclesiae pro fidei nostrae devotione concedimus, ita ut actor aut decimator in rebus Ecclesiae nullus accedat: Ecclesiae vel clericis nullam requirant agentes publici functionem, qui avi vel genitoris aut germani nostri immunitatem meruerunt. Then Read Greg. Turon. IX. 30, and Ibid. V. 29.

Note 218.—Page 99.

Chlotarii Constitutio Generalis, Cap. XI. The passage is given in Note 217. Then read Formula CXLVII: Ergo cognoscat magnitudo seu strenuetas vestra nos inlustre viro illi prumptissima voluntate villa nuncupante illa, sita in pago illo, cum omni merito ex termine suo, in integritate, sicut ab illo aut a fisco nostro fuit possessa vel moderno tempore possidetur, visi fuimus concessisse. Quapropter per praesentem auctoritatem nostram decernimus, quod perpetualiter mansuram esse iubemus, ut ipsa villa illa antedictus vir ille, ut diximus, in omni integritate, cum terris, domibus, aedificiis, acolabus, mancipiis, vineis, silvis, campis, pratis, pascuis, aquis aquarumve decursibus, farinariis, adiacentiis, appendiciis, vel qualibet genus hominum ditioni fisci nostri subditum, qui hibidem commanent, in integra emunitate, absque ullius introitus iudicum de quaslibet causas freda exigendum, perpetualiter habeat concessa: ita ut eam iure proprietario absque ullius expectata iudicum traditione habeat, teneat atque possideat, et suis posteris, Domino adiuvante, ex nostra largitate, aut cui voluerit, ad possedendum relinquat, vel quicquid exinde facere voluerit ex nostro permisso liberam in omnibus habeat potestatem. Et ut haec auctoritas firmior habeatur, manu nostra subter eam decrevimus roborare. This is a good example of the immunity grant.

See also Formulae CXLVIII, CXLIX, CL; and Diplomata Merowing. 2, 4, 9, 15, 28, 31, 38, 54, 55, 63, 69, etc. Kemble's Codex LXXXVII: sit libera ab omnibus saecularibus servitiis, et omnes terrae ad illum pertinentes, exceptis expeditione, pontis et arcis constructione. This is the regular form of immunity in early English records. The landholder was freed from all dues and services, except military service and the duty of repairing bridges and fortifications, — the *trinoda necessitas* as the phrase was. See also Kemble's Codex LVIII, CLXVII, CXCVI, CCVI, CCXIV, CCLXXXVII, and many more. It is useless to multiply these examples.

NOTE 219. — PAGE 99.

Wirtemb. Urkb. CXLV and CXLII (No. 527 of Cod. S. Galli).

NOTE 220. — PAGE 100.

There was an enormous concentration of allodial property during the Carolingian period. It is merely necessary to turn over the documents of the period, to be convinced of this.

An admirable account of the growth of great estates is given by Dr. K. T. von Inama-Sternegg in his work entitled, Die Ausbildung der grossen Grundherrschaften in Deutschland während der Karolingerzeit (Leipzig, 1878, 8°); and in his Wirthschaftsgeschichte (Leipzig, 1879, 8°). We must take the opportunity here to recommend these writings to the student, for his especial consideration.

Dr. von Inama-Sternegg has reasoned conclusively to prove the great antiquity of the system of isolated farms, the *Einzelhofsystem*, and private property in land, *Sondereigenthum*. He has questioned the existence of any community of land, *Feldgemeinschaft*, in the ancient marks, *Markgenossenschaften*. He calls them *Markgenossenschaften ohne Feldgemeinschaft*. He holds that the agricultural community of the Middle Ages is, as a rule, a community of tenants and serfs; that it has been a community of tenants and serfs from the earliest period of its history. These conclusions seem to us to be sound and true. We recommend them, accordingly, to our readers; and take the opportunity, at the same time, to express our respect for their advocate, and also our gratitude for the kind encouragement he has extended to an unknown writer in a distant land.

Note 221. — Page 101.

Cod. S. Galli 494. Cf. references in Note 213.

Note 222. — Page 101.

The distinction between socage tenures and tenures in villenage, what are now known as copyhold tenures, is clearly drawn in our English law books. It is a distinction based upon essential differences, — differences which have existed from the earliest period of recorded history. So in France and Germany, the distinction between free tenures and tenures in villenage is everywhere clearly drawn. It is everywhere based upon real differences. Without doubt, tenures in villenage were sometimes converted into free tenures, and free tenures were converted into tenures in villenage; but that is no reason why they should not be distinguished one from another. By such conversions one form of tenure was substituted for the other.

It is sometimes argued that we have in the free tenant the ancient allodial proprietor. By others it is argued that the villein tenant was the ancient allodial proprietor. There is quite a controversy, whether ancient allodial property has survived to modern times in the free tenures or in the tenures in villenage. The controversy seems to us a very idle one. When allodial property was converted into a free tenure or a tenure in villenage, it ceased to be allodial property. It no longer comes under the definition given to allodial property. When we have once defined an institution correctly, it survives only so long as it answers to the definition. Neither free tenures nor tenures in villenage answer at all to a definition of allodial property; so it cannot be said that allodial property survives either in the one or the other. The question may be raised whether the mass of allodial proprietors became free tenants or serfs; but the question should be at once laid on the shelf, because we have no statistics in the records to enable us to answer it. Besides, it must not be forgotten that both the free tenants and the serfs must have descended, more or less immediately, from allodial proprietors, inasmuch as allodial proprietorship antedates both free tenancy and serfdom; free tenancy being defined as free holding under proprietorship; serfdom being defined as servile holding under proprietorship; there being no other proprietorship among the early Germans, except that which comes under the definition of allodial proprietorship. Of course we have a feudal proprietorship, but that is not properly speaking proprietorship. It is another form of tenancy under proprietorship. We cannot say that allodial proprietorship survived even in feudal lordships. Properly speaking it survived only in the sovereign over-lordship of the kings and emperors, and, here and there, where there were independent lordships among the people. Allodial proprietorship was a sovereign and independent proprietorship. The allodial proprietor may be very correctly described as a king, within the limits of his estate. He was a judge in disputes arising among his tenants. He was their advocate in causes of dispute with persons outside the estate; and he made war upon his neighbors, if he dared to take the consequences of so doing. His neighbors, however, were his kinsmen, and he was usually on good terms with them. In company with his kinsmen, he with his tenants and they with theirs, he waged war on alien families and clans, with more or less success. The state of the early Germans is best described as a confederation of sovereign proprietors, — *reges vicini*. The territory of the state consisted of the estates of these proprietors. The assembly was an inter-estate convention so to speak, in which the opinion of the best men, or a majority, was law.

All this, however, is very much of a digression. We do not propose to examine here the political constitution of the early state. It is with the land system only that we are concerned.

Note 223. — Page 103.

Tacitus Germ. 32: inter familiam et penates et jura successionum equi traduntur: excipit filius, non ut cetera, maximus natu, sed prout ferox bello et melior. Cf. Germ. 20: heredes tamen successoresque sui cuique liberi, et nullum testamentum. In the first passage the Tencteri are referred to; in the second, the Germans in general.

NOTE 224.—PAGE 103.

See Mr. T. E. Cliffe Leslie's very interesting article on Auvergne in the Fortnightly Review, December, 1874, p. 745.

NOTE 225.—PAGE 104.

See Note 223. See also the Vita S. Benedicti of Baed, § 11 : quomodo terreni parentes quem primum partu fuderint, eum principium liberorum suorum cognoscere et ceteris in particnda sua hereditate praeferendum ducere solent.

With the exception of the passage in Tacitus, this is the earliest reference to the custom of primogeniture which we have found. The passage may, however, refer simply to a preference given to the eldest son in respect to certain items of the inheritance incapable of division, heirlooms for example. So in the Customs of Stretford in Oxfordshire. See Coke upon Littleton, 18. b.

NOTE 226.—PAGE 104.

For the *Hausgesetze*, see J. J. Moser's Familien-Staatsrecht der deutschen Reichstände; also his Persönliches Staatsrecht, and Deutsches Staatsrecht. These works were published towards the end of the last century. The *Hausgesetze* of reigning families in Germany were published at Jena, in 1862. by Hermann Schulze, under the title, Die Hausgesetze der regierenden deutschen Fürstenhäuser.

We have not ourselves had access to these works. We have had to depend upon the account of their contents given by Hermann Schulze in the Appendix to Stobbe's Geschichte der deutschen Rechtsquellen (2 vols., Braunschweig, 1860–64, 8°).

By means of the *Hausgesetze* inheritances were given to males rather than to females; they were made inalienable and indivisible; and the right of succession was conferred upon the eldest son, or the eldest male of the eldest line.

Note 227. — Page 106.

See Note 222.

Note 228. — Page 106.

This may be inferred from the existence of the rules prescribing divisions among heirs, and the absence of exceptions to these rules. Among the Bavarians, for example, we have the rule: *ut fratres hereditatem patris aequaliter dividant.* See Lex Baiw. XIV. Cap. VIII. 1. No exception being made to the application of this rule, we may assume that the rule had a universal application, — that it governed the distribution of all inheritances, whether they were held as independent property or as benefices. The existence at this time of beneficiary holdings is proved by the words *nisi defensor Ecclesiae ipsius per beneficium praestare voluerit ei*, in Lex Baiw. I. Cap. 1.

The *vavassoriae* of Normandy partook of the nature of benefices. They were called *feuda minora*. At the same time they were divisible among the heirs from generation to generation. See Note 210. We may suppose that this was the case with almost all benefices in the early time, in so far as they were held with a right of inheritance. We may regard the Norman *vavassoriae* as typical examples of ancient beneficiary holdings. The rule of indivisibility of fiefs was introduced afterwards.

Note 229. — Page 106.

The principle of indivisibility of fiefs being recognized, the question arose which of the heirs shall have the inheritance. The first answer to this question would be, that he who was best qualified to hold and administer it ought to have it. Then the question would arise which of the heirs is best qualified. In order to settle this frequently very difficult question, and the disputes arising in regard to it, it would be necessary to adopt a rule of succession. The rule which, in the long run, would be most satisfactory, would be the rule of primogeniture; and that was the rule generally adopted. We are told that the earliest *Hausgesetze* now extant belong to the fourteenth century, and are simply rules against divisions of family property, — *Untheilbarkeitsverordnungen.* See Stobbe's Geschichte der Deutschen Rechtsquellen, II. pp. 501–502. The rule of indivisibility being recognized and adopted, the rule of primogeniture follows as a natural result, almost inevitably, as the means of preventing disputes among heirs upon the question of succession.

Note 230. — Page 106.

Take, for example, the *varassoria* called *le fief au Rosel* at Quettehou, of which we have a detailed account dating from the beginning of the fifteenth century. It consisted of sixty-six acres of land, and it was divided among more than thirty-nine persons. That would give a little more than an acre and a half to the individual, on an average. With such limited inheritances it is not likely that the *varassores* were persons of any distinction or influence.

See Delisle's Études sur la Classe Agricole en Normandie, pp. 33–34.

Note 231. — Page 108.

Already in the time of Tacitus the people were beginning to group themselves in followings, — *Gefolgschaften*. They gave up their estates and became companions of a chief or king. They received from him arms and horses, and they lived with him as members of his household. Then there arose a competition between the chiefs and kings, to obtain the greatest number of personal adherents, and various and great were the inducements offered to the people at large, to lead them to give up their independence See Germ. 13, 14. The result was, that all but the wealthiest and most powerful of the allodial proprietors became dependants. Then the number of dependants became, in many cases, so great that it was impossible to maintain all of them as retainers in the household. They were, consequently, distributed into two classes, — a class of retainers in the household, and a class of beneficiaries. Then a struggle for wealth and power began between the lords and the beneficiaries.

The lords discovered that their estates must either be increased or remain undivided, and the beneficiaries came to the same conclusion. As long as there was plenty of land, estates were increased and divided; but as soon as land became scarce, and further conquests were impossible, the lords began to adopt the principle that inheritances must not be divided. The beneficiaries followed their example. The feudal system was the result. It was only among the lower orders of tenants that divisions among heirs continued to be made. It was among the lower orders of tenants only that the clan system continued its existence. While the lords and the higher class of tenants became rich and powerful, pauperism and servitude increased beneath them. The number of discontents grew constantly larger and larger, and the number was increased by the accession of the disinherited members of the upper classes. The feudal system became more and more intolerable, until the lower classes were stirred to revolt, and it was overthrown more or less completely everywhere. It is in England only that the practice of disinheriting all but one heir is still tolerated by an indulgent populace. The lower classes are gathered into the manufacturing centres. The disinherited members of the upper classes take refuge in the professions. The land remains still in the hands of comparatively few persons, as in the Middle Ages. How long this condition of things may last remains to be seen. It can hardly last very long. The number of people who consider it intolerable seems to be increasing day by day. With the abolition of indivisible estates a fundamental cause of feudalism will be removed. Given indivisible estates and an increasing population, the result will be dependence upon landlords and personal adherence to them. The ultimate result will be a form of feudalism.

THE student who desires to review the literature of our subject will find the following list of authors and titles serviceable.

ACHENBACH, H. — Die Haubergsgenossenschaften des Siegerlandes. Ein Beitrag zur Darstellung der deutschen Flur- und Agrar-Verfassung. Bonn. 1863. 8°.

ADAMS, H. B. — The Germanic Origin of New England Towns. Johns Hopkins University Studies in Historical and Political Science. II. Baltimore, 1882. 8°.

ALLEN, W. F. — Community of Land in New England. In the Nation, Vol. 26, p. 22, No. 654, Jan. 10, 1878.

ALLEN, W. F. — Rural Classes of England in the Thirteenth Century. Madison, Wisconsin, 1874.

——— Peasant Communities in France, and Origin of the Freeholders [in England]. A pamphlet without imprint.

——— English Cottagers of the Middle Ages. Pamphlet without imprint.

AMIRA, KARL V. — Erbfolge und Verwandschafts-Gliederung nach den alt-niederdeutschen Rechten. München, 1874. 8°.

ANDERSON, JOSEPH. — The Orkneyinga Saga, with Notes and an Introduction. Edinburgh, 1873. 8°.

ANTON, K. G. — Geschichte der teutschen Landwirthschaft. 3 vols. Görliz, 1799-1802. 8°.

ARNOLD, WILHELM. — Ansiedelungen und Wanderungen deutscher Stämme. Marburg, 1875. 8°.

——— Deutsche Urzeit. 3d edition. Gotha, 1881. 8°.

BEAUNE, HENRI. — Introduction à l'Étude Historique du Droit Coutumier Français jusqu'à la Rédaction officielle des Coutumes. Lyon, 1880. 8°.

BECK. — Beschreibung des Regierungsbezirkes Trier. Bd. I. contains an account of the *Gehöferschaften*. Trier, 1868.

BETHMANN-HOLLWEG, M. A. v. — Der germanisch-romanisch Civilprozess im Mittelalter. 3 vols. Bonn, 1868-74. 8°.

BLACKSTONE, SIR WILLIAM. — Commentaries on the Laws of England. We have used the 16th edition, with Notes by John Taylor Coleridge. 4 vols. London, 1825. 8°.

BLUNTSCHLI, J. C. — Ueber die Landgemeinden. Kritische Ueberschau der deutschen Gesetzgebung und Rechtswissenschaft. Bd. I. 1853.

——— Die Wirthschaftliche Rechtsordnung der deutschen Dörfer. Kritische Ueberschau der deutschen Gesetzgebung und Rechtswissenschaft. Bd. II. 1855.

——— Staats- und Rechtsgeschichte der Stadt und Landschaft Zürich. 2d edition. 2 vols. Zürich, 1856. 8°.

BINDING, CARL. — Das Burgundisch-Romanische Königreich (von 443 bis 532 N. Chr.). Leipzig, 1868. 8°.

BODMANN, F. J. — Rheingauischer Alterthümer. Mainz, 1819. 4°.

BORCHGRAVE, ÉMIL DE. — Histoire des Colonies Belges qui s'établirent en Allemagne pendant la Douzième et le Treizième Siècle. Bruxelles, 1865.

—— Essai Historique sur les Colonies Belges qui s'établirent en Hongrie et en Transsylvanie. Bruxelles, 1871.

BRANTS, VICTOR. — Essai Historique sur la Condition des Classes Rurales en Belgique. Louvain, Paris, 1880. 8°.

BRIESEN, CONSTANTIN V. — Urkundliche Geschichte des Kreises Merzig. With an account of the Gehöferschaften. Saarlouis, 1863. 8°.

BRODRICK, G. C. — The Law and Custom of Primogeniture. Systems of Land Tenure in various Countries. IX. Published by the Cobden Club. London, 1876. 8°.

BRUNNER, HEINRICH. — Das Anglonormannische Erbfolgsystem. Zur Geschichte der Parentelen Ordnung. Leipzig, 1869. 8°.

—— Zur Rechtsgeschichte der Römischen und Germanischen Urkunde. Berlin, 1880. 8°.

BÜCHER, KARL. — Das Ureigenthum, von Émile de Laveleye. Authorized translation, with amplifications. Leipzig, 1879. 8°.

COKE, SIR EDWARD. — Upon Littleton. We have used the edition with Hardgrave's and Butler's Notes. 2 vols. Philadelphia, 1853. 8°.

COULANGES, FUSTEL DE. — Histoire des Institutions Politiques de l'Ancienne France. I. Paris, 1875. 8°.

—— Étude sur la Propriété à Sparte. Mémoire lu à l'Académie des Sciences Morales et Politiques. Nov.-Déc. 1879. In the Séances; in the Journal des Savants, 1880; and separately, Paris, 1880. 8°.

DAHN, FELIX. — Die Könige der Germanen. 6 vols. München, Würzburg, 1861-71. 8°.

DARESTE DE LA CHAVANNE, C. — Histoire des Classes Agricoles en France depuis Saint Louis jusqu'à Louis XVI. Paris, 1854. 8°.

DARESTE, R. — Les Anciennes Lois Suédoises. Journal des Savants. Sept., Oct., 1880.

—— Anciennes Lois de Danemark. Journal des Savants. Fév. 1881.

NOTES AND REFERENCES. 255

DARESTE, R. — Les Anciennes Lois de la Norvège. Journal des Savants. April, Mai, 1881.

DASENT, G. W. — The Story of Burnt Njal, or Life in Iceland at the End of the Tenth Century. 2 vols. London, 1861. 8°.

DELISLE, LÉOPOLD. — Études sur la Condition de la Classe Agricole, et l'État de l'Agriculture, au Moyen Age. Évreux, 1851. 8°.

DIGBY, K. E. — Introduction to the History of the Law of Real Property. Oxford, 1875. 8°.

EICHHORN, K. F. — Deutsche Staats- und Rechtsgeschichte. 5th edition. 4 vols. Göttingen, 1843. 8°.

ELLIS, HENRY. — General Introduction to Domesday Book. In Domesday III.; or 2 vols., London, 1833. 8°.

ELTON, CHARLES. — The Tenures of Kent. Oxford, London, 1867. 8°.

——— The Law of Commons and Waste Lands. London, 1868. 8°.

——— The Law of Copyholds and Customary Tenures. London, 1874. 8°.

——— Observations on the Bill for the Improvement of Commons, 1876. London, 1876. 8°.

——— Origins of English History. London, 1882. 8°.

——— Custom and Tenant-Right. London, 1882. 8°.

ERHARDT, LOUIS. — Aelteste germanische Staatenbildung. Leipzig, 1879. 8°.

——— Entstehung des deutschen Königthums, von Heinrich von Sybel. Göttingische gelehrte Anzeigen. 27 Sept., 1882.

FENTON, JOHN. — The Right of Pre-emption in Village Communities. The Antiquary, No. 21, Vol. IV., Sept., 1881.

FINLASON, W. F. — History of the Law of Tenures of Land in England. London, 1870. 8°.

FISHER, JOSEPH. — The History of Landholding in England. In the Proceedings of the Royal Historical Society, and in the Humboldt Library, No. 27. New York, 1881. 8°.

FREEMAN, E. A. — The Norman Conquest. 6 vols. Oxford, 1867-79. 8°.

FREEMAN, E. A. — The Growth of the English Constitution from the earliest Times. London, 1872. 8°. A third edition, with notes. 1876. 8°.

G. A. (GRANT ALLEN?).— Old English Clans. Cornhill Magazine. Sept. 1881.

GAUPP, ERNST THEODOR. — Die germanischen Ansiedelungen und Landtheilungen in den Provinzen des römischen Westreiches. Breslau, 1844. 8°.

GEFFROY, M. A. — L'Island avant le Christianism. Mémoires présentés par divers Savants à l'Académie des Inscriptions et Belles-Lettres. 1re Série, Tom. VI. 1864.

GIERKE, O. F. — Das deutsche Genossenschaftsrecht. Erster Band. Rechtsgeschichte der deutschen Genossenschaft. Berlin, 1868. 8°.

GOMME, G. LAURENCE. — Nottingham Borough Records. The Antiquary, No. 40, Vol. VII., April, 1883.

GRIMM, JACOB. — Deutsche Rechtsalterthümer. 2d edition. Göttingen, 1854. 8°.

GUÉRARD, B. — Polyptique de l'Abbé Irminon. Prolégomènes. Paris, 1844. 4°.

GUIZOT, F. P. G. — Essais sur l'Histoire de France. 11th edition. Paris, 1866. 8°.

HALLAM, HENRY. — View of the State of Europe during the Middle Ages. 10th edition. 3 vols. London, 1853. 8°.

HANSSEN, GEORG. — Agrarhistorische Abhandlungen, 1835–79. Leipzig. 1880. 8°.

——— Agrarhistorische Fragmente zur Erkentniss der deutsche Feldmarkverfassung von der Urzeit bis zur Aufhebung der Feldgemeinschaft. Zeitschrift für die gesammte Staatswissenschaft. Jahrg. 36 and 38.

——— Untersuchungen über das Hofsystem in Mittelalter, von Dr. K. T. von Inama-Sternegg. Göttingische gelehrte Anzeigen. 1873, 1. p. 921.

HAXTHAUSEN, AUGUST V. — Ueber die Agrarverfassung in Norddeutschland. Berlin, 1829. 8°.

——— Ueber die Agrarverfassung in den Fürstenthümer Paderborn und Corvey. Berlin, 1829. 8°.

HAXTHAUSEN, AUGUST V. — Die ländliche Verfassung der Provinz Ost- und West-Preussen. Königsberg, 1839.

——— Ursprung und Grundlagen der Verfassung in den ehemals Slavischen Ländern Deutschlands. Berlin, 1842. 8°.

HENSLER, ANDREAS. — Die Gewere. Weimar, 1872. 8°.

HISELY, J. J. — Essai sur l'Origine et le Développement des Libertés des Waldstetten, Uri, Schwyz, Unterwalden. Published in 3 parts, by the Société d'Histoire de la Suisse Romande. Lausanne, 1838–43. 8°.

HOLMES, O. W., JR. — The Common Law. Boston, 1881. 8°.

HOSKYNS, C. WREN. — The Land Laws of England. Systems of Land Tenure in various Countries. II. Published by the Cobden Club. London, 1876. 8°.

INAMA-STERNEGG, K. T. v. — Untersuchungen über das Hofsystem im Mittelalter. Innsbruck, 1872. 8°.

——— Die Entwickelung der deutschen Alpendörfer. Ein Wirthschaftsgeschichtlicher Essay. Historisches Taschenbuch. 5 Folge, 4 Jahrgang. Leipzig, 1874.

——— Die Ausbildung der grossen Grundherrschaften in Deutschland wärend der Karolinger Zeit. Leipzig, 1878. 8°.

——— Deutsche Wirthschaftsgeschichte bis zum Schluss der Karolingerperiode. I. Leipzig, 1879. 8°.

——— Die Quellen der deutschen Wirthschaftsgeschichte. Novemberheft des Jahrganges 1876 der Sitzungsberichte der Phil.-Hist. Classe der Kais. Akademie der Wissenschaften. Wien, 1877. 8°.

JACOBI, VICTOR. — Agrarwesen des Altenburgischen Osterlandes. First printed in the Leipziger Zeitung; then reprinted under the title, Slaven- und Teutschthum. Hannover, 1845. 8°.

JAHN, ALBERT. — Die Geschichte der Burgundionen und Burgundiens, bis zum Ende der I. Dynastie. 2 vols. Halle, 1874. 8°.

JASTROW, IGNAZ. — Zur Strafrechtlichen Stellung der Sklaven bei Deutschen und Angelsachsen. Breslau, 1878. 8°.

——— Ueber das Eigenthum an und von Sclaven nach deutschen Volksrechten. Forschungen zur deutschen Geschichte, XIX. p. 626. Göttingen, 1879. 8°.

17

KEMBLE, J. M. — The Saxons in England. First edition. London, 1848. Second edition, 1876. 8°.

KINDLINGER, NIKLAS. — Geschichte der deutschen Hörigkeit, inbesondere der sogenannten Leibeigenschaft. Berlin, 1819. 8°.

KOHLER, JOSEPH. — Émile de Laveleye, das Ureigenthum. Vierteljahresschrift für Gesetzgebung und Rechtswissenschaft. Bd. XXIII. p. 24. (Neue Folge, Bd. IV.) 1881.

KOVALEWSKY, MAXIMUS. — Umriss einer Geschichte der Zerstückelung der Feldgemeinschaft in Canton Waadt. Zurich, 1877.

LABOULAYE, E. R. L. — Histoire du Droit de Propriété Foncière en Occident. Paris, 1839. 8°.

LAING, SAMUEL. — The Heimskringla. A Chronicle of the Kings of Norway. From the Icelandic of Snorro Sturleson. With a Preliminary Dissertation. 3 vols. London, 1844. 8°.

LANDAU, GEORG. — Die Territorien in Bezug auf ihre Bildung und ihre Entwicklung. Hamburg, Gotha, 1854. 8°.

——— Das Salgut. Kassel, 1862. 8°.

LAPPENBERG, J. M. — History of England under the Anglo-Saxon Kings. Translated from the German (Hamburg, 1834) by Benjamin Thorpe. 2 vols. London, 1845. 8°. There is a new edition in Bohn's Series.

LAVELEYE, ÉMILE DE. — De la Propriété et de ses Formes Primitives. Paris, 1874. 8°.

LEAKE, STEPHEN MARTIN. — An Elementary Digest of the Law of Property in Land. London, 1874. 8°.

LEHUÉROU, J. M. — Histoire des Institutions Mérovingiennes et Carolingiennes. 2 vols. Paris, 1843. 8°.

LEO, HEINRICH. — Upon the Rectitudines Singularum Personarum. Halle, 1842. 8°.

LEWIS, W. — Die Successionsordnung des Deutschen Rechts. Vierteljahrschrift für Gesetzgebung und Rechts-Wissenschaft. IX. München, 1867.

LODGE, H. CABOT. — An Essay on Land-Law, in Essays in Anglo-Saxon Law. Boston, 1876. 8°.

MAINE, SIR HENRY SUMNER. — Ancient Law. Its Connection with the Early History of Society, and its Relation to Modern Ideas. London, 1861. 8°.

MAINE, SIR HENRY SUMNER. — Village Communities in the East and West. London, 1871. 8°. There are later editions with additional essays.

———— Lectures on the Early History of Institutions. London, 1875. 8°.

———— Dissertations on Early Law and Custom. London, 1883. 8°.

MAJER, J. C. — Teutsche Erbfolge in Lehen- und Stammgütern. Stuttgart, 1801. 8°.

———— Gemeinrechtliche Erbfolge-Ordnung. Stuttgart, 1805. 8°.

MARSHALL. — A Review of the Reports of the Board of Agriculture from the Southern Department of England. York, 1817.

———— A Review of the Reports of the Board of Agriculture from the Midland Department of England. York, 1815. Or else see the Reports themselves. They were printed towards the end of the last century, under the superintendence of Sir John Sinclair.

MAURER, G. L. v. — Einleitung zur Geschichte der Mark- Hof- Dorf-, und Stadt-Verfassung. München, 1854. 8°.

———— Geschichte der Markenverfassung in Deutschland. Erlangen, 1856. 8°.

———— Geschichte der Fronhöfe, der Bauernhöfe und der Hofverfassung in Deutschland. 4 vols. Erlangen, 1862–63. 8°.

———— Geschichte der Dorfverfassung in Deutschland. 2 vols. Erlangen, 1865–66. 8°.

MAURER, KONRAD. — Die Entstehung des isländischen Staats und seiner Verfassung. München, 1852. 8°.

———— Ueber Angelsächsische Rechtsverhältnisse. Kritische Ueberschau der deutschen Gesetzgebung und Rechtswissenschaft. I, II. 1853–55.

———— Island von seiner ersten Entdeckung bis zum Untergange des Freistaats. München, 1874. 8°.

MEITZEN, AUGUST. — Cod. Dipl. Siles. Bd. 4. Einleitung. With maps of villages. Breslau, 1863. 4°.

———— Der Boden und die Landwirthschaftlichen Verhältnisse des Preussischen Staates. 4 vols. Agrarverfassung in Vol. I. Berlin, 1868. 4°.

MEITZEN, AUGUST. — Die Ausbreitung der Deutschen in Deutschland, und ihre Besiedelung der Slavengebiete. Jahrbücher für Nationalökonomie und Statistik. XVII. Jahrgang, 1. Bd.. pp. 1-59.

——— Der älteste Anbau der Deutschen. A review of Inama-Sternegg's Wirthschaftsgeschichte. Jahrbücher für Nationalökonomie und Statistik. Neue Folge, Bd. II. Heft I. 1881.

——— Agrarpolitik im engeren Sinne. Landeskultur-Gesetzgebung. In the Handbuch der Politischen Oekonomie edited by Dr. Schönberg. Tübingen, 1881, pp. 669-710.

——— Das Nomadentum der Germanen. Verhandlungen des zweiten Deutschen Geographentages zu Halle. April, 1882.

——— Die Individualwirtschaft der Germanen. Bemerkungen zu Lorenz v. Stein's: Drei Fragen des Grundbesitzes. Jahrbücher für Nationalökonomie und Statistik. Neue Folge, Bd. VI. Heft I.

MIASKOWSKY, AUGUST v. — Die schweizerische Allmend vom XIII Jahrhundert bis zur Gegenwart. Leipzig, 1879. 8°.

MILL, JOHN STUART. — Mr. Maine on Village Communities. In the Fortnightly Review, vol. 15, p. 543, May, 1871.

MÖSER, JUSTUS. — Osnabrückische Geschichte. 3 vols. Berlin, Stettin, 1880-1824. 8°.

MONE, F. J. — Ueber die Allmenden vom 12 bis 16 Jahrhundert. Zeitschrift für die Geschichte des Oberrheins, I. p. 385. Karlsruhe, 1850.

MORGAN, J. F. — England under the Norman Occupation. London, 1858. 8°.

MORIER, R. B. D. — Agrarian Legislation of Prussia during the present Century. Systems of Land Tenure in various Countries. V. Published by the Cobden Club. London, 1876. 8°.

NASSE, E. — The Agricultural Community of the Middle Ages. Translated from the German by Colonel Ouvry. London, 1871. 8°.

——— Village Communities. Contemporary Review, May, 1871.

OLUFSEN. — Bidrag til Oplysning om Danmarks indvortes Forfatning i de aeldre Tider. In the first volume of the Proceedings of the Kopenhagen Academy of Sciences. There is a separate imprint: Kopenhagen, 1821.

REEVES, JOHN. — History of the English Law, from the Time of the Romans to the End of the Reign of Elizabeth. Edited by W. F. Finlason. 3 vols. London, 1869. 8°.

REPORT. — Commons' Inclosure. Ordered to be printed by the House of Commons, August, 1844. Folio.

REPORTS. — Respecting the Tenure of Land in the several Countries of Europe. Printed for the Houses of Parliament. 2 Parts. 1869-70. Folio.

ROBERTSON, E. W. — Historical Essays in Connection with the Land, &c. Edinburgh, 1872. 8°.

ROBINSON, THOMAS. — The Common Law of Kent, or the Customs of Gavelkind, with an Appendix concerning Borough-English. London, 1741. 8°.

ROSCHER, WILHELM. — Ansichten der Volkswirthschaft aus dem geschichtlichen Standpunkte. Leipzig, 1861. 8°.

—— System der Volkswirthschaft. II. Nationalökonomik des Ackerbaues. 6th edition. Stuttgart, 1870. 8°.

ROTH, PAUL. — Geschichte des Beneficialwesens. Erlangen, 1850. 8°.

—— Feudalität und Unterthanverband. Weimar, 1863. 8°.

SAVIGNY, F. C. v. — Geschichte des römischen Rechts im Mittelalter. 2d edition. 7 vols. Heidelberg, 1834. 8°.

—— Das Recht des Besitzes. 6th edition. Giessen, 1837. 8°.

SCHOTT, J. — Ueber die Natur der weiblichen Erbfolge. 1809. 8°.

SCHRÖDER, RICHARD. — Die niederländischen Kolonien in Norddeutschland zur Zeit des Mittelalters. Berlin, 1880. In Virchow's and Holzendorff's Wissenschaftliche Vorträge, XV.

—— Geschichte des ehelichen Güterrechts in Deutschland. Stettin, Danzig, Elbing, 1863. 8°.

—— Die Ausbreitung der Salischen Franken. Zugleich ein Beitrag zur Geschichte der deutschen Feldgemeinschaft. Forschungen zur deutschen Geschichte. Bd. XIX. p. 137.

—— Die Franken und ihr Recht. Weimar, 1881. 8°. Aus: Zeitschrift der Savigny-Stiftung für Rechtsgeschichte.

SCHULZE, H. J. F. — Recht der Erstgeburt in den deutschen Fürstenhäusern. Leipzig, 1851.

SCHWERZ. — Beiträge zur Kentniss der Landwirthschaft in der Gebirgsgegend des Hundsrücken. In Vol. XXVII. of the Möglinsche Annalen der Landwirthschaft, Erstes Stück. This is the first account we have of the *Gehöferschaften*.

SEEBOHM, FREDERIC. — The Land Question. Feudal Tenures. Fortnightly Review, vol. 13, p. 89, Jan., 1870.

—— The English Village Community, examined in its Relations to the Manorial and Tribal Systems. An Essay in Economic History. London, 1883. 8°.

SIEGEL, HEINRICH. — Die Germanische Verwandschaftsberechnung, mit besondere Beziehung auf die Erbenfolge. Giessen, 1853. 8°.

—— Das Deutsche Erbrecht. Heidelberg, 1853. 8°.

SOHM, RUDOLPH. — Die Fränkische Reichs- und Gerichtsverfassung. Weimar, 1871. 8°.

—— La Procédure de la Lex Salica. Traduit et annoté par Marcel Thévenin. Paris, 1873. 8°.

—— Fränkisches Recht und Römisches Recht. Weimar, 1880. 8°. Aus: Zeitschrift der Savigny-Stiftung für Rechtsgeschichte.

—— Zur Geschichte der Auflassung. Festgabe zum Doctor-Jubiläum des Herrn Geheimen Justizrathes Professors Dr. Heinrich Thöl in Göttingen. Strassburg, 1879. 8°.

SOMNER, WILLIAM. — A Treatise of Gavelkind. London, 1660. 8°.

STEIN, LORENZ v. — Drei Fragen des Grundbesitzes und seiner Zukunft. Stuttgart, 1881. 8°.

STOBBE, O. — Geschichte der deutschen Rechtsquellen. 2 vols. Braunschweig, 1860–64. 8°.

STUBBS, WILLIAM. — The Constitutional History of England. Vol. I. Oxford, 1874. 8°.

—— Select Charters. Illustrations of English Constitutional History. Oxford, 1874. 8°.

STÜVE, C. — Wesen und Verfassung der Landgemeinden und des ländlichen Grundbesitzes in Niedersachsen und Westphalen. Jena, 1851. 8°.

Sybel, Heinrich v. — Entstehung des deutschen Königthums. New edition. Frankfurt a. M., 1881. 8°.

Taillar. — Notice sur l'Origine et la Formation des Villages du Nord de la France. Mémoires de la Société d'Agriculture de Douai. 2d series, vol. 6, p. 276.

Taylor, Silas. — The History of Gavelkind. London, 1663. 8°.

Thudichum, Friedrich. — Die Gau- und Markverfassung in Deutschland. Giessen, 1860. 8°.

—— Der altdeutsche Staat. Giessen, 1862. 8°.

Turner, Sharon. — The History of the Anglo-Saxons. 3 vols. London, 1852. 8°.

Tzschoppe, G. A., and Stenzel, G. A. — Urkundensammlung zur Ursprungs der Städte in Schlesien und der Ober-Lausitz. Einleitung. Hamburg, 1832. 4°.

Viollet, Paul. — Caractère collectif des premières Propriétés immobilières. Bibliothèque de l'École des Chartes, vol. 33, p. 451. 1872.

Waitz, Georg. — Deutsche Verfassungsgeschichte. Kiel, 1844. 8°. A second edition was begun in 1865.

—— Die altdeutsche Hufe. Göttingen, 1854.

Wallace, D. Makenzie. — Russian Village Communities. In Macmillan's Magazine, vol. 34, p. 97, June, 1876. Reprinted in the Eclectic Magazine, vol. 84, p. 196.

Wasserschleben, H. — Das Princip der Successionsordnung. Gotha, 1860. 8°.

—— Die germanische Verwandschaftsberechnung und das Prinzip der Erbfolge. Eine Replik. Giessen, 1864. 8°.

Wietersheim, Eduard v. — Geschichte der Volkerwanderung. 4 Bde. Leipzig, 1859-61. 8°. A second edition, edited by Felix Dahn. 2 Bde. Leipzig, 1880-81. 8°.

Williams, Benjamin. — Account of the Officers of a Manor in Oxfordshire. Archaeologia, vol. 33, p. 269. 1850.

—— Remarks on the Hide of Land. Archaeologia, vol. 35, p. 470. 1854.

—— On the Land of Ditmarsh, and the Mark Confederation. Archaeologia, vol. 37, p. 371. 1857.

WILLIAMS, JOSHUA. — Principles of the Law of Real Property. Fifth American, from the twelfth English edition. Philadelphia, 1879. 8°.

—— Rights of Common and other Prescriptive Rights. London, 1880. 8°.

YOUNG, ERNEST. — An Essay on Family Law, in Essays in Anglo-Saxon Law. Boston, 1876. 8°.

ZIMMERLE, LUDWIG. — Deutsche Stammgutssystem. Tübingen, 1857. 8°.

INDEX.

ACRES, 6–7, 80, 131, 134–136.
Adoption, 66, 69–73, 222–226.
Agilofingi, family of the, 32, 185.
Affatimum, 70–73, 223–225.
Agri, (in Caesar IV. 1), 210–211; (in Tacitus Germ. 26), 4–5, 126, 129–133, 231; (in the Annales IV. 72), 211.
Agricultural life, transition from the pastoral to the, 3, 126.
Agriculture, introduction of, 1–3, 126.
Alfred, King, keeps half his forces in the field, half at home, 126; his will, 182–183.
Alienation, right of, 51–56, 66, 73–75, 209–210, 221, 226, 228–229.
Alienations *in casa*, 71, 225–226.
Allodial property, nature of it, 218; concentration of it, 99–101, 102, 105, 216; converted into hereditary tenures, 100, 106, 217; converted into tenures in villenage, 217.
Almend, 138–139, 196; almend formula, 87, 152, 237.
Alod, 35, 58, 171–175, 189.
Ancestor worship, a theory as to its origin, 189.
Ancient houses, 26.
Appropriation of unoccupied land, 13-14, 28, 151, 153, 168, 171–175, 177–178, 193.
Arable lots, occupied according to the number of cultivators, *pro numero cultorum*, 4–6, 14, 16, 27, 129-133, 147–148, 151–152, 172–173, 231; shifted about, 7-8, 138; held in rotation, 10, 83; distribution of them in the free colonies, 80–83, 232.
Authority, too much deference paid to it, 65.
Auvergne, custom of inheritance in, 103, 249.

BAED, his letter to Abp. Ecgbirht, 170; he refers to the custom of primogeniture, 249.
Benefices, 105–108, 250.
Beneficiaries, 106–108, 251.
Bibliography, 111–122, 252–264.
Blood, kinship, as a bond of union, 66, 90, 195.
Boc-land, 170–171, 182.
Borough English, 104.
Boundaries, none in the early time, 12, 17, 19, 23, 148–149 ; how first laid down, 13, 149–150.
Burgundian Law, notable passages from it, 20, 179.

CAESAR, interpretation of his statements, 2, 12, 15, 17–20, 22, 125–126, 135, 148–149, 156–157, 210–211.
Castles, origin of, 159.
Charibert, taxation in the reign of, 98.
Chiefs and kings, in the ancient houses of the nation, 26–27.
Chilperic, the edict of, 48–49, 206, 213, 214, 220, 221 ; taxes in the reign of, 98.
Chlothar I., taxes in the time of, 98, 245.
Chronology, disregarded by the advocates of a primitive communism, 61–65.
Churches, owned in shares, 44, 200–201.
Civic life among the Germans, 93, 240.
Clan relationships and collateral inheritance, 220–221.
Clan system of the Germans, 46, 66, 219–221; dissolution of it, 66–78, 219–231; clan system among tenants, 95, 101.
Classification of collateral heirs, 53–54, 208–209, 220–221; among the ancient Irish, 208.
Clients, 3. See Dependants.
Collateral inheritance and clan relationships, 220–221.
Coloni, 12, 118, 239, 241.
Colonies, of free proprietors, 78–91, 231–234, 237–241; of tenants, dependants, slaves, or serfs, 14–16, 78, 81, 91–94, 124–125, 153–156, 176, 216–217, 233, 234, 238, 246.
Comarcani, 160–161.
Common of piscary and of fowling, 203 ; of estovers, 145.
Common enclosures, 81, 234.
Common lands (undivided property or property held in undivided shares), 36–40, 177–178, 191, 192–197 ; rights of enjoyment in, 193.
Communia, Communiones, 36, 169, 192–193.
Communio proximorum, confinium coheredum, 178.

Communism, none in early times, 40-41, 55-65, 88-89, 212, 217-218; not to be inferred from the word *communis*, 191.
Concentration of allodial property, 99-101, 102, 105, 246.
Conpascua, 190.
Conquest, proprietors made tenants by, 96, 243.
Copyright, early case of, 200.
Cord, *funiculus*, used in measuring off land, 132, 136.
Coulanges, Fustel de, his judgment of the theory of a primitive communism, 217-218.
Curtis, *tun*, 159.
Custom, services fixed by, 11-12; rent fixed by, 11-12, 133-134.

DEISENHOFEN, terraced acres at, 7.
Dependants, clients, 3-4, 128-129; politically free, economically unfree, 4, 128-129; employed as cultivators of the soil, 4, 128-129; their condition little better than that of slaves, 4, 128-129.
Development of the simpler forms of society out of the family, 176-177.
Distributions of land by the chiefs or kings, 169-170, 171.
Divisions of land, how made in the early time, 23; made by chiefs or kings, or their agents, 58, 169-170, 171, 181, 212; made between brothers, 29-30, 179-183; among kinsmen generally, 31-35, 49-50, 186-189, 212; between fathers and sons, 74, 189, 228-229; made by lot, 5, 34-35, 82-84, 188-189, 233.
Documents, titles based upon, 170-171.
Domain lands, 11, 115.
Dues and services, 11-12, 133-134, 146, 246.

EASEMENT or profit *in alieno solo*, 88, 203.
Einzelhöfe, 1, 127, 175, 231, 238; they become Gehöferschaften, 27, 175.
Enclosures, common, 84.
England, law of inheritance in, 182-183; indivisibility of property, 252; fighting for land, 166; consolidated by the conversion of *folc-land* into *boc-land*, 171.
Equality of property, 19-20; found only in the free colonies when first founded, 79-80, 80-89; prevented by the operation of the law of inheritance prescribing division among heirs. 88-89.
Erbe, it has the same root as the word *arbeit*, 21, 173-175; antedates the *Erbegenossenschaft*, 175.
Erbgenossenschaft, Erbschaft, 175, 178-179, 203.
Eviction of tenants prohibited, 94.

FACULTAS, use of the word, 72.
Fagana family, 32, 185.
Family, the elementary group in sociological development, 176-177; among the Germans, 46, 176-177.
Farm buildings, 16, 158-159.
Farmsteads, isolated, 1, 16, 78-79, 124-125, 127, 138, 175-177, 238.
Feudal system, origin of the, 106-108, 162, 241, 252.
Fief au Rosel, 242, 251.
Field-grass system of tillage, *Feldgraswirthschaft*, 8.
Fighting for land, 58, 77, 167-168, 212; among the Bavarians, 20-21, 163-164 ; among the Saxons, 21, 165; among the Franks, 21, 165; among the Alamanni, 21-22, 165-166 ; among the Lombards, 21, 76-77, 166 ; in England, 166.
Fishing, 45, 85, 202-203.
Folc-land, 170-171.
Forest land, 10, 28, 36-39, 61, 85, 144-145, 152, 190-195, 235-237 ; enjoyment of it unregulated, 10, 36, 85, 144-145 ; enjoyment stinted, 37 ; severalties of, 86, 152, 236-237.
Freedmen, 128.
Freemen, as free-lords, considered from the economic point of view, 16-17 ; how they passed their time, 2-3 ; colonies of, 78-94.
Free tenants, 100, 106, 129, 247-248.
Free tenures, origin of, 100, 247-248.
Frisii, private property in land among them in Tacitus's time, 211.
Funiculus, 132-133, 136.
Furlongs, 134-135.

GAVELKIND in Kent, 166, 242.
Gefolgschaften, 251.
Gehöferschaft, 27, 94, 175, 178-179, 238-239, 240-241.
Genealogical relationships, knowledge of, 189.
Genealogies, from the Anglo-Saxon Chronicle, 206.
Gesettes-land, 145.
Gewannen, 134-135.
Gewere (gwerra *or* werra, guerre *or* war), 22, 167-168.
Gewerida, 167.
Grass land, 2, 9, 28, 36, 83-86, 141, 152; enjoyment of it stinted and unstinted, 9, 36-37, 84 ; divided into lots, 9, 84, 86, 142, 152 ; the rotation system applied to it, 9, 143.
Greeks, civic life of the, 93, 210.
Guerra, guerre, 22, 167.

HAUSGESETZE, 104, 249, 250.
Heirs, how described in the early records, 31-35, 184-186; they could always call for a division of the inheritance, 32, 60; their consent required before land could be alienated, 54-56, 71, 209-210, 228.
Herdsmen, 2, 125.
Herold text of Lex Salica De alodis, 33, 187-188.
Hide of land, *hida*, 4, 130-131, 139.
Hindu village community, 155, 203-205.
Hochäcker, in Bavaria, 7, 138.
Holding in common, to be distinguished from communistic holding, 39, 57, 191, 192, 214.
House communities, of proprietors, 161-162, 177, 199-200, 231; of tenants, 94-95, 101, 212.
Houses owned in shares, 41, 199-200.
Hubae, 4, 13, 25, 29, 93, 130, 152, 160, 178, 195, 203, 237-238; indominicatae, 11, 145.
Hubengemeinden, 178-179, 203.
Hunting, 2, 45, 85, 202.

IMMUNITY, grants of, 98-100, 245-246; purchased, 99.
Inama-Sternegg. K. T. v., value of his writings, 246-247.
Independence, of the house-father in the early time, 16-17.
Indivisibility of inheritances, 102-108, 162, 248-252; leads to the adoption of the rule of primogeniture, 102-108, 248-252.
-ing, patronymical syllable, 46-48, 206.
Inheritance, origin of, 21, 173-175; laws of, 30-33, 48-50, 52-54, 59, 182-183, 213, 226, 250; by primogeniture, 103-106, 183, 207-209, 249, 250-251; by ultimogeniture, or Borough English, 101.
Inheritances, earliest forms of, 21-25, 27-28, 151-155; multiplied at first, not divided, 25-26, 29; how they came to be divided, 29-35, 48-56, 58-60, 68 69, 77-78, 88-89, 95, 102, 161-162, 179-189, 195-196, 206-209, 212-215, 219-222, 237-238, 242, 252; how they remained undivided, 25, 31, 33, 36, 38, 46, 52, 59, 66, 78, 213, 214; not to be divided, 102-108, 162, 248-252; in the Hindu village communities, 203-204; women allowed to take them, 66-69, 221-222.
In-land, 145.
Intermixed holdings, 5-6, 134-137.
Intermarriages between clans, 67, 219, 222.
Isolated farmsteads and domains, 1, 16, 78-79, 121-125, 127, 175-177, 238.
Israel, children of, inheritances divided by lot among them, 188.

JURNALIS, the Latin word for *acre*, 6, 135.

KINGS, they distribute the land among the people, 169-170; in the ancient houses, 26-27.
Kinship, as a bond of union, 66, 90, 195, 203.

LANDLORDSHIP and the village community, 215-217. See Proprietorship.
Land-tax in India, 204-205.
Latins, *pecuniosi et locupletes*, 1; prescription among them, 76; civic life among them, 93, 240.
Lex Frisionum, text of the, 187-188.
Lex Salica, De affatomie, 70-73, 223-224, 226, 227; De alodis, 33, 68, 182, 187, 188; De chrenecruda, 220, 221, 225; De eum qui se de parentilla tollere vult, 60, 214; De migrantibus, 50-52, 75-76, 230.
Literature of our Subject, 252-261.
Lot meadows, 9, 84, 142.

MANORIAL system, 177; developed during the period of migrations, 156, 215-216.
Manors and village communities, 215-217.
Mansi, 4, 12, 13, 29, 38, 92, 93, 99, 130, 136, 145, 147, 151-152, 191, 194, 237-238; indominicati, 13.
Markgenossenschaft, 160; ohne Feldgemeinschaft, 246.
Markland, i. e. border land, 13, 16, 153, 159-161.
Marks used in casting lots, 142-143, 234.
Marriages between clans, 67, 219.
Meadows. See Grass land.
Measurement of land, 130-133, 136.
Migratory life, not inconsistent with the development of a manorial system, 156, 215-216.
Mills, owned in shares, 44, 200; run by water, 200.
Mir, the Russian, 243.
Missus, of the chief or king, sent to divide property, 58, 181.
Money, stock used instead of, 122.
Morgen, the German word for *acre*, 6, 135.
Mortgages in the time of Lex Salica, 225.

NAMES, of isolated farmsteads and tenant colonies, 15-16, 157-158; of clan villages, 46-48.
Neighborhood, as a bond of union, 90.
Numen, use of the word, 72, 226.

INDEX. 271

OPEN field system, 137, 143.
Ownership of land, distributive or collective? 38–39, 49–52, 57–58, 60.

PASTORAL life, 1.
Pasture land, 1, 10, 28, 36, 84–85, 144, 190–191, 191; enjoyment stinted and unstinted, 10, 36–37, 85, 144; severalties of, held in common, 86, 235.
Patres of the Latin town, 93.
Patronymical names of places, 46–48.
Pecunia, 72, 226.
Per capita divisions, 33–35.
Personal names in local names, 15–16, 157–158.
Per stirpes divisions, 33–35, 188.
Pictatium, 170.
Ploughing, co-operative, 8–9, 140–141.
Plough-lands, 8–9, 139–141.
Ploughs, 8–9, 80, 139–141.
Poll-taxes in Russia, 243.
Population of the clan villages and tenant colonies, 91.
Possession in early times, 22–23, 82, 169.
Possessions, landed, how described in the early time, 22, 24.
Predominance of the clan villages over the colonies sent out from them, 91.
Pre-emption, the right of, enjoyed by kinsmen and neighbors, 75, 230.
Prescription, 66–67, 75–77, 166, 230.
Primitive communism, theory of a, 40–41, 55–65, 191, 212, 217–218.
Primitive property, possession maintained when necessary by force, 82.
Primogeniture, introduction of, 103–108, 183, 249, 250–251.
Private property in land, found everywhere after the migrations, 57; may have existed in pre-historic times, 211; false theory of its origin, 217.
Profits *à prendre*, 88, 203.
Property consisting of villages of serfs, village communities, 151–155.
Proprietors in the German village, 231.
Proprietorship, landlordship, to be distinguished from tenancy, 63 61, 95–96; how it was in many cases converted into tenancy, 93, 96–97, 100, 213; concentration of it, 99–101, 102, 105, 246; acquired by corporations and communities, 40, 88, 195.

REDISTRIBUTIONS of land, 82, 233.
Rent, early history of, 133–134, 243.
Rents, dues, and services, 11–12, 146.

Representation, principle of, 188, 226.
Revenue system of the Hindu kings, 205.
Rights in land, not acquired from communities, but from individuals, 87–88; rights in common lands, 193; rights of common, 88, 145, 195, 197, 202–203.
Roads and ways, property in them, 41–12, 76, 197–198.
Rod, *virga*, used in measuring land, 133, 136.
Rotation system, 9, 10, 83, 143, 233.

SALIC law. See Lex Salica.
Services, agricultural, 11–12, 126, 146.
Schwyz, commonwealth of, 216.
Serfs, the class of, 4.
Severalties, how held in common, 85–86, 235.
Shareholders, parceners, 186, 231.
Silva communis, 36–39, 61, 190.
Slavery, the transition from the pastoral to the agricultural life affected by means of, 3, 126.
Slaves as cultivators of the soil, 2–3, 79, 126–127, 176; owned in shares, 45, 201; housed slaves (*servi cassati*), 79; household slaves, 92; slaves as tenants, 79, 94.
Socage tenures, 217.
Sondereigenthum, 246.
Sors, patrimonium significat, 35.
Sortes, 35, 133, 189 190.
Sources of information list of, 111–122.
Spatia camporum (in Germania 26), 5, 134–135.
State of the early Germans, 91, 248.
Stock, flocks and herds, 1–3, 13, 23, 25, 26, 27, 29, 122, 123, 125, 138, 141, 157, 161, 176, 211.
Stretford, customs of, 249.
Strips of land, 80.

TACITUS Germania. Interpretation of Cap. XVI. 15, 124–125, 155, 231, 239; of Cap. XXVI. 4–6, 7, 16, 27, 129–133, 134–135, 147–148, 151, 152, 172–173.
Tagwerch, 135, 141.
Taxes, institution of, 97–98; in India, 204–205; in Russia, 213.
Tenancy, to be distinguished from proprietorship, 63–64, 95–96; in perpetuity, 94, 211; hereditary by custom, 94.
Tenant colonies, 11–16, 78, 81, 91–94, 124–125, 143, 153–156, 176, 215–217, 233, 231, 238, 246.

INDEX. 273

Tenants, classes of, 106; how described, 12, 147–148.
Teneteri, rule of inheritance among them, 102–103, 162, 249.
Tenures in perpetuity, origin of, 91, 244; free tenures (socage tenures) and tenures in villenage, 247.
Terraces, 7.
Teutonic village, 231.
Three-field system, 143.
Titles, derived from original grants, 77; based upon the possession of documents, 170–171.
Tothill-fields, battle for land at, 166.
Township system, none in our Southern States, 127.
Tribal systems, German and Irish, 176.
Tribes, genealogical and topical, 90–91.
Tribes of the children of Israel, distributions of land among them, 188.
Tribute and rent, 243.
Trinoda necessitas, 246.
Tun, *curtis*, 159.

ULTIMOGENITURE, Borough English, 104.
Undivided land, rights of property in it, how defined, 28–29, 36–39, 190–197, 213–214; undivided land as a bond of union, 195–196; undivided land not necessarily common property, 214. See Holding.
Universitas, 40, 88.
Unterwalden, commonwealth of, 216.
Unoccupied land regarded as undivided property, 13–14.
Uri, commonwealth of, 216.

VAVASSORIAE, 95, 242, 250, 251.
Vestitio, 167.
Vici locati in Tacitus Germania, 124–125, 155, 239.
Vicini, the right of the, 48–56, 60, 214–215; origin of the right, 52–53.
Vicus vel genealogia, 46, 205.
Village communities, origin of, 177, 215–217; in connection with landlordship and the manorial system, 215–217; in India, 155, 203–205; in Russia, 155, 243.
Village community of the Germans, 231. See Villages of Proprietors.
Villages of proprietors, origin of them, 27, 52, 231; inheritances in them, 27–28; description of them, 46.
Villicus, prepositus, actor, major, 14, 155–156.
Visigoths, divisions of land among them, 49–50, 212.
Vorwere, *allodium*, 171–175.

WATER, rights of property in, 42-43, 198-199; mills run by it, 200.
Wells, ownership of, 43.
Werra, war, 22, 167.
Women, admitted to rights of inheritance in land, 66-69, 221-222.
Wood, right to cut it, 10, 144-145.

ZELOPHEHAD, the daughters of, 67, 188.

University Press: John Wilson & Son, Cambridge.